coming together

relationship ready

the
mindgym

tough love

a different relationship

Free password for The Mind Gym Online with this book

Here is your personal password to become a member of The Mind Gym Online. To join, simply visit www.themindgym.com and enter this code.

TLY2 YZW5

Verdict on The Mind Gym books

Winner of The MCA Management Handbook of the Year award, 2005

Press

'Success without the sweat . . . of practical use not only at work but also at home.' **Financial Times**

'Give your mentality a makeover . . . techniques to deal with everyday situations.' **The Times**

'Hundreds of practical tips and techniques based on applied psychology . . . achieve more, gain energy, avoid negativity, resolve difficult challenges and get more out of your career and life.' **Management Today**

'An indispensable guide to boosting productivity and achieving more at work and at home.' **Guardian**

'Fashionable salons are buzzing with a new kind of drug, and it's called intelligence . . . *The Mind Gym: Wake Your Mind Up* is at the top...' **The Sunday Times**

'*The Mind Gym* is a book that teaches you how to use your brain in new ways . . . Definitely something to think about.' **Independent on Sunday**

'Inventive about techniques to deal with everyday situations.' **The Times**

'Read *The Mind Gym*. It's full of mental exercises to stop you functioning on autopilot.' **The Sun**

'Everyone who is anyone in business seems to be talking about this book. 10/10.' **Irish Times**

'What could be smarter than having a personal trainer for your brain?' **Evening Standard**

'Tasty little exercises to get you thinking quicker than ever before.' **Tatler**

'It's time to indulge yourself – make sure you're equipped with the most luxurious accessories to fit every corner of your life . . . *The Mind Gym* is no.1.' **Eve**

'Brainy ideas to get your grey matter into fifth gear.' **Harpers and Queen**

'One chapter and you'll take over the world.' **Image**

'Life-changing . . . Accesible, fun and fascinating.' **Woman and Home**

'Business book of the week.' **Money Week**

'The usual hogwash.' **Private Eye**

People

'From boardroom to bedroom, this is an invaluable guide to making good relationships great and making bad relationships better. I am bulk ordering it!' **Martha Lane Fox, Co-founder, lastminute.com**

'If every business leader applied the techniques in this book, the UK productivity gap would disappear in a moment.' **Tim Melville-Ross CBE, Chairman of Investors in People, former Director-General of Institute of Directors**

'Revelation, revelation, revelation – I love *The Mind Gym* for all its helpful tips that I use every day and make my life so much easier and more enjoyable; a really super invention.' **Kirstie Allsopp, Presenter, Location, Location, Location**

'This is my kind of gym: you can do it wherever you like, you see the benefits immediately, you're never bored and no communal showers.' **Richard Reed, Co-founder, Innocent drinks**

'Finally, a way to unlock the vast amount of our brain capacity that we all have but few of us ever use, my mind feels more toned already – I love it!' **Sahar Hashemi, Founder, Coffee Republic**

'Got any sense? Want some more? Join The Mind Gym.' **Nick Jones, Founder, Soho House Clubs**

'When it comes to improving our minds, The Mind Gym is the number one brand – you can trust it completely and may even fall in love.' **Rita Clifton, Chairman, Interbrand**

'Whatever jungle you are doing battle with, *The Mind Gym's* tips and techniques are highly likely to give you the confidence and skills to come out victorious' **Dr Sandra Scott, Psychological Consultant on I'm a Celebrity, Get Me Out Of Here!**

'To stimulate, order, de-stress and ultimately secure peace of mind, whether for personal or professional use, this book is a bedside necessity which you can rely on for the best advice.' **Emilia Fox, Actress**

'This is the perfect intelligent and intuitive guide for everyone who wants power, wealth and influence – without bloodshed.' **Simon Sebag-Montefiore, Author**

Professors

'The best psychology turned into neat ideas for living smarter. Credible, imaginative and practical: you can't ask for more.' **Professor Guy Claxton**

'As if by miracle, the Mind Gym turns rigorous academic science into smart advice for everyday living. Not only is this book full of useful practical information, it is also fun to read. Enjoy!' **Dr Ilona Boniwell**

'I am deeply impressed by how *The Mind Gym* makes so clear and accessible complex, deep ideas and research into human relationships. This is both a wise and eminently useable guide.' **Professor Janet Reibstein**

'I am very impressed by the intellectual rigour and academic integrity of this immensely enjoyable and practical book.' **Emeritus Professor Peter Robinson**

'Filled with everyday uses for some of the best psychological research of the last fifty years, this is a must for anyone who is serious about making better use of their mind.' **Professor Ingrid Lunt**

'Packed with helpful directions for people struggling with the challenges of daily living, *The Mind Gym* puts the new positive psychology into practice and offers a multitude of ways to live a strong and healthy life.' **Professor Michael West**

'This is a very well written and well researched book packed with good advice, useful tips, accurate self-assessment questionnaires and helpful practical exercises. It contains 10 times as much information as its rivals and is neatly packed into nicely formed bite-sized pieces.' **Professor Adrian Furnham**

the mindgym

relationships

sphere

SPHERE

First published in Great Britain in 2009 by Sphere

Copyright © 2009 by The Mind Gym

A CIP catalogue record for this book
is available from the British Library.

ISBN 978-1-84744-063-1

Typeset in Avenir
Printed and bound in Great Britain by
Clays Ltd, St Ives plc

Papers used by Sphere are natural, renewable and recyclable
products made from wood grown in sustainable forests and certified
in accordance with the rules of the Forest Stewardship Council.

Mixed Sources
Product group from well-managed
forests and other controlled sources
www.fsc.org Cert no. SGS-COC-004081
© 1996 Forest Stewardship Council
FSC

Sphere
An imprint of
Little, Brown Book Group
100 Victoria Embankment
London EC4Y 0DY

An Hachette Livre UK Company
www.hachettelivre.co.uk

www.littlebrown.co.uk
www.themindgym.com

Contents

Welcome   1

Do I have to read this book?   9

Section 1: Relationship ready

(A)   Right mind   24

(B)   Check your impulse   38

(C)   Cool to be kind   53

(D)   Shy to shine   63

Section 2: Coming together

(E)   Are you listening?   78

(F)   Charm school   94

(G)   Bid for attention   110

(H)   Trust me   123

Section 3: Tough love

(I)   Fight club   140

(J)   Draw the poison   154

(K)   Deal or no deal   169

(L)   I smell trouble   182

(M)   The hardest word   198

Section 4: A different relationship

(N)   Out of a rut   214

(O)   Tough talk   225

(P)   Tricky people   237

(Q)   Graceful exit   251

New beginnings   266

Bibliography   275

Without whom   281

Index   285

Welcome

Relationships make you happy. In one of the largest studies ever conducted on happiness, only one factor distinguished the 'very happy' from the 'moderately happy' and 'unhappy'. It wasn't how rich they are, how beautiful they looked, how optimistically they saw things or even how much chocolate they'd eaten. It was how sociable they were. More good relationships, the research concluded, make you happier.

How we get on with our boss, our colleague in IT, the teacher at our daughter's school, our dad and, of course, our romantic partner, defines our lives. When our relationships are glowing so are we.

The first piece of good news is that, by and large, we decide the terms of those relationships. We can make them glow.

The tricky boss, the rebellious teenager, the nervous date, the nosey mum: our behaviour dictates how they will respond. Choose our words wisely and the relationship will transform: supportive boss, respectful mum. Get it wrong and the relationship will turn sickly sour.

The second piece of good news is that our ability to improve our relationship with one person increases our ability to improve our relationship with all of them. Whereas most advisors tell you either how to win the girl (or boy) or how to win the client, the magic lies in doing both by borrowing what works in one part of our life and applying it to another. And so if you've got one person you get on with then you can have as many friends, fans and fawning clients as you like (as well as one really amazing lover).

The third piece of good news is that this book shows you how.

Science is sexy

Psychology and the related mind sciences are full of glorious insights about how we can improve our relationships by changing the way we think.

Sometimes these insights simply remind us of what we've always suspected: listen more and you'll be liked more (if you're a waiter and you repeat the customer's order word for word, your tip will go up by up to 70%). Sometimes the discoveries will be new but not altogether surprising: forgive and you'll sleep better; hopeful people are more popular. And sometimes the discoveries are at odds with what we'd expect: don't pay someone and they'll spend longer on the task; the small stuff, like how we respond to 'do you want a cup of coffee?' determines the future of our relationship far more than the big stuff ('where shall we live?')

The thing is that most of us don't have the academic appetite to dig out all these amazing insights. And we're way too busy.

That's where The Mind Gym comes in. There is a team of eager psychologists who spend their days finding the very best that psychology and related science can offer. These discoveries are adapted and tested with up to 500,000 people. How come so many? Because The Mind Gym runs 'workouts' (our name for a workshop, being a gym and all) in over 50 countries for big business, including 40% of FTSE 100, as well as little ones. These Mind Gym participants tell us in the workouts, the summits (longer workouts), online and in countless other ways, what has worked for them.

The very best and most popular techniques are sifted, refined, re-tested and have been assembled here in this book, for you.

You'll find some of them will transform your relationships, and others won't work for you at all. This is why, in the next chapter, there's a questionnaire. Fill it in and find out which chapters you will find worth reading and which to skip.

I'm sorry, we haven't met

Maybe you haven't come across The Mind Gym before, in which case here is a crisp introduction.

The Mind Gym was conceived over dinner ten years ago. A dinner, it must be confessed, fuelled by not a little alcohol. The group were talking about trends: music, fashion, what it takes to become a celebrity, and so on. Someone suggested that the 1980s had been the decade of the body – Jane Fonda, jogging, vegetarianism becoming mainstream – and the 1990s the decade of the soul – feng shui, yoga, alternative medicine. What, came the challenge, would the next decade be about?

One of the party offered 'Mind, Body, Soul' and without a moment's reflection everyone agreed that the 2000s would be the decade of the mind. And what to do with this blinding insight? Get ourselves a mind gym.

The next morning the heads were heavier and the enthusiasm of the previous night had dwindled. Still, the idea of a mind gym continued to niggle and over the next year a couple of us travelled, researched and brought together groups of psychologists (including a professor who became our 'Chair of Integrity'), business advisors and other insightful minds to see what a mind gym might do.

The original idea had been to run workouts for the mind in gyms across the country. You might do kick boxing for an hour on Tuesday and then 'conflict handling' on Thursday. We eagerly presented the idea to a number of well known gym chains. They couldn't have been less interested.

With heavy heart we revisited our original plan. There had always been an element about offering The Mind Gym to businesses and our early research suggested that the bite-size workshop, which had been essential for the regular gym members, also had an appeal to companies.

On 1st September 2000, The Mind Gym ran its first ever 90-minute workout: 'body language' at Deutsche Bank.

The early months were tough. In 'dark November' our accountant asked, 'How much more money are you willing to lose before you realise that this isn't going to work?' We thanked him for his advice and ploughed on regardless.

Since then half a million people in over 40 countries have been to The Mind Gym and this series of books, of which this is the third, has been published in 27 languages.

The Mind Gym Foundation has just been launched to help young people achieve more by thinking differently. All the royalties from this book (for which we thank you) will go to this cause.

And still to come: The Mind Gym for prisons, for cruises, for second lifers and who knows what. If you want to be part of this mind expanding future join The Mind Gym online using your free membership password on the inside cover of this book.

Relationship heaven

The way to relationship heaven is paved with good intentions, for sure, but quite a lot else besides.

If you're in one of those luxurious bookshops, browsing with a latte in one hand and keen to save a few quid on books by getting all the best bits without having to buy a copy (given the price of your latte, we can understand why) here are the five things you need to know.

1 Give me security
Deep down, or sometimes very much on the surface, everyone wants to feel secure, loved and appreciated. If a relationship isn't working, one or both of us isn't feeling secure. Chances are it's them. So give them reasons to feel safe being who they are.

In an experiment, a school of pupils was given a test and then teachers were told which of their pupils had high potential. The examiners then left the school and returned a year later. When they came back they discovered that the pupils who had been marked as future stars had lived up to their billing. Their scores had not only risen immediately compared with the rest of their class but had stayed higher. Even their IQ scores, which are normally assumed to be fairly static, had improved significantly.

However, what the teachers didn't know is that the selection of so-called high potential pupils had nothing to do with their test scores. It was done completely at random. This experiment shows how if we believe someone is amazing, they probably will be (and vice versa, alas).

Imagine the best in your lover, boss or younger brother, and watch the relationship flourish.

2 Get fit
We need to be fit to make relationships work. Not necessarily physically in shape, though that helps, but mentally fit (hence, mind gym).

Relationships prosper when at least one party has the energy to think before acting, to control unhelpful impulses, to change their assumptions, to make that little extra effort at the end of a long and painful day. Managing our energy and self-regulation is central to having great relationships.

3 It's a system
If you read on you will uncover hundreds of techniques to use in the moment: how to prevent a disagreement going toxic; how to listen for the real meaning behind words; the formula for building trust swiftly; how to get your apology accepted.

Equally, a relationship is about more than an event or a particular exchange. It is made up from a series of activities, each of which has a knock-on effect. Our opening greeting will direct the rest of the conversation; our first meeting will have a bearing on whether you reply to my email.

There are also thousands of other knock-on events that directly affect our relationship. I have a hangover so am snappy with you and you snap back. I've just had an espresso so I'm buzzing with enthusiasm for your suggestion which fills you with confidence. I heard from Angus that you fancy me so I'm flirty. Our relationships are shaped not just by the history of our experiences together but also by the myriad of experiences we have outside it.

Relationships are part of an ever-evolving system. At any moment we can see only a few of the many inter-connected parts. Thinking about relationships in this systemic way helps us be more patient, more considered and more likely to make the right call about what to do right now.

4 Many me

One Mind Gym member explained how Jim had moved from being her client to her employee, to become her lover, her husband, the father of her daughter, her ex-husband, the primary investor in her new business and now a business supplier.

Whilst most of us haven't been through quite this many turns with the same person, we have been through plenty of smaller shifts from, say, buddy to boss or flatmate to fling to live-in.

Mental agility – the ability to dance between different ways of thinking – helps us have many relationships with the same person, as well as the same relationship with many people. We need to remain authentic (see the last chapter, New beginnings) as well as encouraging the many versions of me, how I am at work, with my best friend, with my mum. The trick lies in knowing when and how to adapt.

5 We choose how we think

At the core of all matters Mind Gym is the belief that we choose how we think far more than we imagine. It's easy to fall into mental habits. When I see Sheila I start to yawn; when you say 'What's for supper...?' I hear 'What have you been doing all day...?'; when I see a lady crying I assume she's sad.

Whilst these are all valid responses, they aren't the only ones. Maybe the lady is crying with relief, or joy, or acting, or she has something in her eye.

We always, always, always have a choice. With choice comes control. And with control comes responsibility.

We are 100% responsible for our relationships. For some this is an unhelpful extra burden – but it's their fault, I'm not doing anything wrong. For others, this is totally liberating – you mean I alone can determine our relationship? Pretty much.

If you are excited about this freedom, read on and discover how to train your mind so your relationships prosper, delight and fulfil your wildest desires.

Do I have to read this book?

No. You don't have to read this book. In fact you shouldn't, at least not from cover to cover.

Much wiser to develop your own relationship workout programme that takes you to the places where you'll get the most benefit and skip the rest.

If you are brimming with confidence you won't get much value from chapter D, Shy to shine; if you're already a skilled negotiator, you won't need the hints in Deal or no deal?, chapter K.

Here are several ways to get the nuggets that will help you most.

Pick 'n' mix

If you want some practical guidance on how you can deal with a stress cadet, then just go straight to the chapter that deals with Tricky people, chapter P. Or, if you're looking for a way to be more entertaining at your next date, or sales conference, head for Charm school, chapter F.

The chapter summaries on page 20 will help you find what you are looking for. Like a book of short stories or a magazine, you can dip in and out as you like; each chapter makes sense by itself.

Read a section

The chapters are grouped into four sections:

- **Relationship ready**
  With our minds in the right place, having great relationships becomes infinitely easier. This section reveals how to get ourselves straight first.

- **Coming together**
  Making strong bonds requires a knack that few of us are born with but all of us can acquire. In 'coming together' we uncover tools and techniques to build longer-lasting relationships.

- **Tough love**
  All relationships have disagreements – they wouldn't be worth having if they didn't. The challenge lies in knowing what to do with them. This section shares the options and helps you pick wisely.

- **A different relationship**
  When we get stuck in a rut we need to do more than stop digging. Discover how to change the course of a relationship so it's heading where we want.

Each section starts with an overview of what you will find within.

Adopt a programme

Follow one of the programmes outlined on pages 13–15. Rather like a fitness workout that is designed to work on strength or stamina, each of these programmes has been developed to address a specific goal.

There's even The Gym Special, like a chef's recommendation: all the basics for building great relationships.

Design your own programme

On pages 17–19 you'll find a questionnaire that will help you design your own journey. The questionnaire is also available online (complete with personalised bookmark). Fill it in and use the results to create a tailor-made programme.

The Mind Gym Online

The Mind Gym Online is open 24/7. It's a place to practise, prepare, share and, if you want, compete. In the Mind Gym Online you can:

- complete the questionnaires in the book and many more for an in-depth analysis of your preferences and how you might choose to adapt. You can also send the questionnaire to friends and colleagues and discover how their views fit with your idea of yourself (scary).

- use specific relationship repair tools to work out how you can apply the best relationship repair techniques to today's thorny challenge.

- share ideas and get top tips from people who've been there already – Mind Gym experts, members and other like-minded folk.

- keep a private record of how you are doing and chart your progress.

To start your membership of The Mind Gym Online, simply visit www.themindgym.com and enter the password on the inside front cover of this book. If you're already a member, simply add this code to your existing profile to unleash a treasure trove of new online experiences.

Wherever you see in the book, you will find something relevant at The Mind Gym Online. But if you don't have access to a computer, don't worry, everything in these pages makes complete sense without any further support.

You now know all you need to get going. If, however, you would like to follow a particular programme, or design your own, read on.

The Mind Gym programmes

Here are three programmes that have been developed to help you get what you want from *The Mind Gym: relationships* as quickly and efficiently as possible. After all, time is of the essence.

1 Relationship essentials
A whistle-stop tour of the essentials for building great relationships: ideal for anyone who wants to get the basics under their belt.

2 Relationship repair kit
What should be a joyous or productive relationship is proving to be anything but. Get equipped to turn things around.

3 Like me, love me, respect me
How to win friends, clients, colleagues and keep them for good.

See pages 13–15 for these routes.

Relationship essentials

A whistle-stop tour of the essentials for building great relationships, ideal for anyone who wants to get the basics under their belt.

Section 1: Relationship ready   **23**

(A) Right mind   24

(B) Check your impulse   38

Cool to be kind   53

Shy to shine   63

Section 2: Coming together   **77**

(E) Are you listening?   78

Charm school   94

(G) Bid for attention   110

Trust me   123

Section 3: Tough love   **139**

(I) Fight club   140

Draw the poison   154

Deal or no deal   169

I smell trouble   182

(M) The hardest word   198

Section 4: A different relationship   **213**

Out of a rut   214

Tough talk   225

Tricky people   237

(Q) Graceful exit   251

New beginnings   266

Relationship repair kit

What should be a joyous or productive relationship is proving to be anything but. Get equipped to turn things around.

Section 1: Relationship ready   **23**

Right mind   24

(B) Check your impulse   38

(C) Cool to be kind   53

Shy to shine   63

Section 2: Coming together   **77**

Are you listening?   78

Charm school   94

(G) Bid for attention   110

Trust me   123

Section 3: Tough love   **139**

(I) Fight club   140

(J) Draw the poison   154

Deal or no deal   169

I smell trouble   182

(M) The hardest word   198

Section 4: A different relationship   **213**

(N) Out of a rut   214

(O) Tough talk   225

Tricky people   237

(Q) Graceful exit   251

New beginnings   266

Like me, love me, respect me

If you want more, and stronger, relationships with friends, clients and colleagues then this is your programme.

Section 1: Relationship ready   **23**

(A) Right mind   24

Check your impulse   38

(C) Cool to be kind   53

(D) Shy to shine   63

Section 2: Coming together   **77**

(E) Are you listening?   78

(F) Charm school   94

Bid for attention   110

(H) Trust me   123

Section 3: Tough love   **139**

Fight club   140

Draw the poison   154

(K) Deal or no deal   169

I smell trouble   182

The hardest word   198

Section 4: A different relationship   **213**

Out of a rut   214

Tough talk   225

Tricky people   237

Graceful exit   251

New beginnings   266

Five steps to design your own programme

Step 1
Fold the section of page 17 to the right of the dotted line back on itself so you can see the circles on page 19 (but nothing else on that page).

Step 2
Complete the questionnaire on page 17. Look through each of the statements that begin 'I wish that' and pick the option that is closest to your view. There are five options:

1 This is already largely true or it's not that important to me
2 This would be nice to have but there are other things I'd prefer to have first
3 Yes please. This would be great
4 Wow. That would be absolutely fantastic. How soon can I have it?
5 I'd give my right arm for this

In order to get a good idea of where to start, try to give a range of scores across the different statements. If everything gets a five then you will be none the wiser.

Step 3
Transfer the score for each question to each of the chapters that are suggested on the next page.

Step 4
Add up the scores for each chapter and write them in the 'Total score' circles. The chapters with the highest score are the ones that you should probably focus on. You are now equipped to design your own programme.

Step 5
You could, for example, start with the chapter with the highest score and then move on to the one with the second highest score and work down your list (where two chapters have the same score, start with the one that comes earlier in the book).

Alternatively, you could calculate your average score (say seven) and develop a programme with all the chapters that scored over seven, starting at the beginning of the book and working through.

If you complete the questionnaire online you can print out a bookmark with your personal programme which will make it even easier to stay on track.

already largely true
nice to have
yes please – great
absolutely fantastic
give my right arm

Fold this portion of the page back on itself and write your score directly into the relevant circle on page 19

I wish that...

	already largely true	nice to have	yes please – great	absolutely fantastic	give my right arm
I was more popular/liked/loved	1	2	3	4	5
I was more respected	1	2	3	4	5
I didn't get into so many arguments	1	2	3	4	5
People were more loyal to me	1	2	3	4	5
I always got on with people at first meeting	1	2	3	4	5
I didn't worry so much about what other people think of me	1	2	3	4	5
We could disagree without fighting	1	2	3	4	5
We got on better	1	2	3	4	5
I knew when to stick at it and when to quit	1	2	3	4	5
I could start afresh	1	2	3	4	5
My relationships lasted for longer	1	2	3	4	5
I knew what to do when it felt like the relationship was turning sour	1	2	3	4	5
I was better at dealing with people who wind me up	1	2	3	4	5
I was quicker at spotting things that aren't quite right	1	2	3	4	5
I could win the argument without the other person feeling that they'd lost	1	2	3	4	5
I felt closer to the people around me	1	2	3	4	5
I could talk about relationship issues more easily	1	2	3	4	5
My relationships had a little more give and a little less take	1	2	3	4	5
I knew how to handle covert conflict	1	2	3	4	5
I didn't feel so put upon	1	2	3	4	5
I could get us out of the rut we're in	1	2	3	4	5
I could move on	1	2	3	4	5
I could end a relationship without burning bridges	1	2	3	4	5
I could build relationships with difficult people just as easily	1	2	3	4	5

Scoring

Transfer your scores for the relevant chapter to the sheet below.

Total
score

(A) Right mind ○ + ○ + ○ = ○

(B) Check your impulse ○ + ○ + ○ = ○

(C) Cool to be kind ○ + ○ + ○ = ○

(D) Shy to shine ○ + ○ + ○ = ○

(E) Are you listening? ○ + ○ + ○ = ○

(F) Charm school ○ + ○ + ○ = ○

(G) Bid for attention ○ + ○ + ○ = ○

(H) Trust me ○ + ○ + ○ = ○

(I) Fight club ○ + ○ + ○ = ○

(J) Draw the poison ○ + ○ + ○ = ○

(K) Deal or no deal ○ + ○ + ○ = ○

(L) I smell trouble ○ + ○ + ○ = ○

(M) The hardest word ○ + ○ + ○ = ○

(N) Out of a rut ○ + ○ + ○ = ○

(O) Tough talk ○ + ○ + ○ = ○

(P) Tricky people ○ + ○ + ○ = ○

(Q) Graceful exit ○ + ○ + ○ = ○

Transfer your score for each question into all the relevant circles on the opposite page 18. When you have finished there should be a number in each circle. For example, if you scored 4 in the first question, put a 4 in the circles on the opposite page 18 in the row for (A) Right mind, (C) Cool to be kind, (E) Are you listening? and (F) Charm school.

A, C, E, F ○
F, H ○
B, J, N ○
H ○
D, E, F ○

A, D ○
B, I, J, N ○
C, E, G, P ○
Q ○
M ○
A, G ○

L, O ○

B, I, J, P ○
L ○

I, K ○
C, G, H ○
O ○

K ○
L, P ○
D, K ○
M, N, O ○
M, P, Q ○
Q ○

P ○

A summary of each chapter

(A) **Right mind**
When our mind is in the right place, relationships flourish. Find out how to get it there.

(B) **Check your impulse**
Keep our emotions in check and we become richer, healthier and have happier relationships. Discover how to get control of your impulses.

(C) **Cool to be kind**
For generosity of mind, warmth of heart and the enlightenment that comes from seeing the world in its sandals, sign-up to this chapter.

(D) **Shy to shine**
Half of the population describe themselves as shy. For those of us keen on a kick-start in confidence, book here.

(E) **Are you listening?**
Give your listening filters a fine tune and find out how to hear what people really mean.

(F) **Charm school**
Discover how to be the person people want more of.

(G) **Bid for attention**
Little things matter a lot. Find out which ones and what to do about them so you're heading for diamond anniversary, not the divorce court.

(H) **Trust me**
Revealed: how to build the DNA of trust so it lasts a lifetime.

(I) **Fight club**
There's more to conflict than fight or flight. Uncover the options so you consistently make the right call on how to handle disagreements.

(J) Draw the poison
Antidotes for the most virulent conflict toxins. Build your own relationship pharmacy for when arguments turn nasty.

(K) Deal or no deal
Uncover the secrets of a cleanly negotiated settlement.

(L) I smell trouble
There's something in the air and it doesn't smell good. Read this blog for tips on dealing with covert conflict.

(M) The hardest word
Sorry can be the hardest word to say and to hear. Explore techniques that help on both sides of an apology.

(N) Out of a rut
The record is stuck, broken and about to be replayed. A chapter for those who feel like they're having the same unproductive exchange over and over and over.

(O) Tough talk
The secret to solving many an intractable problem: dialogue. Find out how to have conversations that generate a happy resolution.

(P) Tricky people
A line-up of life's relationship criminals and the best way to rehabilitate them.

(Q) Graceful exit
Sometimes we don't know when to leave and sometimes we don't know how. This chapter provides answers.

New beginnings
Find out how to put your favourite ideas into practice not just today but every day.

Relationship ready

Whether it's unreasonable clients, disloyal lovers, flaky friends or a lazy team, it's easy to blame others, and so, when the relationship suffers, we conclude: it's not me, it's you.

The trouble is we're usually wrong. Most of the time, it's just as much us. And when it comes to doing anything about it the only thing we can change is ourselves.

To avoid undermining one relationship after another we need to get our mind in the right place. This section reveals how .

We start with the healthy way to look at the world: A – Right mind. Next, how to make the right calls by keeping our emotions under control: B – Check your impulse. Then how to give people what they need: C – Cool to be kind. And finally, how to conquer low confidence: D – Shy to shine.

'Do you know any girl suitable for Tom?' asked a concerned friend.
'Plenty. But is he ready for them, however wonderful?' was the wise reply.

This section is for Tom, and for all of us who find that in at least one part of our life we aren't forming the relationships we want.

(A) Right mind

Do your clients irritate you, your suppliers let you down, or your romantic relationships wither after just a few months? If you find it hard to keep old friends or make new ones, maintain your colleagues' loyalty or stay with the same employer, the chances are that it's because of the way you look at the world.

To discover how, and what to do about it, start with these questions.

How do you see it?

Below are a list of statements. Don't spend too long on each one, simply decide whether, on balance, you generally agree or disagree.

1. Most people seem to like me.	Agree / Disagree
2. I am comfortable about getting close to others.	Agree / Disagree
3. I worry about being alone.	Agree / Disagree
4. People are rarely there when you need them.	Agree / Disagree
5. Other people tend to respect me.	Agree / Disagree
6. I am comfortable depending on others.	Agree / Disagree
7. I tend to worry that romantic partners don't really love me.	Agree / Disagree

8. I find it difficult to trust others.   Agree / Disagree

9. I enjoy close relationships.   Agree / Disagree

10. I worry that others don't value me as   Agree / Disagree
   much as I value them.

Me				You		
Question	Agree	Disagree		Question	Agree	Disagree
1	+2	−2		1	+2	−2
3	−2	+2		3	−2	+2
5	+2	−2		5	+2	−2
7	−2	+2		7	−2	+2
10	+2	−2		10	+2	−2
Total				Total		
		(between −10 and +10)				(between −10 and +10)

What it means

What these results suggest is how you look at your self and how you look at others. Am I ok? Are you ok? (there are only 10 questions so this is more of a suggestion than a conclusive diagnosis).

If the 'me' score is positive (and certainly if it is greater than +2) then you feel pretty good in your own skin. You value yourself and you are likely to agree with the statement 'I'm ok', maybe even 'I'm an all-round good person'.

If the score is negative (and certainly if it is less than −2) then it's the opposite. You probably do not value yourself very highly. You might even agree with the statement 'I'm not ok' or, 'I'm not good enough' or maybe even 'there's a lot that's not quite right with me'.

The same rules apply for the 'you' score, which is about how you see other people. Do you tend to assume that they are ok until they prove otherwise? Or is it more often the other way around:

they need to prove themselves before you are willing to be impressed? The positive score (especially more than +2) suggests you are in the 'you're ok' camp. And a negative score (especially less than –2) suggests you're in the 'you're not ok'.

To make it clear, plot where you are in the following grid:

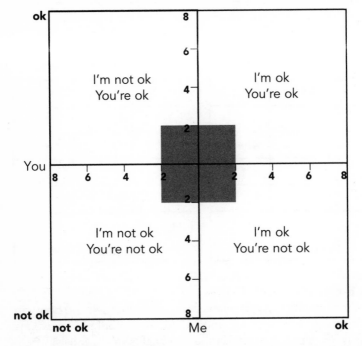

If you are in the shaded box then your position is mere borderline and so it is worth considering the neighbouring box too.

Who's ok?

Position 1: I'm ok, you're ok
This is the best place to be for healthy relationships. With barely a bad egg in sight, people in this position start off with the assumption that everyone – including themselves – is inherently good.

When in this position people tend to be logical and understanding, they take emotion into account, but they're not ruled by it. They're self-aware and tolerant, understanding that people can behave

Right mind

irrationally but looking for the positive motives behind other people's behaviour. When things go wrong they give the benefit of the doubt and do their best to work collaboratively.

People with an I'm ok / you're ok attitude are perceived by others as being open, direct and honest.

If you are in this position you are likely to have a good sense of self-worth and to be trusting of others. As a result, you're likely to be at ease around other people and feel comfortable about having close relationships.

If your relationships aren't working, there's another reason.

Position 2: I'm ok, you're not ok
When people take the I'm ok / you're not ok perspective they experience a sense of superiority. They believe that they're better or smarter than all the idiots around them. People are failing them (in their opinion) and not delivering what they should. And so they criticise and reprimand, zooming in on the failings and shortcomings of others, usually without noticing the errors that they may have made themselves.

Being on the receiving end of people who take the I'm ok / You're not ok position is not pleasant. They can come across as argumentative, sniping and dismissive ('they know best'). As a result people may avoid them, leaving them feeling unsupported – which simply reinforces their view that others are not. Although they come across as high status, people in this position often feel threatened and isolated.

A score that lands you in this position suggests that, while you may feel good about yourself, you don't have a lot of faith in other people at the moment. You may have found that other people are unreliable and so you're protecting yourself by not allowing others to get too close.

This will put other people off forming strong relationships with you.

Person 3: I'm not ok, you're ok
People in this position tend to feel pretty rotten about themselves. They sense that they are at fault, that they are less competent,

successful or significant than other people. They may lack confidence or feel that they don't fit in.

They are continually on the lookout for evidence of their own shortcomings highlighting the areas where they compare unfavourably with others – 'he is cleverer, more stylish or fitter than me' – whilst ignoring the fact that they themselves may be streets ahead in other areas.

People who get stuck in this position can start to feel helpless and, as a result, they tend to let opportunities pass them by.

To those around them, people who take this position can be exhausting. Compliant, lacking in confidence and short on motivation, they can seem dependent, vulnerable and a bit weak. And whilst friendly, they can be hyper negative complainers who can never get enough support and encouragement. A bit of a victim.

If your score puts you in this position you're probably being very hard on yourself right now, whilst putting others on pedestals. You may think that you would feel happy if only you could get people around you to respond properly to you. But in this state of mind you won't. And whatever support they do give you, it still won't be enough.

Person 4: I'm not ok, you're not ok
I'm not ok / you're not ok is not a nice place to be. People who are here have usually been dragged here by others (uncaring parents, cruel lovers, bullying employers), or events may have damaged their faith in people and left them feeling helpless.

If you know your Winnie-the-Pooh, think Eyore.

When holding the 'I'm not ok / you're not ok' attitude people expect the worst – they expect to fail, they expect to be let down. This becomes a self-fulfilling prophecy (as they seek out the pitfalls) and a self-reinforcing one (see, I knew they'd let me down).

People in this position are low on confidence and high on negativity, pessimism and cynicism. Being around them can be a demoralising experience.

If you're in this position, you don't have high hopes of others and you're not feeling good about yourself, either. As a result, you tend to reject others as a way of protecting yourself from being hurt.

A–ok
When we are being kind to ourselves and generous spirited with others, relationships are likely to flourish; we're much more likely to solve problems than apportion blame, take responsibility rather than play the victim, deal with the issue instead of giving up.

Ideally we'd spend all of our time in I'm ok / you're ok. In reality most of us move around the quadrants as we get buffeted by events, situations and people. Equally, we all have an anchor quadrant, one where we spend most of our time.

If your current mood and situation is fairly typical then the place you've plotted is likely to be fairly representative. If not, come back to the questionnaire another time.

Knowing where we are is half the journey. Knowing what to do about it is the next challenge.

5 tips for getting into 'I'm ok'

The motto here is 'I see the best in me'. Here are five practical ways to help live the motto and restore faith in yourself.

1. Talk yourself up
Write down 20 things you've done well in the last month. Review the list. What does this tell you that you're good at (other than writing lists)? Try to find at least 10 significant things.

Keep a diary every day of 5 things you've done well from the momentous (at least momentous for you: worked out hard in the gym, won the account) to the miniature (mowed the lawn, completed the Su Doku). And once a week look at the list and identify 10 more things that you're good at.

Writing it down may seem unnecessary. It isn't. Those who do the writing report a much bigger benefit, especially if they stick at it. If you want to move out of 'I'm not ok', get a notebook and start scribbling.

Even better is to write down the part you played in making these good things happen. So if I've written 'had a good workout in the gym' – I need to add, for example, 'this happened because I set myself the goal to leave work at 6.30 pm, I avoided the strong temptation to crawl home to the sofa and instead reminded myself how good I would feel.' Psychologist Christopher Peterson found that explicitly acknowledging our part in making good things happen helps shift us to a more I'm ok way of thinking.

2. Focus on solutions
When the problem seems big, it's easy to feel helpless. Work on what you can do that will make a difference, however small. Then do it. Concentrating on action (and then recognising when we've completed it) is a productive way for all of us to appreciate our value a little bit more.

3. Do what you do best
As one successful entrepreneur explained, 'I worked out what I like doing and then found someone to pay me to do it'.

The kitchen, the pitch (football or client), designing or dancing, most of us have somewhere to shine. Our challenge is to spend more time there.

Write down the five places or things you do where you are at your best. And then work out how you can reorganise your life so you spend more time doing them.

4. Hear the praise
There are people out there who like you, rate you and appreciate you. They may not be making this completely obvious and so you may not be picking up their signals. From the smiling lady on the bus to the client who doesn't complain (which is rather out of character for him) look out for the small signs that have large meanings about the good you're spreading.

Praise: not always so clear

5. Minimise the rubbish
Things go wrong. They do to all of us. The difference is in how we think about them.

To get into 'I'm ok', put the rubbish in the bin. This means seeing negative experiences as temporary – one missed deadline, the occasional memory lapse – and specific to a particular situation – playing squash with Roger, last year's performance review.

It also means making little of these daily upsets. So what if you forgot to buy milk? Or source the data? Does it really matter?

Getting stuck

In The Mind Gym workout on fixing relationships, John talked about the relationship he had with a colleague in his team. He felt this person had let him down – customers calls weren't returned, goals weren't met, processes weren't followed. He felt this guy was not ok and that's how he started to treat him – so much so that, even when a piece of work was completed well, he'd focus on the weak points. He found himself becoming slightly aggressive in conversation with him, until finally the colleague got the message and quit. When John reflected back on the story he realised that the person was actually making quite good progress but, stuck in the I'm ok / you're not ok attitude, John wasn't able to respond positively.

---

5 tips for getting into 'You're ok'

'I always prefer to believe the best of everybody, it saves so much trouble.' Rudyard Kipling

The motto we need is 'Give people the benefit of the doubt'. Here are five practical ways to turn this aspiration into reality.

1. Alternative, positive explanation
Assume the best realistic motivation of the other person's behaviour. They are hopeless rather than cunning, nervous rather than angry, shy rather than rude, under pressure rather than vindictive.

The habit of guessing at someone's intention from even the smallest behaviours can get us into serious trouble. If it's too hard coming up with the best possible explanation, then simply try not coming up with any interpretation at all. Note their behaviour and move on.

2. Look for the good
It's easy to concentrate on what's wrong with people. Try focusing on what's good about them. Everyone has great qualities, which are often the reasons why we like them in the first place. Consciously think about what's good about the other person when you're talking with them (and writing to them). By itself, this will help improve your relationship.

3. Be patient
Two examples don't make a pattern. We all make mistakes, especially when we're trying to change. It's easy and tempting to seize on a transgression and hold it up to prove (at least to your self) what's wrong with them. Easy but unhelpful. Just wait and look for the positive acts too.

4. Lower your expectations
Do people often let you down? Maybe your expectations are so high that they always will. This doesn't mean that you have to accept shoddy work or friends who don't show up when they say they would. It does, however, suggest that your consistently high standards may be damaging your relationships.

5. Forgive
If you can't lower your expectations, at least forgive quickly and easily. Otherwise you will spend much of your energy feeling angry or upset about people letting you down, which isn't much fun. Forgiveness doesn't mean excusing what happened in the past, instead it allows the relationship to move on. See chapter M – The hardest word, for more.

When 'they' don't want you to change
After a while people become accustomed to how we are and they get used to behaving with us in a certain way. There may be some kind of positive payoff in it for them. If we decide to change the way we behave, it will change things for them too. As a result, there may be upset.

For example – perhaps you've always had a negative view of yourself and a positive view of others (I'm not ok / you're ok). You may have been super attentive to those around you. People will have got used to that – they may have come to see it as your way of demonstrating love. And so, when your behaviour changes and you stop being so clingy they may experience a sense of loss. Your demonstrations of love may have given them a boost. Your attentiveness may have made their life a little easier. As a result they may find themselves feeling resistant to the changes at the same time as being glad that you are feeling better about yourself.

So, be aware that you may encounter ambivalence and be prepared to offer reassurance to those around you.

When it all began

Where our views of the world come from no one knows for sure. Most of the psychologists place it in our childhood. Oliver James argues that the greatest influence is between 0 and 3 years old. Others leave it slightly later.

John Bowlby, the psychologist who led the work on attachment theory (see below), said it is based on our experience with our caregivers. These are the people we look to for protection, comfort and support. From the way they respond to our needs we build up a picture of how the world of relationships works – a template which we then use to interpret new relationships. We start to make assumptions about what we can expect from others, and even what we deserve. And based on these expectations, from a very early age we develop strategies and ways of responding to other people.

Getting attached

Why do some of us keep moving on, at work, in love, from one country to the next, one profession to another? And others of us seem to have a firm base from which we go out and explore, and to which we confidently return.

The answer lies in security. In particular, how secure we feel in our relationships. Psychological research, called attachment theory, helps explain why.

Imagine you are in the playground and you observe four children.

The first is happily playing. He looks over at his father every now and then and occasionally goes over to show him something he's found. But most of the time he's playing away, welcoming other boys and girls to his game when they're interested but not too bothered when they get distracted and leave.

The second is staying close to a woman, his mum or maybe a nanny or other carer. He is holding onto her hand and when a dog comes near he tries to hide behind her legs. When no one else is close he goes to play in the sandpit, but he doesn't go far and he keeps looking over to make sure that she's still there.

And then there's the third little boy. He's wondering around on the far side of the playground and when other children come close and try to play he pretty much ignores them. You're worried for a moment that he's been left alone and lost his parents until you hear a voice behind you shouting 'Freddie, where are you?'

Finally, there's a boy you can't make out what's going on. One moment he's like the second boy, clinging to

Lone Ranger?

his dad. The next moment he is like the third boy, wondering off on his own adventures seemingly oblivious to everyone else around him.

The first boy has secure relationships. The second is anxious about relationships. The third is relationship avoidant. And the fourth fearful.

These modes are based on desire for intimacy and desire for independence and are generally aligned with our 'ok' profile:

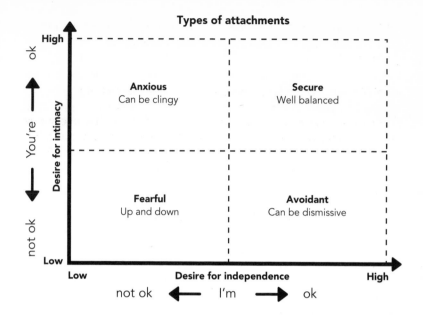

Types of attachments

The pattern in the playground continues throughout our adult life.

Know any single men just turned 40? There's a good chance they're 'avoidant'. Any single women approaching 40 who keep being chucked because they're too keen? Probably relationship 'anxious' and going out with men who are 'avoidant' (messy). It will be similar in the office. The woman in accounts who has been there forever and doubles as office mum is likely to be relationship 'anxious'. The woman who everyone wants as a mentor but who is too busy with clients to take them all on could well be relationship secure. And the woman who everyone thinks is tough and rarely comes out for office socials: probably avoidant.

What are you? Your position in the ok corral earlier is a good guide.
• I'm ok / you're ok = secure
• I'm ok / you're not ok = avoidant
• I'm not ok / you're ok = anxious
• I'm not ok / you're not ok = fearful

If that doesn't seem to work for you, look at the pattern of relationships in your life, or at least one area of your life (eg, family or love or clients). Are these characterised by intimacy, eg, do old clients still invite you out, are you close to your brothers or sisters?

And how independent are you? Do you flourish when you're left to your own devices and resent being given advice?

Once we realise where we are it's a lot easier to appreciate that it's us, not them. With that insight we're well on the way. If you're not secure but want to be then look at what's holding you back and think about how to change it, starting with how to become more 'I'm ok, you're ok'.

This is a big step and it will involve taking risks that are going to feel uncomfortable. Avoidant people will find it hard to commit to someone and stick with them especially when times are tough (which, inevitably, they will be). Anxious people will find it difficult to stay away and just get on with things regardless of the people around them (at least for now). This is difficult but necessary if we're going to build relationships that last. The trick is to take one small step at a time.

Enough about me

The 'I'm ok / you're ok' mindsets and the matching attachment theory (secure, anxious, avoidant and fearful) help us see how we think about relationships. This means that we can choose to think differently in order to have better, longer lasting relationships. And they are helpful in another way too.

The models also explain other people's behaviour and so give us important clues about how we should treat them if we want to get on with them. For tips on how to spot the styles of your clients, boss, mother, lover or ex-best friend, and what to do about it, sign up at The Mind Gym online using your free personal membership number on the inside cover of this book.

And finally, from Woody Allen for those who are still thinking 'it's them not me' . . .

'Doctor, my brother thinks he's a chicken.'
'Well bring him in to see me.'
'I would, but we need the eggs.'

I SPY Think of a category of people you know, eg, colleagues, clients, friends from college, suppliers. Write down everyone you know in this category (don't miss anyone significant out) putting them into one of the three columns:

People I think are great	People I think are ok	People I don't rate

Look at which columns are longest.

(a) Consider the strengths of the people in the second and third column (maybe even write them down) and see how many you can honestly shift to the left.

(b) Looking at those in the second and third columns, what do you think they are in terms of 'I'm ok / you're ok'? Does that help you think about them differently (eg, maybe they're being slightly aggressive because they have a 'you're not ok' outlook)?

Those with a 'you're ok' attitude are likely to have the longest lists in the first two columns, ideally with the first being the longest of all. See what you can do in terms of your perceptions to build longer lists on the left.

TRY The next time you catch yourself slipping into a negative 'I'm ok/ you're not ok' response – stop. Think like an actor and ask yourself 'What's my motivation at this precise moment? What judgements am I making about the other person?' You may find yourself surprised by what's behind your actions and spot that you are actually contributing to the problem. Now ask yourself what you can do to move out of the negative position.

(B) Check your impulse

Like most subjects, the ancient Greeks had plenty to say about self-control. But the Homer who can really teach us about managing our emotions and thoughts is not the poet of classical times, but the beer-guzzling, doughnut-dunking guy with the big yellow head: Homer Simpson.

Homer appeals to us so much because there is a little part of us which is Homer Simpson, with his bumbling inability to forgo temptation, to eat whatever is close at hand, and to marry cocktail waitresses in Las Vegas. Ok, perhaps not the last one, but you get the drift. In fact, this similarity between Homer Simpson and many of us led George Bush senior to say, 'We need a nation closer to the Waltons than to the Simpsons.'

What Homer lacks is familiar to all of us – the ability to exert control over our responses, to pursue specific goals and live up to specific standards. And this can deeply affect our relationships. We see or hear something we don't like and we respond in a way that exacerbates the situation. We agree to do the washing up or stop the spending sprees, but a favourite TV programme or fantastic pair of shoes get in the way. We intend to be loyal and faithful and yet find ourselves gossiping or double-crossing.

In all these cases, the extra glass of wine, the chocolate éclair begging to be eaten or even the attractive old flame contacted through Friends Reunited, self-control is often the difference between success and failure. This chapter looks at the benefits of self-control, what makes it so hard and ways we can enhance our own ability to control ourselves.

Where's the fun in that?

'I generally avoid temptation, unless I can't resist it,' quipped Mae West, which may explain why she had such a turbulent love life: two husbands, one a secret and one she refused to share a bedroom with, and quite a few other lovers besides.

If only for self-regulation

A high-flying senior manager, who was being coached at The Mind Gym, talked about his relationship with a peer, 'when he says certain things I go from 0 to 60 in an instant. I want to ring his f***ing neck'. He went on to explain that he had got into fierce arguments with this colleague whom he felt was being completely unreasonable and positively obstructive. The peer may well be aggressive and provocative but that's irrelevant. For this particular senior manager, his inability to self-regulate was getting in the way of his career. Unless he could change he wasn't going to make it to the top.

There are plenty of psychology experiments that show how self-regulation lies at the heart of great relationships, not just those at work but in all parts of our lives. For example:

- high levels of self-regulation are linked to successful relationships and less conflict.
- leaders at work who are skilled in self-control are rated as more trustworthy, fair and consistent by their employees.
- the biggest difference in profitability of partners in a management consultancy was their ability to self-regulate.
- children who self-regulate successfully are more popular with their peers.
- skilled self-regulators are also less likely to engage in anti-social behaviour. They're more resistant to addictions and eating disorders.

Lots of benefits. How do we get them?

Do you walk the line?

Find out how fit your self-regulation muscle is by choosing the most accurate option for each of the following questions:

---

1 You promised to look after your friend's flat. Then you are invited away for the weekend. You:

A Give the plants a thorough watering and pack your bags.
B Find someone else to mind the flat.
C Regretfully decline. You've made a commitment.

---

2 You exercise:

A Rarely
B Occasionally
C Regularly

---

3 You're preparing a presentation for tomorrow morning. Then a friend you haven't seen in ages rings to say they'll be in town for the night. You:

A Go out. You can wing it tomorrow.
B Sketch out some ideas on the presentation and then head out. You'll miss some of the fun, but you will be partly prepared.
C Stay in. You'd rather forgo the good times and do a first-rate job.

---

4 You've put yourself on a diet and are having dinner at a friend's house. They offer you a delicious pudding that's strictly forbidden. You say 'no' but they insist. Do you:

A Cave in quickly – after all it would be rude to refuse.
B Hold out for a while, and then say you'll have a small one. Compromise is the best option here.
C Politely stand your ground. A 'no' is a 'no'.

---

5 You have been married for one year. Then an old flame invites you out for a drink. You:

A Can't wait. You are already out the door.
B Aren't sure. Well, maybe a chat over a coffee would be ok.
C Say no.

---

6 You prefer:

A Excitement
B A balance
C Routine

---

7 A work colleague snaps at you. You:

A Snap back.
B Bite your tongue, but feel angry for the rest of the day.
C Ask them if there is something they would like to talk about.

8 You prefer to do things:

A On the spur of the moment
B With a general direction
C Only after careful consideration

9 You receive some very upsetting news on your way to work. For the rest of the day you:

A Are a mess. You spend the day surrounded by consoling workmates.
B Generally have it under control, but feel quietly upset.
C Carry on, business as usual.

10 You prefer the saying:

A The only way to get rid of temptation is to yield to it. (Oscar Wilde)
B What makes resisting temptation difficult is that you don't want to discourage it completely. (Franklin P. Jones)
C If passion drives you let reason hold the reigns. (Benjamin Franklin)

Now add up your total.
As = 0
Bs = 1
Cs = 2

0–6: Footloose

You can resist everything but temptation. For you, tomorrow can take care of itself. The only difficulty with living in the here and now is the morning after. And no matter how quickly you move, rash decisions have a way of catching up. As charming as your impetuous behaviour may be, it is bound to cause some problems in your relationships. From saying things in the heat of the moment, to letting friends down when a better offer comes along – charm will only get you so far.

7–14: Step forward

We all have our foibles. And while you are generally very good at resisting temptation, there can be certain offers you find hard to refuse. So while you aren't exactly a model of self-restraint, you aren't completely out of control either. You just let yourself go off the rails once in a while. How these moments of weakness impact on your relationships depends on the nature and degree of your crimes. If flirtatiousness is your frailty, then your romantic relationships will likely suffer. And your relationships at work won't be helped if flexible deadlines become your habit.

15–21: Feet on the ground

You are in control of your appetites and wants. Not the reverse. Because you can hold your desires, needs and impulses in check you tend to be effective in achieving whatever you set out to do. Not only are people with high self-control generally happier, more successful and healthier – they also tend to enjoy more satisfying relationships, experience less conflict and have better family cohesion. The drawbacks? None supported by evidence. It seems that, like intelligence, with self-control the positive payouts just keep on coming. Just don't start giving into your whims and fancies now. Strength in self-control can be maintained only with continuous vigilance.

Flood warning

In serious conflicts, or if we have short tempers, we can feel overwhelmed both emotionally and physically, which is called flooding.

In this state we may feel righteous indignation ('I don't have to put up with this') or like innocent victims ('He's picking on me, again'). Our body is in a state of distress: pounding heart, sweating, taking shorter and shorter breaths, and either lots of movement or going statue-still. When our heart rate exceeds 100 beats per minute we won't be able to take in what anyone else is saying, no matter how hard we try.

When we're in this state the first thing to do is stop whatever is going on, otherwise we'll explode. Find an excuse and take a break, which should last at least 20 minutes.

To return to a more relaxed state we may listen to music, walk the dog, or think of something completely different – preferably soothing and calm. Equally importantly, we need to avoid letting our mind return to the argument and rethinking all the righteous indignation or innocent-victim views we had a few moments earlier.

Only once the physical and emotional state has passed should we return to the other person, either to explain what has happened or to renew the conversation in a different, more controlled way. The first thing to do when the flooding starts is get out. Only when it's over should we come back to repair the damage.

1. Mr Muscle

The remarkably good news about self-regulation is that it is like a muscle: if we build it in one area of our life it will be stronger in all other areas too.

This is very rare. For example, if we build our reaction speed playing 'grand theft auto' it won't make any difference to our reaction speed when we're driving to the supermarket. Solving top level Su Doku will have no discernible impact on our ability to add up the cost of what's in our basket. And hours spent devoted to Tetris won't help you one jot when it comes to working out how to make best use of the space in the cupboards when you get home.

Most mental exercises (sometimes called brain training) are like that – the gains are specific to the domain in which the skill is learnt.

Self-regulation is a glorious exception. It can be developed and improved in one area and then used in every other. Exercise makes it stronger and practise will make us more skilled at using it. Like a muscle it can also be exhausted – a fact that supermarket designers know only too well. Take a young child shopping and see how many times you can resist 'please can we have this' before you finally give way. That's why sweets are by the checkout.

World champion athletes and meditating gurus are models of self-regulation. It can take a lifetime to reach this state and most who try never get there. And most of us won't even try.

What we can do is create our own less life-consuming regime for building self-regulation. Here are a few suggestions.

Starter class

1 Sit up straight at your desk whenever you remember.
2 Postpone your first cup of coffee or tea by an extra 15 mins every day.
3 When you're on the train or bus, for 5 minutes concentrate on a single thing – whether it be a word in an advertisment or a mark on the floor.
4 Keep a record of everything you eat for a week.
5 Sit quietly and do nothing for an hour at lunch or in the evening (not with your partner, unless you've agreed to first)

Intermediate

1 Give up something that is bad for you that you enjoy, eg, caffeine, white sugar, saturated fats. If giving it up completely is too hard, restrict it to the weekends only.
2 Take up something that requires dedication and regular attention, eg, learning to touch type, working out in the gym and stick to your regime.

Gorge on self-control

3 Stop snacking – eat only at meal times.
4 Change the way you breathe so that your diaphragm rises and falls as opposed to your chest.
5 Sit stationary without moving a single muscle for 15 minutes (another one for the bus).

Advanced class

1 Take up meditation.
2 Spend 30 minutes reflecting on a single word.
3 Write a daily blog of at least 200 words. The self-regulation involves keeping it going without missing a day.
4 Run a marathon.
5 Get out of bed on the first bleep of the alarm clock.

Stop slouching

Three groups of research participants were assigned three different self-regulation tasks for two weeks.

Check your impulse

One group were asked to improve their posture as often as they remembered to do so. The second made consistent attempts to improve their mood, turning gloomy emotions into good ones whenever possible. The third kept a food diary for two weeks – not altering their eating habits, but simply recording intake.

At the end of the week all three groups were better at self-regulating. And not just with the task they had worked on. They had improved their self-regulation skills overall.

2. Jam tomorrow

Toddlers have no understanding of self-regulation. They will scream and scream until their needs are met or they are convincingly distracted: 'Look the garden's all dark and there's no one out there (because it's 3 am) but maybe there are some stars. Let's take a look.'

We improve as we get older based on our experience. If our parent promises a reward for self-control and delivers, we improve our self-regulation. But if they don't deliver, even when we've kept our side of the bargain, we learn that it's not in our interest to control ourselves. Our childhood experiences have a big impact on how well we self-regulate in later life and for some of us this means we have to do some serious unlearning.

One way we can strengthen our ability to delay gratification is by imagining the consequences of our actions, the jam tomorrow.

When my computer freezes and I feel like smashing it to pieces, I hold myself back by thinking about (a) having to pick up the pieces (b) buying a new computer (c) confessing that I lost my temper with a machine (d) realising that I will never, ever recover those documents (e) all of the above.

This may happen in an instant of a moment but it is enough to make me self-regulate.

The trick lies in setting up a mental trip wire so that just as we're about to lose it, we fast forward in our mind to an hour or a week later and imagine the consequences – best to imagine the very worst consequences. And, hopefully, this will be enough to hold us back.

So next time you're about to shout at your loved one, 'you bleedin' idiot' think about the silence at the kitchen table that evening and the cold shoulder in bed afterwards.

Why something has to give

Sometimes when we work hard at resisting temptation in one area, we lose control in another. This has led some psychologists to believe that all efforts at self-control may involve the same underlying mechanism. This could explain why dieting can make you short-tempered and coping with stress can lead you to start smoking again.

This theory was tested in an experiment where participants signed up for what they thought was a study on taste perception. When they arrived they were seated in front of a table stacked with two types of food. One was a plate of chocolate chip cookies, decorated with chocolate candies. The other was a stack of white and red radishes.

Half of the participants were assigned the radishes, the other the cookies. They were then asked to work on a difficult puzzle. Unbeknownst to them, the puzzle was unsolvable. Those who had to eat radishes instead of the cookies subsequently quit faster on the puzzles than those who did not.

It seems that at any given moment, the more effort you put in resisting temptation in one area, the less will you have left to cope in another. Which is another good reason for getting going on building the self-regulation muscle now, ready for a testing day.

---

3. Silver lining

We can't feel our way into thinking differently but we can think our way into changing how we feel.

In an experiment, the first group of people were given no instructions and left to respond normally to a series of photographs. The second group was encouraged to attach alternative, positive interpretations to the scenes (to 'reframe' their responses). The experimenters then measured their emotional reactions.

For example, one of the photographs showed a woman weeping at a funeral. Rather than responding with the thought 'that's so sad', the viewers in the second group were asked to consider a positive response – 'weeping is a natural and healthy part of the grieving process'. The results showed that, when they thought differently, the subjects also felt differently.

If, at the critical moment, we think of a positive alternative explanation, we can stop the bad feelings taking over and may even transform them into positive emotions. The reason our partner is shouting at us is not because they are angry or blaming us but because they are frightened, confused and don't know what to do. In fact, they're probably asking for help.

This can be really hard, particularly when we're going through a rough time in a relationship. But it's worth persisting. The research shows that people who deliberately focus on the positive element in a situation, not only end up happier but also find it much easier to self-regulate.

The ironic processes of mental control

Ever started to worry you can't fall asleep and then found getting to sleep harder still? Or tried deliberately not to think of the colour red? Doesn't work, does it? That's because of what pschologists call the 'ironic processes of mental control'. When we try and suppress something our brain responds in two ways. First, it starts monitoring for the unwanted thought (Am I still awake? Am I thinking of the colour red?). Then it suppresses the thought if it starts to emerge.

The ironic bit comes in the fact that the monitoring process makes the thought far more accessible. So in fact you think more about being awake or seeing red, than you would do otherwise. Many a dieter has spotted this flaw: trying to banish food from your mind because you know you can't have any, makes it fill your every waking thought. And, of course, poor old Basil Fawlty when he continuously reminds himself 'Don't mention the war', finds he can do very little else.

We can avoid the ironic process by resolving to do something rather than to not do something. Simply replace negative resolutions with positive ones to ensure much better self-regulation success.

Instead of:	Try:
I must not smoke.	I want fit healthy lungs.
I must not eat chocolate.	I want balanced blood sugar.
I must not email that old flame on Friends Reunited.	I want to stay married.
I must not drink so much.	I love waking up feeling energetic.

4. Talk to the page

A group of recently enrolled students were spilt into two groups. One group were asked to write about how they were finding life at college. The others were told to write about unrelated topics. Both groups wrote for three consecutive days. At the end of the study results showed that those students who wrote about their thoughts and feelings subsequently got better grades. They also turned up at the health centre less often.

As well as stimulating self-expression, by giving greater attention to their emotions the students gained insights about the casual connections behind everyday events and what they could do about them.

Subsequent studies have also shown that letting it all hang out on the page can make us more self-aware and better self-regulators.

A partnership of unequals

The experimental evidence suggests that it is the combined level of self-control in a relationship that predicts the longevity of a partnership. So, if at least one of you has the will of steel, there might be enough for both of you to flourish together.

5. Vivid intentions

Two groups of students were to write an essay. The first group were asked to think in advance about where and when they were going to do the essay. The second group were just left to get on with it. The results were pretty unequivocal: 75% of the students who considered where and when they'd do the task completed their essay – as opposed to 33% of the others.

So how does this work? Peter Gollwitzer, a psychologist researching self-regulation, suggests that by creating implementation intentions (vividly imagining what I'll do in a situation I can anticipate happening) we make the task easier for ourselves. Our actions are more automatic and therefore they require less energy. We also have less need to self-regulate as we've already decided what we're going to do.

Tom, a workout participant, told how he spotted a pattern in his dealings with the union representatives at work. He felt passionately about equitable pay and so when the union representatives asked for more than he thought was fair, he would become defensive and the discussions would end badly. Before the next meeting he took some time to reflect and create the implementation intention: 'When the trade union representatives bring up pay, I will listen and respond calmly.' Very simple. And it worked.

Think about something that you have been putting off. Now imagine in detail where, when and how you will do it. The more detail the better: the exact time of day, where you're sitting, what will have just happened, how you're likely to be feeling. When the time comes, take the action you envisaged (and see how accurate your prediction was).

6. Stop digging

If you have a problem with booze, don't hang out in bars.

Think back to the screaming baby who needs distracting. This technique is the same, only for adults. Spot where and when you most frequently lose it and avoid these situations.

One couple who found that their evening discussions repeatedly spiralled into arguments, imposed a watershed on their conversations. No serious stuff after 9 pm. It worked a treat.

Where does all the anger go?

When the red mist descends, or the aroma of the donut shop wafts our way, it takes a lot of effort to resist. Even when we succeed we may still feel pent-up emotions. The ideal option is metaphorically to throw them to the wind, imagine them being cast away to some foreign land. The creative version of 'so what?'

If that doesn't work, try strong physical exercise. It's hard to feel anything other than exhaustion after a punishing run. Or go for an indulgent distraction on TV or at the cinema.

Chatting with friends in similar situations also helps normalise the situation – 'So your husband only calls once a day when he's away at a conference; yes, I worry too.'

And we can still get angry. Self-control gives us a window of opportunity in which to weigh the options. For example, 'I think the best way to get the builder to finish the job is to show him how angry I am' vs. 'Getting angry won't get him to work any harder, instead I need to agree a project plan'. Whichever way the decision goes – whether we go crazy or go organised – at least we know we're acting out of choice, rather than simply caving into cravings.

There's more than one way to self-regulate

Remember the manager who went from 0–60 faster than a Ferrari? He combined several techniques to overcome his anger.

First, he worked on spotting the triggers, ie, what were the kinds of things that his colleague said that turned him red. Secondly, he explored all the different ways that he could respond. He came up with 20 or 30 (ask questions, explore criteria for a successful outcome, etc), rather than the two he had imagined (capitulate, argue). Then he decided on his implementation intentions, ie, what he would do when his colleague next produced the red rag. And finally, he explored all the positive reasons why his colleague was behaving in this way: maybe he felt left out (the colleague was based in the US and the rest of the team in the UK), maybe he was worried that his career had hit a dead end, maybe he was having a tough time at home, and so on. In fact a long list of reasons why the best response was to listen, empathise and explore rather than to attack back.

The result: a restored relationship and a promotion.

PY Think about someone you admire, or someone who's reached the top of their game. Whether it's a celebrity, a great leader, or your mum, consider the times they may have delayed gratification to get where they are.

Sports heroes are well-documented self-regulators. Jonny Wilkinson famously returned to the field after a match when he had missed a kick, and kept practising until it was dark. Paula Radcliffe, Tiger Woods, Rafael Nadal indeed almost any top performing athlete will have exceptional self-regulation.

When you read interviews or biographies look out for examples of self-restraint. They aren't always apparent (because they aren't especially compelling) but if you read between the lines, you'll find them.

RY Practise self-control one small step at a time.

For one week think about the amount of water you drink. Every time you reach for the diet coke or a juice, take a pause and pour a glass of water instead.

When the crowded bus zooms past without stopping, walk to the next stop thinking about how the exercise is doing you good. And if you're feeling super-generous, at least the people on board will get to their destination sooner.

After a week you'll be on your way to a ballerina's posture and the patience of a fully hydrated Zen master. Persist and you will build an all powerful self-regulation muscle. The relationship benefits will be immense.

(C) Cool to be kind

In the 1992 film *White Men Can't Jump*, Woody Harrelson plays Billy, a basketball player. We join him in bed with his girlfriend, Gloria (Rosie Perez), where the conversation goes something like this:

Gloria: Honey? My mouth is dry. Honey, I'm thirsty.

Billy: There you go honey. (He hands her a glass of water.)

Gloria: When I said I was thirsty, it doesn't mean I want a glass of water.

Billy: It doesn't?

Gloria: You're missing the whole point of me saying I'm thirsty. If I have a problem, you're not supposed to solve it. Men always make the mistake of thinking they can solve a woman's problem. It makes them feel omnipotent.

Billy: Omnipotent? Did you have a bad dream?

Gloria: It's a way of controlling a woman.

Billy: Bringing them a glass of water?

Gloria: Yes. See, if I'm thirsty I don't want a glass of water. I want you to sympathise. I want you to say, Gloria, I too know what it feels like to be thirsty. I too have had a dry mouth. I want you to connect with me through sharing and understanding the concept of dry-mouthedness.

Poor old Billy. He may be a hot shot on the basketball court, but when it comes to the art of empathy, he's a real rookie.

A boy named 'empathy'

The gender stereotypes suggest that girls are good at empathy and boys are not. There is precious little scientific evidence to support this. The truth is that regardless of our gender, most of us would have much stronger relationships if we made empathy into a regular habit.

The challenge is that we naturally see things from our perspective. And then we stop. And so we respond to other people as if we were in their shoes, rather than to them as individuals with very different needs, wants and footwear.

Kinder with fiction

Novel thinking

The more fiction a person reads, the more empathy they have and the better they perform on tests of social understanding and awareness. By contrast, reading more non-fiction, fact-based books shows the opposite association.

In a study conducted by Raymond Mar and colleagues, the more novels adults read, the higher they scored on measures of social awareness and tests of empathy – for example, being able to recognise a person's emotions from a picture showing their eyes only, or being able to take another person's perspective.

I'm right

Psychologists use the term 'myside bias' to describe what happens when we get irrationally attached to our own point of view and so fail to see things from anyone else's perspective.

If I believe that Maya is usually late for work, I will notice when she's even a minute late and yet not notice or bother when Frank, who I rate for his punctuality, is half an hour late because he has been caught on a delayed train (poor fellow).

I will give extra weight to information that supports my view (called 'confirming evidence') and ignore or dismiss any facts that might contradict my stance. The thing is that we all know people who do this (your dad? Mine too) but most of us don't realise how much we do it ourselves. Usually hundreds of times every day.

In an experiment, a group of Democrats and a group of Republicans were shown the same videos of George W. Bush and John Kerry (the Democratic presidential candidate at the time). In both cases the party leaders were telling some questionable truths based on information given to the groups. Each group found the leader of their party much more honest and easier to defend and the other side's leader far more dishonest.

Each to their own

You have a view too?

The first step to empathy is to recognise that my view isn't the only one or even necessarily the right one. Maybe there isn't a 'right' view. For the sake of building strong relationships, it may be your view, however misguided, that matters most.

And so before I start saying or doing whatever springs to mind, I would do well to imagine what you're thinking and how you're feeling just now.

Which is easier said than done.

Meta-mirror on the wall

The meta-mirror was developed in 1988 by Robert Dilts as a way of getting inside someone else's head and so seeing a situation more objectively.

The meta-mirror works by getting us to observe what's going on from three different perspectives, rather like the film *Vantage Point* or a range of novels from Wilkie Collins' *Moonstone* to Julian Barnes' *Talking It Over* and Ian Pears' *An Instance of the the Fingerpost*.

The three perspectives or perceptual positions are:
1. Our own
2. The other person's
3. That of an objective observer

Using the meta-mirror we shift our camera position to give ourselves different views on the same situation. We even mimic the other person's physical behaviour (do they slouch, or stride, or simper) to help imagine we are them and so see the situation as they would.

 This is how it works (an audio version is available at The Mind Gym online when you sign up using your free personal password on the inside cover of this book).

First off, make yourself comfortable and relax. Breathe in through your nose deeply right into your stomach and then slowly out again through your mouth, counting slowly to 10 while you do so. Repeat this twice more.

Now think of someone you want to empathise with and the situation you're both in together. Ideally choose a real episode or, failing that, one that is likely to take place. Work through the following three stages in turn.

1. Enter the 'me' zone.
In this first phase of the meta-mirror we explore our own view of the world. It's time to indulge and also to probe.

Imagine the situation and picture the other person there with you.

What do you see? What can you hear? What can you feel? Any smells? Imagine that each of your senses is super sensitive (you have a bionic eye, bionic ear, etc), what else do you see and hear? Immerse yourself in this situation.

Now describe what you are doing. Are you shouting or listening? What's your body posture? What are you saying?

At this moment, what are you, honestly, thinking and feeling about their behaviour? And about them as a person? And what would you most like to say or do to them?

And what do you think the other person is thinking and feeling about you?

Pause with this set of thoughts.

2. Step into their shoes
Now you are going to look at the world through the other person's eyes.

Imagine you're Robert De Niro preparing for a part.

Think about the physical characteristics of this person: how do they cross their arms? How do they walk? How do they sit in a chair? With what speed, volume and tone do they speak? Do they suck their bottom lip or play with their nails or have any other physical characteristics? Think about their attitudes and the language they use to express them.

Stand the way the other person stands; walk the way they walk; sit the way they sit; breathe as they breathe. Take on as much of their physical personality as you can.

Now play the episode again from the start but this time 'in character'. Keeping as close as you can to the other person's physicality, notice how you react to the situation. Explore the feelings, intentions and hopes that you experience. Notice the tactics that you use. Ask yourself these questions:

What do you see? What can you hear?

Someone else's shoes

Now describe what you are doing. And how you are feeling.

What do you notice about the other person (ie, the person who is 'you' in the real world)?

At this moment, what are you thinking and feeling about their behaviour? And about them as a person? And what would you most like to say or do to them?

And what do you think the other person is thinking and feeling about you?

Pause with this set of thoughts and, if it helps, write them down.

3. Adopt the 'wise observer' position
In phase three, we become an impartial and wise observer.

In order to do this we imagine ourselves as an independent, concerned, and very intelligent fly on the wall who has seen a million scenes just like this and given wise advice on many occasions on how to increase understanding and empathy. In this role, replay the scenario in your head so that you can see and hear both parties as if you were standing next to them. Then answer the following questions:

Based on what you are seeing, what is each person thinking? And feeling?

What advice would you give the person from phase one (that's the real you) in order to understand the other person better?

What would you advise them to say or do differently in order to show greater empathy and build a stronger relationship?

4. Back to you
Now we step back into our own shoes. Take a look over the answers and see what insights there are about how the other person is feeling. How can you use these to understand them better and build a stronger connection?

Thinking yourself smart

You can't just become cleverer by thinking that you're cleverer. Or can you?

Two psychologists went to a football match. They behaved very well until they found themselves surrounded by a crowd of football hooligans. Shortly afterwards, one of the psychologists saw a beer can on the floor and kicked it as hard as he could. Slightly embarrassed, the psychologists started to wonder what had prompted this out-of-character behaviour.

So, as psychologists do, they set up an experiment to test whether, if we are primed in a particular way, our thinking and behaviour will change.

In this experiment, one group of people were asked to imagine that they were university professors. First, they wrote a list of all the attributes they associated with being a professor: clever, expert, highly respected for their intellect. Then they were asked to imagine that these attributes applied to them. A second group was asked to imagine that they were football hooligans (the list went along the lines of: stupid, lazy, bored, angry).

They were then asked 60 general knowledge questions taken from Trivial Pursuit. Having taken into account general intelligence levels, the group that scored themselves as 'professors' outperformed the 'hooligans' by a very significant 92% to 71%.

It appears that simply by shifting our perspective we can make ourselves more intelligent.

Mirror, Mirror

A recent neuroscience study has offered hope to couch potatoes everywhere. It appears that a type of brain cell called 'mirror neurons' respond in the same way whether we perform an action ourselves, or witness that same action being performed by someone else.

Neuroscientist Christian Keysers and his colleagues examined 'tactile empathy' or, how we experience the feeling of someone being touched. The researchers observed that the same area of the brain was activated whether participants were actually being touched or simply looking at a picture of someone being touched in the same spot.

Research into the mirror neuron has important implications for our understanding of empathy as it begins to explain how we can instinctively understand other people's actions and thoughts.

Cool to be kind

It's good to limit the myside bias and even better to see things from the other person's perspective but the real dividends come when we demonstrate kindness.

Kindness pays double
The good news about kindness is that it pays a double benefit. There are obvious benefits for the receiver but, as the science shows, there are significant gains for the giver as well.

Research from a leading psychologist at Stanford University showed that performing random acts of kindness increases the level of positive emotion the giver feels. The study asked people to do five acts of kindness. It didn't have to be to the same person or the same thing – they could choose whatever they wanted. One group had to spread their kind acts over the course of a week, the other group was given the challenge of doing all five kind acts in a single day. Whilst both groups reported a significant uplift in how they felt, those people who had to do the five kind things on a single day recorded the greatest increase. So, if you're going to be kind save it up for a single day of the week and really confuse your colleagues.

How kind
Most of us would describe ourselves as being kind when the opportunity presents itself. By this we mean that if we're asked for help or to do something considerate, we would generally do so. This is a passive kindness – base camp.

The next level is random acts of kindness to strangers, say offering our seat to a pregnant woman on the train or helping someone carry their suitcase down the stairs. Here we spot the need and proactively respond. A great gesture and the right thing to do. However there is more to kindness than helping old ladies across the road.

Joann Jones recalls this lesson in kindness. 'During my second year of nursing school our professor gave us a quiz. I breezed through the questions until I read the last one: "What is the first name of the woman who cleans the school?" Surely this was a joke. I had seen the cleaning woman several times, but how would I know her name? I handed in my paper, leaving the last question blank. Before the class ended, one student asked if the last question would count toward our grade. "Absolutely," the professor said. "In your careers, you will meet many people. All are significant. They deserve your attention and care, even if all you do is smile and say hello." I've never forgotten that lesson. I also learned her name was Dorothy.'

Your colleague comes in elated as they've won a big contract. Do you caution against over-celebrating, after all it's a complicated deal that is going to be hard to deliver? Or do you feel a twinge of envy, you're going to have to work even harder to look good? Or do you take some of the credit, as the proposal was a carbon copy of one you'd done before? The kind response is what psychologists call active-constructive. Here, we support, take an interest and share in the good feelings. There'll be plenty of time later for friendly warnings.

The next stage is getting into the habit of being kind. In the experiment where people decided to do five random acts of kindness on a particular day each week, they described a funny thing happening. They say that they became much more aware of kindness and started to make adjustments to being kinder on the other days of the week too.

The same idea sits behind a very powerful concept in helping people to act safely at work and at home: active caring. This encourages people to focus not on what's wrong – most organisations report accidents – and instead concentrate on caring for someone. This could be anything from setting a ladder straight, mopping up some water on the canteen floor, or reminding a colleague to put their seat belt on. The shift away from looking at what's not quite right to looking for opportunities to care for others seems to make a big difference. Safety compliance in a manufacturing plant that introduced active care went from 68% to 78%.

Being romantic is a form of active care. For your anniversary you plan a trip round five places you went to when you were first dating. Or you create an album with memories of each month/year you've been together. Equally, there are everyday delights, bringing home her favourite cheese or filling his car up with petrol, that are small but symbolic signs of actively caring.

'Today I bent the truth to be kind, and I have no regret, for I am far surer of what is kind than I am of what is true.' Robert Brault

Meanwhile back in the bedroom.

So, now we've got the idea of empathy, let's replay that conversation between Billy and Gloria, after Billy has adopted these ideas.

Gloria: I'm thirsty.

Billy: I hear what you say, honey. It's so hard to get to sleep when you're thirsty. Being thirsty is the worst. What can I do?

Gloria: Nothing, don't worry. I just need to get some water. Want some?

Billy: Thanks, honey.

Gloria: There you go.

Billy: Thanks [drinks]. Ohh, that feels good, doesn't it?

Gloria: Sure does. [Pause] Honey?

Billy: What baby?

Gloria: Come here. [fade to black]

Obviously it doesn't make for nearly such an edgy scene. But sometime edgy's not what you're after.

(D) Shy to shine

Fifty per cent of people describe themselves as lacking in social confidence and a whopping 98% of us say we've felt shy at some time or another. Its good to know that in this crowded room we're not alone.

Most of us who are shy actually appear perfectly confident in social situations, which is why we don't spot all those other shy people, any more than they spot us. We are 'shy extraverts' or 'privately shy'. Shyness is our little secret.

Many public figures are shy extraverts, well known for their public ease and private reticence. Actors and comedians are famed for it. Julie Allen, who played alongside John Belushi in the movie *Animal House*, spoke of her surprise when the famous hellraiser turned out to be shy and vulnerable:

'Rather than being a confident established star, he seemed nervous about meeting everyone, about fitting in.'

Surprisingly, many politicians are cripplingly shy too. Keith Joseph, who was Margaret Thatcher's Secretary of State for Education and closest advisor, would often be physically sick before giving a speech.

Brad Pitt is also reported to be shy, as are Victoria Wood, Tom Hanks, Michelle Pfeiffer and David Letterman. Ella Fitzgerald was shy, so was Alec Guiness.

It seems that it's one thing to function well in a highly structured environment, while playing a prescribed role or delivering a prepared speech, but quite another to feel confident in a less controlled or more intimate situation. In social environments where there aren't any rules, or where it's not obvious what behaviour is expected, these high-functioning shy people often struggle.

To cover their anxiety, many of the privately shy have learned how to fake it. And so convincing is their socially relaxed shtick that even those close to them might not suspect what they are really feeling. When it all gets too much they often protest that they're 'tired', to explain why they are not being outgoing and funny. Inside, though, their confidence has abandoned them.

Shades of shy

'No one can make you feel inferior without your consent', Eleanor Roosevelt

So what do we really mean when we use the word 'shy'? It's a term that gets applied to a whole range of social anxieties; from the mild apprehensiveness we feel when we walk into a room full of strangers, to the crippling self-consciousness that can seriously disadvantage those who suffer from it. If we're going to address our shyness, it helps to have a more precise understanding of what kind of shyness we're suffering from.

The research has identified three types of shyness: 'situational' (it only occurs in certain, specific situations) 'transitional' (it kicks in at a time of change, and then passes when we get comfortable) and 'pervasive' (it's a pretty permanent feature in our life).

1. Not now

Situational shyness has a nasty habit of showing up at exactly the wrong time.

Dan's been hit by a migraine and he can't make the pitch presentation. You thought you were just there to answer questions but now you've got ten minutes to get up to speed before the very

You can run...

valuable and notoriously tricky potential client arrives. As you walk through the door you're told that his boss is there too, a high-profile big hitter who, you can't help noticing, is also drop-dead gorgeous.

Sweating yet?

You'd need nerves of steel not to feel a twinge of anxiety in this nightmare scenario. It contains many of the common situations that press our shyness buttons: having to perform in front of a group, having to think on our feet, needing to impress someone in authority, knowing that others are depending on our performance, wanting to dazzle someone extremely cute. Even if we're normally outgoing we are likely find ourselves struggling in situations like these.

Gerry, a confident lawyer with a good line in witty conversation, admitted that his situational shyness was prompted by girlfriends' mothers. He was always terrified he would make a bad impression. And so, when one day his new girlfriend's mother showed up unannounced, he panicked and made a dash for the bathroom. Minutes later he heard the bathroom door open. His girlfriend's mother had arrived to use the loo, only to find a strange man crouching fully clothed in the bath. On this occasion he was right, he didn't make a good impression.

Whether it's meeting new people in a bar, the room going silent just as we're about to tell a risky joke or mum turning up at work (or Sports Day), most of us have situations that turn us shy.

How to beat it

1. Change the rules
The first step is to spot exactly where and when this happens. Does your confidence collapse every time you make a presentation, or just when you present to your boss? Do you clam up in front of every stranger you meet or just the attractive ones? Get specific.

Next, picture yourself in the precise situation and notice the thoughts that come into your head. They're probably critical and negative: 'I'll look like an idiot', 'I'll bore them to death'. Now look for conflicting evidence.

The client reviewing your pitch wants to appoint the right people to do the project. If they are looking critical or asking tough questions it's only because they want to make the right decision. They may be worried that they could look stupid later, but they are very unlikely to want to make you look foolish.

Convert the negative assumptions into positive ones and the shyness will evaporate. And if that doesn't work, minimise their importance – they're just people.

2. Recognise shyness in others
It's not just me. Pretty much everyone at this party knows only a few people and they're almost certainly feeling just as shy as I am. Yes, there is that guy who is chatting and laughing with everyone, but there's also those two girls who look like they're hiding in the corner and that bloke in the sharp suit who's all by himself. I'll go and see if he's all right.

3. Look at similar situations where you weren't shy
When the facilitator in a training course announces, 'Now we're going to do a role play' many or us just want to curl up into a ball and disappear. Yet we may be happy holding forth in the pub or putting on a show at our daughter's fifth birthday party. And if you can keep the attention of a group of 5 year olds, you have nothing to fear from a collection of middle-aged executives.

Many of us get shy in the presence of greatness, or the corporate substitute, seniority (the two are, of course, quite different but in respect to shyness they can have much the same effect). Think of all the impressive/senior people you've met. Pick out one with whom you didn't feel especially shy. What was different?

Think about how you felt and what you did: spoke slower, stood up straight; saw them as an interesting person more than an important one; liked them. See what attitudes and behaviours you can borrow from the time it worked and apply to those situations where the shyness is still creeping in.

> **Do you come here often?**
>
> The psychologist Albert Ellis, dubbed 'the grandfather of Cognitive Behavioural Therapy' was painfully shy around women in his youth. In an attempt to get over his fear of failure, he visited the Bronx Botanical Garden every day for a month. He sat on a bench and spoke to every woman he saw. His 130 attempts at conversation did not lead to true love. But that wasn't the point. He proved to himself that rejection, though unpleasant, was not unbearable. There was no need to 'awfulise' it. 'Nobody vomited and ran away, ' he wrote. 'Nobody called the cops.'

2. I've mislaid my mojo

First day at school, starting a new job, arriving in a new country, after a divorce: transitional shyness grabs us during times of change.

Our confidence plummets and we feel like we're floundering. Faced with a barrage of new experiences, new people and unfamiliar situations, we lose our bearings. We feel and act shy.

This kind of bashfulness is a common response to insecure or unpredictable situations. But what to do?

How to beat it

1. It's just a phase
Recognise that this is simply a transitional stage. It's going to pass – keep telling yourself that even in the darkest moments. It won't feel like it until afterwards. But once you've got your mojo back it will be hard to recall that it ever went away.

2. Count the benefits
Your lack of assertiveness in this new environment may make it easier for others to approach you (far better than being overwhelming and scaring the life out of them). You'll be reflective rather than impulsive, so less likely to get off on the wrong foot. Holding back and staying low key will give you a chance to watch

and analyse the new situation so you'll get a better understanding of your place in it.

Transitional shyness is essentially a safety mechanism, giving us time to acclimatise until we've got the measure of the situation – as the saying goes, only fools rush in.

3. I'm shy

Do you describe yourself as 'a shy person'? Individuals who see their shyness as part of their personality – rather than something that comes over them now and again – are described as having pervasive shyness. If that sounds like you then you probably feel anxious in most social situations and you don't see that changing any time soon. After all, you've felt shy for as long as you can remember. You consider your shyness to be part of who you are – even if others don't see you that way. Indeed, you may consider yourself to be the shyest person you know.

How to beat it
First of all, ask if you want to beat it. Some of us are happily shy – it makes us a good listener, an astute observer of social situations, a tactful friend, an insightful colleague. It may give you room to breathe and space to think. It can feel good being the power behind the scene.

There are plenty of self-proclaimed shy people who have achieved great success – what's to worry about.

If, however, you don't feel quite like that, don't despair. There's plenty we can do to alleviate the effects of shyness.

1. Conversation card
To pre-empt anxious conversations: prepare.

Bob Monkhouse had his own book of jokes that he would keep adding to and borrowing from. No wonder he lasted 20 years in showbiz.

Why not create a series of conversation cards: interesting facts, stories, anecdotes, adventures or whatever else appeals? Have a read before you go out and update with new gems when you get back home. If someone tells you a particularly good tale, well, it could have happened to you.

2. People like me

If your shyness makes you feel isolated, find people who share a passion. Volunteering for social projects is a low risk way of meeting people who will be warm, welcoming and keen to talk about the work they're doing. This will also help us feel we belong and get rid of feelings of difference or isolation.

3. Accept the discomfort

Actors who are starting out in their training, carry out an exercise to desensitise themselves to the audience's gaze. An actor is instructed to sit at the front of the room and do nothing. The rest of the group then stares at her in silence. They stare and stare. And then they stare some more. After what probably feels like an eternity of extreme discomfort, the actor suddenly begins to relax. They have broken through the pain barrier, faced the demon and found it to be harmless.

The discomfort is part of the journey through personality shyness.

If we're nervous with strangers then it pays to strike up a conversation with someone we're not likely to see again: the supermarket checkout person, the taxi driver, someone else who's been waiting for ages at the bus stop. If we hate walking into groups of people then we should make it clear when accepting an invitation that we can only stay for a limited time. When there, we should set ourselves a challenge, say to talk to four people, then leave.

How did it go? Usually the fear is far greater than the reality. This should make it easier next time.

Why so shy?

Some of us know we're shy but we're not quite sure why. Discovering the cause helps us take the right kind of remedial action.

So, if you think you're shy and want to know the root cause, answer the following questionnaire, giving each of the four options in each question a score on a scale between 1 and 5, where 1= not at all the case, and 5=absolutely true. There is an electronic version of this at The Mind Gym online with more comprehensive explanations for your profile. It also saves having to do the maths. See inside cover for your free password and details for how to join.

I am at ease when:

A I know what is expected of me
B I'm just having a casual chat
C I'm with someone who is happy to dominate the conversation
D No one is looking

At a dinner party I am likely to:

A Ask the host how I can help and spend half the night in the kitchen
B Deflect the conversation on to others by asking lots of questions
C Rely on everyone else to keep the conversation going
D Worry about whether I am making a good impression

I am unnerved by:

A Having to think on my feet
B Being asked questions that are too personal
C Witty banter
D An audience

When in conversation with others I tend to:

A Stick to topics I know
B Keep the conversation light
C Not know what to say
D Wonder what they are thinking about me

My great strengths are:

A Being fully prepared
B Independence
C Modesty
D Spotting when somethings wrong

The trait I least like in others is:

A Inconsistency
B Being intrusive
C Impatience
D Judging people

Others probably don't know that I:

A Am not as confident as I appear
B Feel nervous about letting people get too close to me
C Want to be outgoing, but find it hard to express myself
D Am always worried about making a fool of myself

I am likely to think:

A I need to get a grip on the situation
B Don't stand so close to me
C Still waters run deep
D If only . . .

Others are likely to describe me as:

A Controlling
B Guarded
C Timid
D Distracted

What keeps me awake at night?

A Not feeling ready for tomorrow
B Having spoken too freely earlier today
C All the things I should have said but didn't
D Something I did that was really embarrassing

Total up

Add up your total score for each letter:

A [   ]   B [   ]   C [   ]   D [   ]

A > 35: Need control

People who score high on As have probably found a niche for themselves. They have one or two clearly defined roles, whether it is as schoolteacher or solicitor, as Milly's mummy or a magistrate. When they're in those roles, other people experience them as being confident, collected and convivial. This is because they're in control.

But, like the forceful boss who doesn't know where to put himself at the golf club drinks, when they move outside their comfort zone, they're unsure how to behave and how to relate to people around them. In ambiguous or unstructured situations they often feel riddled with angst, anxiety and apprehension.

Best advice is to take some risks and not care too much about the consequences. Go fly a kite or something you've never done before and don't worry if you're no good at it; let someone else do something that you would normally do yourself; have some fun.

B > 35: Lack of trust

People who scored high on Bs tend to keep their distance. At the heart of this shyness is a lack of trust born from a fear of being hurt if they let others get too close. They are more likely than the other groups to have experienced rejection, neglect or bullying, and so their shyness becomes a shelter, allowing them to avoid exposing themselves or risking the fallout from unhappy relationships.

Some life experiences cast a long shadow. That, in turn, means we don't give ourselves the chance to challenge old assumptions.

The best motto is: that was then, this is now.

Try telling close friends more about yourself; show them how you feel, reveal personal foibles, share the odd secret. No need to go overboard, just one small revelation at a time, so if they do let you down it doesn't really matter. Personal disclosure will not only help the shyness fall off, it will also endear you to people who felt they didn't know you before.

C > 35: Tongue tied

Inhibition is at the root of this shyness.

Those of us who score high in Cs tend to believe that other people are quick to judge us and that their judgements are often unfair and incorrect. As a result, we feel that things go wrong when people see us so it's safer to be invisible and keep out of the limelight.

This may be because we're trying to hide something (eg, our sexual preference, our geekiness, our ignorance or lack of intellect), or because we deliberately put forward an external persona that is different from our 'real' self (eg, I want people to think I'm rebellious but actually I'm really conventional). Or it may be simply that we find it hard to express ourselves (we are witty but we get flustered easily and so it comes out all wrong).

We will probably have a small group of friends and colleagues who appreciate us despite our inhibitions but the shyness comes on when we have to talk with people we don't know well. This is immensely frustrating as we'd like to be seen and appreciated for who we are.

Best advice: remember that other people's judgements say more about them than they do about you. One person's gullible is another's trusting, ditto caring/pushover, honest/insensitive, flexible/unpredictable and so on. Be true to yourself and others will learn to get to know you. Worry not if they don't get there first time, they usually will in due course. And if they don't what are the consequences? Not much.

The alternative is a lifetime of being misunderstood.

D > 35: My fault
Self-criticism fuels this shyness.

If I have a high score for D then I've probably got a commentary in my head telling me about all the things that I'm doing wrong: you shouldn't have used her nickname, that joke was a bit off colour, you sounded really old and out-of-date when you said that, you should have opened the door for him, and on, and on. Blah, blah. It's a load of nonsense but still it comes.

One snip too far

We spend much of the time either worrying that we're going to do or say something inappropriate or reflecting back on what we think we did that was embarrassing. And because we're so critical of ourselves, we assume others are just as critical of us when, in truth, they almost certainly haven't noticed (they're much too busy thinking about whether they're doing the right thing).

Best advice: quieten the inner critic by concentrating on what is going on outside your head. This may be the conversation, the specific words the other person is using, the way their lips move or anything else that is actually happening. Our minds can't focus externally and internally at the same time. Ask a question. Give a compliment. Talk about the weather. Listen to the sound of their voice. Anything that distracts you from the inner critic.

> ### So what if I'm nuts?
>
> Albert Ellis prescribed 'shame attacking' experiences to his shy patients. In one exercise he would ask them to walk up to a random person on the street and say: 'I just got out of the loony bin, what year is it?' The aim was to learn not to feel ashamed 'when they look at you like you're off your rocker, which they think you are'.

At the heart of shyness is fear. Fear of looking stupid, getting it wrong, being misjudged and so on. And so the cure for shyness lies in losing the fear. This may be by realising that most other people are feeling the same, or by worrying less what others think (and realising that most of them aren't thinking about us at all), or by deciding that mistakes don't really matter, they're just a part of learning.

Most of us will never lose our shyness completely, which is no bad thing. Modesty is a virtue. But we can start to lose the debilitating elements one emboldening step at a time.

I SPY Look out for other people's shyness: when do they look away or go quiet? Because we usually notice people who want to be noticed, we miss the shy ones. However, once we start looking out for shy people we'll see them everywhere, being slightly awkward, or quiet, or avoiding situations where they may have to perform in public. Can you spot the 50% of your colleagues and friends who lack social confidence? Go and have a chat with them. They'll appreciate it.

I TRY Pick a situation in which you wish you could be less shy. Try the following five steps.

1. Imagine what it would be like if you felt confident: what would you do, say, how would you move, what would your posture be like? Take on the posture and voice of you being confident.

2. Imagine what the other person or people might be thinking

(a) about themselves (b) about the situation, the subject or (c) about anything else that may be on their mind, eg, the impact of the cost of energy or what their teenage son screamed at them as they left the house.

3. Prepare what you might say. Practise saying it out loud as many times as you can face. Verbalising ideas helps spot which ones come across well and which are best kept to ourselves.

4. When you're with the other person, concentrate on what they're saying. If you feel yourself get distracted, focus on their lips, their eyes, the tone of their voice or even their scent, if you're that close.

5. Assume the best. It's easy to imagine that the other person is bored when in fact they're thinking deeply about what we're saying, or laughing at us when they're laughing with us.

Coming together

The arts, science and business are full of examples of successful pairings: Gilbert and George, Crick and Watson, Lennon and McCartney, Ben and Jerry, and, of course, Sooty and Sweep.

This section deals with how to get and stay connected with people who matter to us.

We start with E – Are you listening? Discover that there's more to being a great listener than you'll have heard. The magic formula for great connections is to be interested and interesting, and so to F – Charm school, for those of us who could do with a charisma boost. G – Bid for attention, reveals how by looking after the small, everyday stuff we transform our chances of relationship prosperity. Finally, H – Trust me, unveils the secrets to building trust and keeping it.

For those who are interested in not just the power of attraction but also how to keep it going, this is the section for you.

$\textcircled{E}$ **Are you listening?**

'At a friend's birthday I was sat next to this woman I knew but didn't like much. In order to make the evening more entertaining, I thought I'd play a game,' explains a friend of The Mind Gym.

'Given that she is very talkative I decided to see if I could last the whole evening without actually saying a word. Nodding, smiling, noises like "ah-ha", "mmm-hmm", "ohh" were allowed but nothing you could find in a dictionary.

'At this dinner no one turned to the person on their other side and so I was stuck with this woman for almost three hours. And during those three hours I didn't say a single word. I was rather impressed that I'd managed to keep it up (and enjoyed the evening a whole lot more as a result).

'But the biggest surprise was still to come. As my dinner companion got up to leave, she kissed me on both cheeks and announced: "It was lovely sitting next to you. I'd forgotten quite how interesting you are."'

The amazing power of listening: it doesn't just make other people feel good – it can make us seem more interesting too.

Most people enjoy talking and being listened to more than listening and being talked to, which is why, for example, the more successful corporate conferences leave plenty of opportunity for discussion in small groups.

One behaviour that improves our relationship enormously, is listening. So, if it's so beneficial, what can we do to reap the rewards?

Was that a yes?

I hear you

Recent research suggests the 'back-channel responses' we make while others are speaking (nodding, saying yes, ah-ha, mmmm etc) may mean different things to different people, particularly people of a different gender. Apparently men tend to perceive these responses as signalling agreement, whereas women see them as indicating that the other person is involved with what they are saying. This could explain why women frequently complain that men don't seem to be listening to them – whereas men are bemused by women who appear to be agreeing with them, but turn out to be thinking quite the opposite.

The art of listening

'A good listener is usually thinking of something else,' quipped the American playwright Kin Hubbard. He might have added, a great listener is thinking of nothing else.

The first of four tenets:

1. Focus
Our mind finds it easy to head off course, thinking about what we are going to say, or forming an opinion on the other person's opinion, or wondering what's causing that humming sound, is it a hum or more of a buzz. I bet it's the air conditioning.

The hardest and most vital part of great listening is to concentrate.

Alas, there aren't many short cuts – if we try hard we will succeed and if we're lazy, relying on the speaker to keep us entertained, most of the time we won't. Unless we live in a sitcom.

Here are a few techniques to help:

- Red hot people. Not so much hot totty as people that wind us up before they even start, so we are already thinking 'I wonder what rubbish they're going to come out with now'.

  'In my monthly reviews with my manager I would just switch off and ignore the drivel she would spew out,' explained a Mind Gym member. I believed that she was determined to find fault whatever, so there was no point in listening. On further probing about his manager's motivation, he accepted that she might be providing some useful advice in amongst the criticism. He then set himself the challenge of digging out the nuggets, which required listening acutely. Unsurprisingly, the relationship started to improve after this.

  It's easy to block people out because they've disappointed or annoyed us before. But a mistake. There's usually something to glean if we're willing to give them our attention.

- Write it down. Taking notes keeps us focused on the content, just as long as we don't get so engrossed in our scribbling that we stop paying attention and start doodling instead (a rather visible sign that we're not listening). The problem with note taking is that it breaks eye contact so whilst a few notes are a glorious and quite flattering thing, taking quasi-dictation will deaden the connection and lower our status.

- Lose the other stuff. The row with your partner, the analysis that has to be in by end of day, the boss's fury, the overdraft. All matter but none of them matter now. Park them and come back after this conversation is over.

- Re-wire the hot buttons. 'But' (as in this work is good but...), 'You don't understand', 'I know about this because...' are just a few of the phrases that tend to turn off our listening switch and turn on our argument preparation mode. Psychologists call it a 'click-whirr' when a word or phrase casues our mind to move from one state to another without us noticing.

Imagine that these phrases are like the names on door bells, with wiring directly to our brain. For each hot phrase, imagine unscrewing the buzzer and mentally cutting the wires on these words and then replacing the bell. So next time the button is pressed nothing happens and we carry on listening as before.

- Allow distractions to come and go without paying them too much attention. Don't get annoyed with yourself if you get distracted, just notice it has happened and focus on what you were doing before.

2. Facts
This is the moment to take on the mantle of Columbo, Morse, Holmes, Miss Marple or DI Tennyson. The challenge with pure listening is to keep to the facts, constantly seeking out more information and so deferring judgement.

Once we can tell the difference between what's actually happening (the objective behaviour) and what we are thinking about what's happening (our interpretations) we're ready. I observe reality when I say that James uses eye contact when we talk. I am interpreting my experience when I say James is very thoughtful and intense in conversation. Pure listening demands masses of observation and collecting facts before making any assumptions.

In responses it plays to stay in neutral. Try replacing the words 'right' and 'wrong' with the phrase, 'works for me because...' or 'doesn't work for me because...' As in 'the idea of hot-desking in the office doesn't work for me because...' This way we invite further discussion rather than closing down the conversation by judging an idea as bad.

Talk less, sell more

Twelve of Kodak's top salespeople were asked to identify five accounts in which they were not making sales because, in their judgement, the customer had no needs to which they or their company could add value.

Sales coach Neil Rackham observed them on a typical call with these clients and discovered that on average the calls

---

were only 15 minutes long and focused on sharing the latest products Kodak had added since their last catch-up call.

When asked about why they didn't spend more time in understanding the customer, the salespeople would reply along the lines of: there was no point because there was no opportunity to make a sale.

Rackham's team then asked them quite deliberately not to mention a single Kodak product and just spend the whole call investing time asking questions to understand customer's issues, problems and needs. To their surprise, in over half of the accounts the salespeople found new needs that neither they nor their customer had suspected. Even better, these calls ultimately led to over $1m of new business.

3. Questions

Architect: What do you want for your living area?
Client: I'd like it to be open plan.
Architect: All of it?
Client: Yes. Except for the study which needs to be separate so I can work in peace.
Architect: To what extent have you thought about the effect of kitchen smells on soft furnishings?
Client: Not much. That's a good point.
Architect: If there was a cost effective way to keep the smells out, would you be interested?
Client: I suppose I would.

Carry on questioning. Make sure you've heard what was said. Then dig for more information. This is the route to full understanding of the facts. There is a faintly irritating management mantra that goes: 'assume' makes an 'ass' out of 'u' and 'me'. Questions are the way to turn an ass into a thoroughbred.

Best to start with open questions (where there are a range of options), then use clarifying questions (to check understanding) and hypothetical questions (to help the other person to think through the implications of what they're saying). This is the pattern used by the architect above.

Fixed-option questions (is your favourite colour red, green or yellow?) are risky as they invite another option (actually none of those, it's lilac). The respondent may feel less understood because we haven't included their option, or, worse, that we're trying to force them to think like us (who would dream of such a thing?).

Even riskier are closed questions, where the answer is Yes/No, unless we're trying to pin them down. Beware: they're also the easiest to ask. Know what I mean?

Why do patients sue doctors?

The reason why patients sue their doctor is not because they haven't got better, or the accuracy of the doctor's diagnosis, or their track record with patient mortality, or the type of illness that they specialise in. Although the patient doing the suing might imagine it is any one (or all) of these.

A study by medical researchers in the US revealed that the most accurate way to predict whether a doctor would be sued was nothing to do with their medical skills – it was how much time they spent with their patients. The results were unequivocal: those doctors who had never been sued were also the ones who spent longest with their patients. On average they spent three minutes more than their colleagues who had been sued. The extra time meant that patients felt they were listened to and given attention, rather than simply being 'processed'. As a result they felt more satisfied and less likely to find fault with their treatment, however faulty that treatment might be.

---

4. The unsaid
There's more than words to what people say.

- It's easy to be put off by the messenger. They may not look the part but this doesn't mean that what they say isn't just as valuable. Blind auditions for orchestras produce surprising results – more slight, female brass players, for example. The reason is that conductors assume that great brass players need to have big lungs and so have an unconscious (we presume) preference for large men.

It's easy to dismiss them for their prejudice, however, there are many experiments that show how we all do this every day. Our challenge is to listen to what they say without judging the content regardless of how the messenger, looks, dresses or slouches.

- Listen between the lines.

  Try changing the way you say 'this is a great report' to mean each of the following:
  – This report really is great.
  – This report is far from great.
  – This particular report is great, in contrast to most reports.
  – This would be great as a report but would make a lousy presentation.
  – I am delighted that this is a great report.
  – I am sad/annoyed/frustrated that this is a great report.
  – This report may be great but I don't really care.

  And so on.

  When we listen to the tone and look out for the body language, we learn far more.

  In a test when the instructor says a single word (eg, 'maybe', 'thanks', 'terrible') with different para-language (tone, timbre, rhythm, volume) and body language, it was found that the impact on the audience was 7% for the word, 38% for the para-language and 55% for body language. As words becomes sentences, paragraphs and speeches, the influence of the words grows relative to the others. Nevertheless, the non-verbal elements still play an important role.

- Spot the shadow meanings. Wealthy, well off, rich, prosperous, financially secure, loaded, rolling in it, affluent – on the surface all mean the same thing but the implications are decidedly different. As well as their usual definition, they have 'shadow meanings', or nuances that reveal more about what the speaker is saying.

- What's missing? The undermining of politicians from their own side often comes by what is left unsaid. When in 2008 Foreign Secretary David Miliband wrote an article about the need to renew the Labour Government's message it was widely interpreted as an attack on Prime Minister Gordon Brown. Nothing in the article suggested this. The conclusion was because of what wasn't said: Mr Brown wasn't mentioned by name in the article.

It's harder to spot what the other person didn't say or left out, but this can be where we find the crucial clues.

Is your listening filtered?

Pure listening is at the core of good listening, but it isn't the whole story. When we listen we often use filters, which can be extremely helpful or extremely damaging, depending on which ones we use and when. To spot your natural filter, complete this short questionnaire, choosing the most accurate option for each question.

1 Your partner has a breakfast meeting and oversleeps. They say: 'I'll never make it in time.' You say:

A It is ridiculous to set a meeting so early.
B What a start to the day.
C How can you be sure you won't make it?
D What will it take to get there on time?

2 Your friend's house sale falls through for a second time. They say: 'Why does this always happen to me?' You say:

A Unlucky.
B You must feel utterly frustrated.
C How does twice become always?
D How can you avoid having this happen again?

3 Your greatest strength is:

A Enthusiasm
B Empathy
C Honesty
D Problem-solving

4 Your colleague gets passed over for promotion again. They say: 'I think the boss doesn't like me.' You say:

A How unfair of them to put personal preference over professional capability.
B I can understand how upset that must make you feel.
C What evidence do you have that your boss doesn't like you?
D How are you going to raise your profile so you don't get passed over again?

5 **Your friend asks someone out and is turned down. They say: 'I am such a loser.' You say:**

A They don't know what they are missing.
B You sound really disappointed.
C How does one rejection make you a loser?
D Is there anyone else you fancy?

6 **Others are more likely to describe you as:**

A Loyal
B Understanding
C Realistic
D Helpful

7 **Your friend has been looking for a job for months without success. They say 'I will never find work.' You say:**

A The job market is impossible.
B You must feel thoroughly frustrated.
C How is your pessimism going to help you find the right job?
D What's your next move?

8 **Your friend says: 'I really must lose some weight.' You say:**

A You are perfect as you are.
B You seem down on yourself.
C Why must you?
D How do you plan to go about it?

9 **A close colleague tells you their new manager is exceptionally rude. You say:**

A I know what you mean.
B Sounds like you aren't too keen on them.
C They have just started. Have you given them a chance?
D How are you going to cope?

10 A good friend:

A Is a personal cheerleader.
B Always a shoulder to cry on to.
C Tells you the facts.
D Helps you solve problems.

What is your total for each letter?

A [   ]   B [   ]   C [   ]   D [   ]

Mainly As: Generous listener
A: I'm not going to be able to hit the deadline.

B: Oh my goodness, what a nightmare, poor you.

I see

The ideal best friend. You are on their side, supportive, listening, agreeing and finding the most positive interpretation for whatever they say. You make plenty of sympathetic statements (and soothing noises) that validate their point of view. You don't challenge, as your priority is to make them feel cared for and valued.

As a result, people tend to like you and see you as loyal. They are inclined to share things with you, confident that you will be a helpful ally.

The research suggests, however, that we are less attracted to those who see us in a wholly flattering light. While people do look for sympathy that is in line with their positive self-image, they also seek unfavourable feedback that is consistent with their more negative views of themselves.

There is further evidence that couples feel more committed to one another, and friends share higher regard, when they see each other as they see themselves, rather than the rose-tinted version.

How to be a good generous listener:

- Pick out the pieces of what they've said that you can agree with, and tell them that you do.
- Find a positive explanation for what they've said and offer it.
- If necessary re-interpret what they've said making it more favourable.

A Mind Gym member recalled admitting over a family lunch that she'd once tried horse meat on a trip abroad. Her brother replied, 'I think that anyone who's eaten horse meat should be shot.' The generous listener in her responded, 'I agree that it's very important that we treat animals with care.'

Good to use when the other person is:

- More powerful than you
- Angry or in a seriously bad mood
- Feels unfairly judged by others
- Distressed
- Trying to get a rise out of you

Watch out for:

- Over-use, or you will lose their respect
- Being seen as all things to all people/two-faced

Mainly Bs: Empathetic listener
A: I'm not going to be able to hit the deadline.
B: I can see that you're very worried about this.

The perfect counsellor. You want to understand what is going on at an emotional level and to help the other person express how they feel.

By encouraging people to open up you build trust and deepen your relationships. As you rarely take a judgemental stance, others feel that they can share what they are experiencing at that moment, whether fear, anger, confusion or pride. They often come away from conversations with you feeling acknowledged and understood.

While this is a particularly good approach in the heat of the moment – to allow others to let off steam or express disappointments – it tends to be more helpful in dealing with the consequences, rather than the causes, of problems.

How to be a good empathetic listener:

- Repeat what you've heard using slightly different words, to show you've understood.
- Ask open questions: What happened next? How do you feel about this?
- Nod and mirror expressions.
- Give broad and largely vague views rather than specific recommendations.

'In my office there's someone everyone goes to when they've got a problem, like an office mum only he's a bloke,' explained a Mind

Gym participant. He almost certainly does a lot of empathetic listening.

Good to use when the other person is:

- Emotional (teary, angry, sad, exasperated or anything else that is out of the ordinary for them).
- Unable to express what they're feeling/caught up in themselves.
- Feeling that no one understands them.

Watch out for:

- Using this filter alone, it will calm the waters but won't help change the the current.
- Misreading the other person's emotions, which could make things worse (I'm not angry, I'm scared). Questions are safer.
- Being deceived – are the waterworks coming out to distract you from the facts?

Mainly Cs: The critical listener

A: I'm not going to be able to hit the deadline.
B: If you knew this, why didn't you tell someone before?

As critic you're looking for flaws, you question the details, you're challenging, discriminating and sometimes you're downright picky. But often with good reason. Think of a barrister, or a discerning shopper – they need to know they've got all the facts, so they're looking for contradictions and gaps in the argument.

This means that when others leap to illogical conclusions, make mountains out of molehills or swing from one extreme to another, you cut to the chase. As a sensible friend, you aren't one to indulge in drama. You stick to the facts by highlighting distorted, faulty or irrational thoughts.

For those of our friends whose unhelpful thinking increases their stress and anxiety (or chances of getting anything done), this approach is particularly beneficial. And for those trying to hoodwink, they're not going to get past you.

Do be gentle in your approach. This type of listening can appear cold, impatient or unkind. If you overplay your hand, you may end up right but alone.

How to be a good critical listener:

- Keep asking questions until you are completely clear what they're saying, and so are they.
- Then ask hypothetical questions to test that they've thought through the implications of what they're saying.
- Look for inconsistencies and, when you spot something that doesn't seem to fit, ask for an explanation.
- Keep calm. If you seem aggressive then emotion is likely to cloud their response as well as your thinking.

'I had a friend who asked me if I could get them a job here," explained a Mind Gym member who worked in a small business. "I suspected that he was desperate for any job and that working here wouldn't have suited them, or us. Rather than say this outright, I asked him a series of direct questions about what he really wanted, what he thought he was good at and what he thought a job here would be like. It became clear to him that he wouldn't get what he wanted here and he ended up thanking me very much for the advice even though I hadn't recommended anything, just asked questions.'

Good to use when the other person is:

- Trying to convince or sell you something.
- Confused or confusing.
- Less important than getting the right result.

Watch out for:

- Coming across as not listening because you seem to be on the attack.
- Exhausting the other person.
- Damaging the relationship.

Mainly Ds: The solution-focused listener
A: I'm not going to be able to hit the deadline.
B: How can you re-organise your other priorities in order to deliver on this project?

You'd make a great inventor, or project manager. You're eager to keep things moving forward. You're inquiring and questioning but always positive and focused towards a solution.

As a solution-focused listener you concentrate on how to solve a problem, rather than its effects or the circumstances that led up to it. Not one to dwell on difficulties or to fret about feelings, you would rather get on with whatever needs to be done to make things better. Cool in a crisis, others can count on you to get them through the stickiest of situations.

While some are keen to wallow in self-pity, you are making course and setting sail. Be careful that you don't put them off with impossible goals; keep them small, specific and behavioural. Rather than 'be more confident' choose something concrete like 'to say something at the next staff meeting'.

How to be a good solution-focused listener:

- Ask questions along the lines of 'What would need to happen for this problem to be resolved?' or even, 'So what are you going to do?'
- Offer practical suggestions. If you're unsure of the reception, frame them as questions: 'What would happen if you tried...?'
- Don't be put off if your suggestions are rejected, but try to find out why the other person doesn't think they'd work. It will help hone your next bit of advice.
- Get the other person to be specific about what will be done and by when.

'I'm fed up with the fact that no one takes responsibility around here,' explained a newly appointed head of a local authority, 'so now each time someone comes to me with a problem I ask them what they're going to do about it. The first few times people resisted, saying it was someone else's department. I just kept asking the same question: so, what are you going to do about it? Eventually they got the message.'

Good to use when the other person is:

- Stuck in a rut and doesn't know what to do.
- Stopping you or the team from making progress.
- Being persistently negative or defeatist.
- Ducking responsibility.

Watch out for:

- Rushing to the solution before you've understood the problem.
- Ignoring how the other person is feeling, especially if they need to be part of the solution.
- Assuming the other person wants a solution rather than just to be heard.

Filter magic

Where listening often goes wrong is that we use the wrong filter. He suggests what to do whereas what she wants is a sympathetic ear. Sound familiar?

The very greatest listening comes by using the right filters in the right situation, like a light engineer who uses different filters to create just the right effect.

Your partner comes home exhausted and exasperated after a long and largely unproductive week. You might start with generous listening (they've been really unfair to you at the office, they just don't appreciate what they've got) or empathetic listening (you must be absolutely knackered, sit down and relax). Over supper, as they start to explain what's gone on, you might switch to pure listening (which client cancelled the contract? What reasons did they give? Are there other clients who have also cancelled?).

The next day, you're boiling the kettle and the work subject comes up again. You try critical listening (why is it that your clients are cancelling and no one else's?) before moving on to solution-focused listening (what can you learn from the most successful people in the team?).

The magic lies in your listening agility: knowing when to use pure listening and when to apply one of the filters.

What you need is a good listening to

Learning to listen can spark off a quiet revolution in our relationships. Once we turn our attention on to the other person we tend to find that relations start to improve. Low tech, calorie free, and as cheap as chips, good listening really is a miracle cure for many of our relationship woes.

SPY Listen out for the listening styles that different people adopt in different kinds of conversations. What would happen if they used another style?

TRY Choose someone close to you – someone you often find yourself in conflict with. Next time you meet them, deliberately use the generous listening technique.

(F) Charm school

'I remember being teased at school about being boring. It was devastating. I swore that it would never happen again.' So confessed one of The Mind Gym's most requested coaches. He quickly taught himself how to be interesting and has been much admired for his easy charm ever since.

Charisma is not something we're born with. It's something we learn. If you want to be the person everyone wants more of, welcome to 10 quick lessons at charm school.

Lesson one: Hope

The top 100 best-selling singles ever in UK are dominated by optimistic songs. No Bob Dylan or James Taylor. Instead 'She loves you' (The Beatles), 'You're the one that I want' (John Travolta and Olivia Newton John), 'Anything is possible' (Will Young), 'Love is all around' (Wet Wet Wet) all make it into the top 12. We want to feel that the future can be better and so sign up for songs, and people, who give us hope.

Optimists outperform pessimists in political elections, sales and social connections (for more on the power of optimism, see *The Mind Gym: wake your mind up*, chapter A, Lucky you) because hope tends to attract and absolute conviction attracts, well, almost absolutely.

'Smile and the world smiles with you', may not be in the top 100 but it is a sentiment that runs through the blood of most charismatic people. It's not that they don't have dark days, it's just that they don't advertise them.

Lesson two: Passion

When we show how much we care, our passion and commitment draws others in. It's hard to fake and so whether we are excited about saving the planet, getting to the top of the league, the latest fashion tips, freshwater fishing or fine art, it pays to talk about subjects we care about. I have to talk about something tedious, dig out an angle that matters to you.

One Mind Gym member was told to give a talk on a new performance management system at work, which he found deeply dull. So, instead, he talked about how he had helped his daughter to transform her grades at school, about which he felt extremely passionately, and only at the end showed how this linked to the new system.

In the sitcom *Only Fools and Horses* Del Boy was the typical lovable rogue – obsessed with a making a fast buck and possessed of an indefatigable optimism. No matter how dodgy his track record, people still signed up to his hare-brained schemes. They were swept along by his passion and enthusiasm. Rodney, his morose and cautious brother, tended to have the opposite effect.

When it comes to igniting interest, downbeat doesn't cut it. Passion trumps every time.

Lesson three: Connection

Entrainment occurs when we move together, in flow, as one. My movements match your movements, my rhythm is in sync with yours, we laugh together at the same volume, we use similar words, we even make hand gestures at the same time. We may experience this when we see an old friend and find ourselves finishing off each other's stories or guffawing at the same mad memories.

It's a lovely feeling when it happens naturally. Usually, however, we need to give it a nudge.

We do this by matching the other person in some of the following ways:

- Speaking at the same volume, pace, tempo, rhythm
- Reflecting similar body language, eg, legs crossed, gesticulating hands
- Sharing similar belief and values
- Making statements or giving views that the audience is sure to agree with.

We can tell when we've made a strong connection because, when we start to laugh, so does the other person, or when we sit up, so do they. Once we've got to this stage, we're ready to lead.

For more on connecting, see *The Mind Gym: wake your mind up*, chapter H.

Entraining a nation

Colonel Oliver North was accused of underhand skulduggery in the Iran–Contra affair, when the United States appeared to have been supporting terrorists in Nicaragua. He had been tried by the media for a year before the Congressional hearing and, in most people's eyes, it was not a question of whether he was guilty, just about how guilty. Yet he won round the nation and became, for many, a hero.

He did this by establishing entrainment with the people of America. He established entrainment by making statement after statement of incontrovertible truths. He started with 'My best friend is my wife Betsy, to whom I have been married for 19 years...' (and there she was looking loyal behind him) and continued on with his biography, 'I came to the National Security Council six years ago', and then to his recent experience, 'I would not be frank with you if I did not admit that the last several months have been difficult for me and my family.'

In each case, the audience had to agree that he was telling

---

the truth. He also made his very unusual experiences (being vilified in the media) sound like ones we could all connect with – difficult for me and my family (we've all had that feeling).

Lesson four: Concentration

With the hope, the passion and the connection, we should be fully involved in the conversation. It's certainly a bad sign if we start to bore ourselves. Equally, it's vital that every cell in our system is engaged in the topic of our choice.

Whether it's the tired salesman making the same pitch for the fifth time or the cheeky deceit from our nephew about what time he normally goes to bed, we tend to pick up inconsistencies between what is said and how it's said pretty quickly.

Congruence occurs when all the non-verbal signs are aligned with what is being said – think Norman Schwarzkopf, Jamie Oliver, Anita Roddick. The secret to congruence is:

• Concentrate on the conversation
• Speak about subjects we care about
• Believe in what we're saying
• Relax the body, enjoying the experience
• Maintain a low, natural breathing rate.

Lesson five: Impact words

The power of charismatic communication comes not in changing the way people think but in changing the way they feel. Whilst we can tickle them or ply them with caffeine, the safest and most powerful way to change how people feel is with words.

In general, charismatic language is dominated by three forms of words that tend to be absent in general conversation:

• Words that express emotion: upset, determined, excited, concerned, happy, passionate, nervous, thrilled.
• Words that evoke sounds, smells or other physical sensations: smack, blossom, clunk, grating, crash, whoop, chill.

- Descriptive words that are used to create a picture in the listener's mind: immense, slender, towering, shimmering.

Jimmy Carter and Ronald Reagan both held the office of US President. The former lasted one turbulent term. The latter was the first US President to serve two full terms since Dwight Eisenhower, thirty years earlier. He was also known as the great communicator. To see why, compare these two extracts taken from speeches made at the same reunion of past presidents.

To make the point, impact words and phrases are underlined.

Charm school professor

Ronald Reagan:
'No doubt many visitors will stand in the replica of my oval office. Perhaps they will <u>sense</u> a little of the <u>loneliness</u> that comes with decision-making on a global scale, or the <u>stabbing</u> pain inflicted by a terrorist bomb <u>half a world away</u>, or the <u>dreaded sound</u> of the telephone in the middle of the night with news of <u>hostile actions</u>. They will also feel some of the <u>immense pride</u> that comes to any president in that office as he comes into daily contact with <u>American heroes</u> whose <u>faith</u> in themselves, their mission, and their mandate is a <u>never ending source of emotional renewal</u>.'

Failed to graduate

Jimmy Carter:
'Let me point out that we still have some unanswered questions: how to provide good health care for all our people, homes for those who don't have a place to dwell, better education for our children. These are the kind of things that make a <u>common tie</u> among all us presidents who have served.

I would say parenthetically that one of the things that brings former presidents closest together is the extremely <u>onerous</u> and <u>burdensome</u> task of <u>begging</u> for enough money to build a presidential library from private sources, not from the government, and then turn it over to the federal government in perpetuity as a repository for the records of our great nation.'

Ronald Regan uses 10 impact words and phrases, Jimmy Carter, just four. No wonder he comprehensively outperformed Jimmy Carter. That said, Reagan also famously declared 'You can tell a lot about a fellow's character by the way he eats his jellybeans' though unfortunately he didn't tell us exactly what you could learn, or how.

In Britain, a number of well-known personalities grab our attention by the ears with their rich, colourful language. The politician, Boris Johnson, for example:

'The Lib Dems are not just empty. They are a void within a vacuum surrounded by a vast inanition.'

'He's lost the plot, people tell me. He's drifting rudderless in the wide Sargasso Sea of New Labour's ideological vacuum.'

And the writer Jeanette Winterson:

'Book collecting is an obsession, an occupation, a disease, an addiction, a fascination, an absurdity, a fate. It is not a hobby. Those who do it must do it. Those who do not do it think of it as a cousin of stamp collecting, a sister of the trophy cabinet, bastard of a sound bank account and a weak mind.'

And the rich description of comedian Russell Brand about what he puts in his hair:

'Mostly orphans' tears, old clock parts, lizards tails, spit, the concept of freedom; all up there, all shooshed up right nice and tight, like a bonfire that's never actually burned... it mutters follicular oddities into my mind.'

We might not want to get quite that fruity in a budget meeting or even on a second date, but there's no doubt that, from Cyrano de Bergerac to Will Smith's smooth-talking matchmaker in the movie *Hitch*, a way with words is definitely the way for strong heart to win fair maiden (or hunky bloke).

Choosing our words carefully has never been so resonant.

Lesson 6: Be generous

How was your weekend? Fine.

How was your weekend? I had to work.

How was your weekend? We went to the park, which was just at that perfect moment when the leaves are turning a tangy orange and the wind is cool enough to make you glad you've got a scarf. And we had a brisk invigorating walk, almost a stomp, and just as we were getting tired and almost back at the car we found this little tea shop we'd never noticed before with the best flapjacks I've ever eaten.

It's easy to imagine that the three responses above are from people who had different weekends but that isn't necessarily so. Many of us can reduce the gamut of emotions to 'fine' or 'ok'. The interesting person offers anything but. Instead they tend to be generous with their answer, sharing specifics about what happened, giving colour and flavour with incidental detail (tangy orange) and a degree of disclosure about how they felt.

Next time someone asks, 'how are you?', what will you say?

Just one look

Good looking

You've made your judgement about me faster than you can think, in a tenth of a second.

University students were asked to look at photographs of actors' faces for just 100 milliseconds then rate them for attractiveness, likeability, competence, trustworthiness, and aggressiveness. Another group of students were left to look at the photos for as long as they wished. The ratings for both groups were very similar, with the strongest correlation for trustworthiness. And the results stayed like this, even when the first group was given longer to look at the photos.

Before we walk into a room or stand up in front of an audience, it pays to think ourselves into the person we want to be. If you want to be trusted, remember all the trustworthy things you've done; if you want to be assertive, bring to mind all the times you've taken the lead. If it's your wisdom you want them to see, proudly remember all excellent decisions you've made. It feels good too.

Lesson 7: Remember when

Can you think of a time when you couldn't stop yourself smiling, when you were so happy that you were beaming joy and everyone could see it? When was that? What was going on?

Or can you think of a time when you had to make a very difficult decision, and it was really tricky, but you made a call and it was the right one? Can you remember what you considered? What made you finally know you'd done the right thing?

Or the time when you had a really delighted client who was over the moon with the work you'd done? What did they say? What had you done that so impressed them?

These are called elicitation questions because they are designed to elicit an emotion, usually a positive one. If you answered the questions, rather than skim reading them, then you would have brought back into your conscious mind a scene when you felt pretty good. As you recalled the scene, the chances are that you will have felt more positive, right here, right now as you're reading this book.

We can also use questions about the future to elicit emotions: what would happen on your perfect holiday? Who do you most admire? What do you enjoy most? What's your favourite food?

In a similar way, we can guide other people's feelings by referring to near-universal situations.

Do you remember the feeling of fear and excitement when you had stabilisers on your first bicycle and you were pedalling away and then you realised that no one was holding on to the back? That thrill as you discovered that were upright and straight and going forward and you were doing it all yourself. (Well, that's how I feel now, standing before you at this, our inaugural . . .)

What was the lead up to Christmas like in your house when you were a child? Do you remember opening up the last few days on the advent calendar and knowing that your parents had now bought the presents, that the destiny of what you'd get had been determined, but not knowing what they'd bought and really wanting to know and just wishing it wasn't still 21st and that the next few days would just rush by? (This is what we want our customers to feel when they realise that by buying a . . .)

Whether it's curiosity, pride, desire, hope or determination, stimulating memories is a reliable way to stimulate emotions. As feelings tend to lead thoughts, this is a powerful way to engage and entrain.

Lesson 8: Story time

When Barack Obama was running for the Democratic nomination he came under attack because of the fiery comments from his pastor, Rev Jeremiah Wright. His poll ratings were falling, his opponent Hillary Clinton had dismissed Obama's loyalty with 'I wouldn't have Wright as my pastor', and the campaign was in danger of losing momentum.

Top of the class

Senator Obama gave a remarkable speech that defused the issue, re-ignited his campaign and touched 85% of Americans. The speech is packed with examples of impact words, passion, hope (one of his books is called *The Audacity of Hope*) and universal experiences to create entrainment. He concludes his speech in the following way:

'There is one story in particular that I'd like to leave you with today – a story I told when I had the great honor of speaking on Dr King's birthday at his home church, Ebenezer Baptist, in Atlanta.

There is a young, twenty-three-year-old white woman named Ashley Baia who organized for our campaign in Florence, South Carolina. She had been working to organize a mostly African–American community since the beginning of this campaign, and one day she was at a roundtable discussion where everyone went around telling their story and why they were there.

And Ashley said that when she was nine years old, her mother got cancer. And because she had to miss days of work, she was let go and lost her health care. They had to file for bankruptcy, and thats when Ashley decided that she had to do something to help her mom.

She knew that food was one of their most expensive costs, and so Ashley convinced her mother that what she really liked and really wanted to eat more than anything else was mustard and relish sandwiches. Because that was the cheapest way to eat.

She did this for a year until her mom got better, and she told everyone at the roundtable that the reason she joined our campaign was so that she could help the millions of other children in the country who want and need to help their parents too.

Now Ashley might have made a different choice. Perhaps somebody told her along the way that the source of her mother's problems were blacks who were on welfare and too lazy to work, or Hispanics who were coming into the country illegally. But she didn't. She sought out allies in her fight against injustice.

Anyway, Ashley finishes her story and then goes around the room and asks everyone else why they're supporting the campaign. They all have different stories and reasons. Many bring up a specific issue. And finally they come to this elderly black man who's been sitting there quietly the entire time. And Ashley asks him why he's there. And he does not bring up a specific issue. He does not say health care or the economy. He does not say education or the war. He does not say that he was there because of Barack Obama. He simply says to everyone in the room, "I am here because of Ashley."

"I'm here because of Ashley." By itself, that single moment of recognition between that young white girl and that old black man is not enough. It is not enough to give health care to the sick, or jobs to the jobless, or education to our children.

But it is where we start. It is where our union grows stronger. And as so many generations have come to realize over the course of the 221 years since a band of patriots signed that document in Philadelphia, that is where the perfection begins.'

Two stories, one within another, beautifully told, that, entwined together, helped turn a nation. At the kernel is the story of Ashley saving her mother but around it is the story of the quiet, elderly black man.

It's often said that we all have a book in us. True or not, we all have plenty of stories to tell. The trouble is that often we don't tell them as stories. So, to get us going in the right direction, here are the four vital elements in any story.

1 A protagonist
This is the lead character, the hero.

During the story the protagonist goes on a journey. It may be a literal journey – as in *The Wizard of Oz* when Dorothy travels from Kansas to The Land of Oz. Or it could be a symbolic journey, which takes the protagonist to a new understanding, or teaches them something. (Having started out dissatisfied with her life in Kansas, the journey to Oz teaches Dorothy that 'There's no place like home'.)

In the case of Obama's stories, the protagonist is (a) Ashley (b) the black man (who remains nameless, playing in some ways the role of Everyman).

2 A predicament
To get a story going our protagonist needs to be faced with a challenging situation that forces them to take action or make a choice. Something that will get our audience wondering: 'What's going to happen next?' The more unpredictable the outcome, the more engrossed the audience will be.

Ashley's mother got cancer, lost her job and they had to file for bankruptcy. At the roundtable, they were discussing why they had signed up for the Obama campaign.

3 The narrative
This is where we show what happened and how. We add detail and emotion to enrich the story.

The writer E. M. Forster put it like this: 'The queen died; the king died. That's plot. The queen died, the king died of a broken heart – that's narrative.'

Ashley convinced her mother that she loved mustard and relish sandwiches. The elderly black man was 'sitting there quietly the entire time'.

4 Finally the outcome, the denouement, the resolution
Here we bring all the elements together in a way that resolves your protagonist's predicament and ends the journey. Ashley's mother survived and the old black man signed up because of Ashley – a tentative connection to build bonds across the racial divide.

In a world of business clichés and opinionated conversation it's easy to be bland and forgettable. If we want to be interesting we'd do well to pepper our conversation with stories.

Lesson 9: Surprise

In the movie *Dead Poets Society* Robin Williams gets attention by making a dramatic entrance. The first time he meets his new students, he enters the classroom, walks straight through it without saying a word, and exits by the door at the back of the room. The students are nonplussed, but intrigued. When, almost as an afterthought, he sticks his head back round the door and invites them to follow him, they do just that. They're hooked. That's entrainment in action.

Going beyond the obvious, suggesting and/or doing the unexpected is at the heart of entrainment.

Political fable has it that Russian leader Nikita Khrushchev took off his shoe and banged it on the table at the UN when irritated by a speech from the then British Prime Minister, Harold Macmillan.

Celebrity gossip reports that Johnny Depp, when asked by a journalist what he thought of the Iraq war, replied, 'Who cares? I'm just a f***king actor.'

In both cases these highly charismatic people captured attention by doing and saying something that no one had anticipated. Even Tom Cruise, leaping on to Oprah's sofa and bouncing up and down to declare his love of Katie Holmes – well, he got attention. Unconventional responses to familiar situations grab our attention and stay in our memory.

Lesson 10: Put me at the centre

'There was once a pirate queen called Amy.'

'And did she have a freckle on her left cheek too?'

'Sure she did and curly brown hair and sparkling brown eyes. And she was very, very brave.'

Captive audience

Children are enchanted when a storyteller gives the hero or heroine their name and plenty of other characteristics. The adult version is slightly more subtle, but only slightly.

- Give the protagonist some of the positive characteristics of the person with whom we want to build a relationship. It usually pays to sprinkle a little flattery 'Just like you, Jasper was always open to new ideas.'

- Draw comparisons between the details of the story and episodes in their personal history. For example: 'It was just like the time you took Jan rowing on the lake and you saw the storm coming and...'

- Use expansive body language that includes the listener. Perhaps a touch on the arm, direct eye contact, a raised eyebrow, an open palm facing towards them or a cheeky smile.

- At key junctures, ask them what they think happened next. Or ask them to consider what they would do in this situation. Listen generously and point out how their suggestions fit with the next stage in the story.

- Get your listener physically involved. Ask them to do something – for example, you might ask them to help you out with an explanation. If you're trying to describe a shape you might say – 'Hold out your left hand as a clenched fist, thumb at the top, now lay your right hand flat over the top: that was petty much the shape it formed when...'

- Animate the scene you are describing by making it concrete. Act it out with whatever items you have to hand – 'The coffee pot represents the farmer and the cards in your wallet all his dogs, then take this sugar bowl, that represents...' Even use their possessions as props – 'May I borrow your fork for a moment?'

- Use their name. It sounds obvious but it makes us feel good to be acknowledged by name. 'The challenge, Justine, is how to get all the delegates there on time...' Don't over do it, though – keep it real. Like all these techniques, it can have the opposite effect when it's overdone.

End of term

Well, there's the bell and here endeth the lessons. All pretty easy in principle but perhaps a little harder to remember when we're anxious to be liked and admired. It gets much easier with practice.

So, here's some homework.

PY Next time you hear someone telling a good story, note it down. You never know when it may come in useful.

Practise storytelling by keeping a journal. Each evening, describe an episode that happened during the day using the story structure.

Next time you watch a good film, take a few moments to decide who is the protagonist. What's their predicament? What happened in the narrative? How was the story resolved? Getting used to the spotting the structure of great stories helps us develop our own.

RY Energy attracts. When someone is fizzing with life we take notice. Actors know all about energy; they use exercises to get themselves fired up before they go on stage. Next time you're about to meet someone you want to infect with your passion, try this actor's warm up. (If you have a history of neck or back trouble, you'll want to select judiciously from this list.) Once you start moving each element should take 15–30 seconds.

- Stand up with your legs half a metre apart and hands by your sides.
- Drop your head on to your chest and let it roll from side to side. Let your head feel heavy and your neck feel loose.

- Raise your hands and shake them vigorously, as though you are trying to dry them. Then add your arms and shake them from below the elbow.
- Rotate your arms as though you are a windmill or a slightly crazed air traffic controller. Circle them in one direction, then the other.
- Raise one leg and shake it like you are trying to shake off a dog that's grabbed your foot. Repeat with the other leg.
- Scrunch your face up as tight as you can. Imagine you've just bitten into a lemon. Then let it relax.
- Sing a scale. If you can't sing, repeat the word 'La', starting very low and deep, and working up to a high pitch. Then go back down again.
- Push your lips out, let them go loose, and blow through them. Let them vibrate as if they're made of rubber.
- Hop from foot to foot as though you are walking across hot coals.
- If you felt a drop in energy on any of the exercises, go back and repeat it, twice as forcefully.

Your body will now be full of energy and you'll be firing on all cylinders. Go sock it to them.

Impact words
Prepare by making a list of low impact words. Now write down at least three high-impact alternatives for each one.

Here are a few low impact words to get you going. If these aren't words you often use, make sure you include your personal favourites in your own list.

- Say/said – announced, proclaimed, shouted, enthused, wept, whispered, assumed, pronounced, suggested, exclaimed, pondered, considered, and so on.
- Good
- Fine
- Maybe
- Hi
- How are you?

And a few negative words, we could all live without for a day:

- But
- No
- Never
- Nothing
- Wrong
- Can't

You could also make a list of 20 words that you are fond of and would like to use more often. And use them.

(G) Bid for attention

Have you ever tried to trace back a broken relationship to work out when it started to go wrong? Was it the time when you scratched his car (honestly, you could barely see it) and didn't tell him for weeks? Or when he went on a stag weekend even though he knew you had to go to hospital? Or when . . .

Whatever you came up with, you're probably wrong. How can we be so sure? Because it's not the high drama and the grand passions that make or break our relationships – it's the small stuff; the almost imperceptible micro signals that we give out constantly throughout the day.

The relationship may have started to go wrong months earlier when he asked:

'Do you fancy a coffee?'

Surprising though it may sound, how you replied to this question may have sealed this relationship's fate. Because how we respond to the thousands of apparently trivial comments people make every day, determines what happens to relationships far more than the big events.

Indeed, so vital are these tiny signals to the health of our relationships that observing them in the arguments of a married couple for just 15 minutes can provide a prediction of future divorce with over 90% accuracy.

Psychologists call these signals 'bids' and if that word makes you think of a poker game or an auction room, then you're on the right track. A bid is something that invites a response. Often we don't notice how we are responding – until it is too late, that is, and we are left wondering why our relationship is unravelling.

The good news is that these micro signals (or 'bids') are very easy to spot and pretty easy to change. So if we know where to look and are willing to make a little effort, we'll never again need to go in search of the origin of the broken relationship.

How to stay married
In the early 1980s psychologist John Gottman was wondering why some married couples stayed together while others broke apart. While he won't have been the first person to ask that question, he is the only one who went on to raise millions of dollars to build an apartment in Chicago filled with hidden cameras and microphones, in an attempt to find out.

In his Big Brother-style house, Professor Gottman watched closely as a series of couples went about their daily interactions. He didn't know what he was looking for, but he was expecting something more than the routine chit-chat of everyday life.

'Anything interesting in the paper?'
'Nah, usual old stuff. Some old lady got mugged on her way out the door...'

After a while of watching this trivia Professor Gottman was on the point of giving up. Then he took a closer look and, like a forensic detective, he found the answer he was looking for lay in the tiny details of those apparently inconsequential exchanges. Banal as they seemed on the surface, at another level they were highly nuanced emotional exchanges.

The impact of Gottman's work was enormous. Based on his insights a whole new approach to marriage counselling was developed. His findings provide the psychology behind the advice in this chapter.

Do sweat the small stuff

Picture the scene. Your partner / boss / colleague / best mate / prospective lover is sitting in front of their computer. They're working. Or perhaps they're pretending to work, in fact they're updating their Facebook page or reading their emails – you know them better than us, you choose.

Now imagine yourself entering the room. Hear yourself asking:

'Do you fancy a coffee?'

So, what happens next?

Your friend could choose to respond in one of three ways:

It must be love

1. They could acknowledge your offer and reply to it in a positive way
'That's really kind, I'll have it black with lots of sugar. ' Or 'Thanks, but I'm ok right now.'

In psychologist's speak this is called a 'turning towards response' or a 'towards bid'.

2. They could acknowledge it in a negative way
'Your coffee is disgusting, I'll do it myself' or 'You want to make me a coffee? What do you want in return?'

Unsurprisingly, this is called an 'against bid'.

3. Or they could just stay silent, or reply by changing the subject
'There's this new film out about the life of the flamingo.'

This is called an 'away from' bid. By replying they acknowledge that you've spoken, but they don't engage with what you've said. In effect they ignore your bid.

Whatever response they choose will determine what you do next. But only the first one is likely to encourage you to make another bid. Faced with an 'against' or 'away from' response we're more likely to make an unconscious mental note not to bother asking next time.

Positive bids create a virtuous cycle. When we make a 'towards bid', the bidder feels good about themselves. As a result they are more likely to make more bids which, in turn, lead to more positive interactions (and more offers of coffee).

The research shows that, when we use plenty of the 'turning towards' bids, the effect on our relationships is enormous:

- We're less likely to get divorced (see box for details)
- Our children will have a better time. When parents are in a relationship full of positive bids there is less conflict. Children from these families are more attentive and are likely to perform better at school
- Siblings (in particular those of different genders) who turn towards one another in conversations are more likely to have a close, supportive and satisfying relationship
- Work teams achieve more. A 3:1 ratio of positive to negative responses will deliver significantly greater productivity than teams with a lower ratio
- We laugh more, feel greater affection and are more likely to be interested in other people's discussions
- We get more sex. Ok, there's no research to prove this yet but, given everything else, it makes sense

Overall, the research is unequivocal: people who respond positively to other's bids have healthier, happier and much more successful relationships.

So, what's not to love?

Divorce predictor

Couples where the exchanges are predominantly 'towards' stay together. In fact, there is even a magic ratio. If we manage a ratio of 5:1 positive (towards) responses to negative (away from or against) responses, we're likely to have a healthy, long-lasting partnership.

Again the research comes from Professor Gottman. In 1992 he

---

teamed up with two mathematicians to test this model. They recruited 700 couples who had just received their marriage licences. The researchers then videotaped a 15-minute conversation between the husband and wife of each couple and counted the number of positive and negative interactions. Then, based on the 5:1 ratio, they predicted whether each couple would stay together or divorce.

Ten years later, Gottman and his colleagues got in touch with each of the couples to determine the accuracy of their original predictions. The results were stunning. They had predicted divorce with 94% accuracy – based on scoring the couples' interactions for just 15 minutes.

The research also revealed a gender difference. Men who are headed for divorce generally turn away from their wives' bids 82% of the time. Whereas husbands in stable relationships only ignore their wives' bids 19% of the time.

Women use turning-away responses slightly less often. Wives who were heading for the divorce courts ignored their husbands' bids 50% of the time, as opposed to those in stable relationships who ignored their husbands' bids 14% of the time.

Is there any down side to this business of positive bids? Well, yes, it is possible to go a little too far. The mathematical modelling in Gottman's study suggests that, once the ratio of positive to negative responses goes above 13:1, the positive responses become diluted and devalued in the eyes of the recipient. It's like being on the receiving end of one of those hyperactive dogs who slobber all over your face every time you enter the room. Too much of this particular thing can be overwhelming. It may also feel phoney or patronising. But really, since most of us find it tough hitting the 5:1 mark, overdoing it is unlikely to be a problem.

Whose bid is it anyway?

Turning towards
In improvised comedy there is only one rule: however outlandish the suggestion, the players never contradict each other.

For example, one player might open with: 'Maggie got up on Monday morning and went out to her car.' The next player could add to that with: 'And she drove to the airport where she caught a plane to Morocco.' Or 'And on her car seat she found a briefcase full of fifty pound notes.' These are positive responses that build on the opening bid.

The second player cannot say: 'Actually it was Sunday and Maggie didn't own a car.' That's a negative, or turning against bid. It doesn't develop the story. It also feels like a slap in the face to the person making the bid.

The same rule applies to healthy relationships. The positive bid may be as simple as a laugh or a knowing smile. It may be a phrase or question. But whatever form it takes, this positive response reassures the bidder that we have heard and accepted what they say (even if we don't necessarily agree with it).

Psychologists have identified four types of turning towards response. A healthy relationship will have a mix of all of them:

- Nearly Passive: The friendly grunt, an affirming 'uh-huh' or a gesture of acknowledgement – a nod, or a smile. (Note: this is a 'friendly' grunt, not the 'just go away and leave me alone' grunt favoured by moody teenagers.)

- Low Energy: A few words of acknowledgement: 'ok', 'sure', or a question to clarify the bid: 'Sorry?'; 'come again?'

- Attentive: Now we're getting involved. These responses involve sharing opinions, thoughts and feelings: express empathy, offer an insight, a joke, a question. Actions like a goodnight kiss or a handshake are also attentive responses.

- High Energy: As above, but even bigger – with more energy, full attention and eye contact. These are usually enthusiastic responses ('Wow, congratulations!'). High energy responses are often physical (big hugs, sloppy kisses etc), and loud (hearty laughs, giggles).

High energy responses have the most positive impact – when you get this kind of reaction you really know that you've been heard. But remember the experience of being greeted by the sloppy dog – too much of this kind of positive attention can be exhausting, particularly if the recipient is a rather shy person.

Three ways to keep your bids going towards:
1. Always respond by showing that you've heard what has been said – even if you want to change the subject. 'I'm so glad that you've found a flat that you like, that must be a weight off your mind. I've just finished a new draft of the report, so if you've got a moment...' etc.

2. Open every conversation with a positive bid. In his research Gottman found in over 90% of cases he could accurately predict the outcome of a 15-minute conversation based on what he heard in the first three minutes. If those first minutes were full of negativity, blame and criticism, the outcome would be negative as well. And vice versa.

3. Even when you vehemently disagree, say what you like about their suggestions first ('I like the fact you're being totally up front, I appreciate how passionately you feel about this issue') before presenting your case.

How could you say that to me?

Turning against
Turning against is always unpleasant. Yes, we get a response to our bid, but we may well wish we hadn't. Mocking, ridiculing, belittling and making sarcastic comments about the bid or the bidder are all turning against responses. And they always make the other person feel bad.

There is little to recommend turning against except for the short and very temporary release of anger, frustration or denial. It's a bit like running up a bill on a particularly expensive credit card, where we get a brief 'hit' from what we've bought and months or years of pain as we try to pay off the debt. The exception is when we want the other person to feel bad (and annoyed with us) as part of some complex negotiation or because we're keen to get them out of our life, no matter what – in which case a turn against may be just the ticket.

Here are six familiar 'turn-against' responses. Unless you're more angelic than most, prepare to wince:

- Contemptuous: A contemptuous response to: 'Shall we ask for directions?' is: 'We wouldn't need to if you could just read the map.' Ouch.

- Belligerent: Someone is spoiling for a fight. So when friend B asks: 'Do you want to see a film? ' Friend A replies 'Do you really think I have time for a movie? Don't you realise how busy I am?' It's pretty obvious where the conversation is going.

- Contradictory: 'I think you'll find there's a better way to tie a bin bag...', 'Leave it alone, let me do it' or the supremely irritating: 'Actually I think you'll find it's pronounced...' are all contradictory responses. They're designed to get a reaction, ideally 'I'm sorry, you're right' but usually something rather less savoury.

- Domineering: These responses are made to assert authority and force the other person to withdraw, retreat or submit. Eg, Daughter: 'My dream is to be on *Dragon's Den*.' Mother: 'Don't be ridiculous. You're not nearly clever enough.'

- Character attack: 'I didn't quite understand what Michael meant in the meeting today', gets the turning-against response: 'Of course not, you weren't paying attention – as usual.' 'You always', 'you shouldn't have', 'you never' are amongst the early warning signals. More in chapter J – Draw the poison.

- Defensive: Me: 'I can't find my book.' My lover: 'Well, don't look at me!' The respondent is going on the offensive to evade responsibility.

When someone turns against us, we feel undervalued. If we do hang on in there, we'll probably stop making further bids. That'll effectively put an end to the interaction and damage the relationship. If the other person is in a position of power (aggressive boss) we may suppress our emotions to avoid conflict and the relationship will become one based on fear.

> **'I'll get my coat...'**
>
> Prince Philip is famous for his 'gaffes', many of which come in the form of turning-against bids. In one particularly jaw-dropping example he allegedly informed a 13-year-old schoolboy that he was too fat to be an astronaut. The 13-year-old was described as 'stocky' by the Prince. Having been reduced to tears by the comment he later responded with admirable aplomb: 'I don't want to be an astronaut anyway, I want to be an actor.'

Three ways to avoid turning against:

1. Pause. Count to five in your head. Slowly. If that doesn't work, explain that you want to take a breather to calm down. And, no, storming out with a slammed door doesn't count.

2. Repeat what the other person has said, or summarise it favourably, and check you've understood correctly. Often we turn against when we have seized hold of the wrong end of their stick.

3. Report on what is going on. 'I notice that we are both raising our voices in this discussion about who is cooking dinner. How can we answer this question calmly?' Psychologists call this reported observation. It is based on the principle that if we name what is going on, we have a better chance of choosing to do things differently to prevent the bad outcome.

In all cases think of the credit card. The short-term gain is rarely going to be greater than the long-term pain.

I'm sorry, did you say something?

Turning away

We 'turn away' when we ignore a bid or act preoccupied or uninterested. There may be a reason why we are being unresponsive; we might be feeling irritated or our attention may be elsewhere. But whatever our conscious motivation, turning away from a bid indicates that we have disengaged from the relationship. The outcome is not going to be good.

Research shows that when people repeatedly ignore or dismiss each other's bids, they become hostile and defensive. And the sad fact is that most people turn away without even knowing they are doing it.

So, what do turning-away responses look like? They can occur in three different ways:

- Silence: Let's say we're searching the Internet, or cooking, or driving. We're engrossed and, to be honest, we're not really interested in whatever's going on around us. So we zone out and try to ignore any bids coming our way. No-one wants 'the silent treatment' so to the other person this feel like a snub. The trouble is that if they keep trying we're as likely to turn against (Can't you see I'm busy?) as turn towards, (Sorry, I was completely away there, what did you say?).

- Dismissive: When we ignore the substance of what they're saying and either focus on some incidental detail: she had nice finger nails; or reframe the issue (Yes, yes, but the real issue is...); or minimise its importance (Does it matter?).

- Switching: Changing the subject either by announcing a new and irrelevant piece of information (It says here that penguins can do first degree algebra; I feel like going for a walk). Or the deliberate non sequitur: Dad: Did you finish your homework? Son: What are you cooking for supper?

In Gottman's research turning away is more common than turning against but the effects are frighteningly similar.

Pass the salt, would you?

During a dinner-hour conversation, stable couples engage one another as many as 100 times in 10 minutes, whereas those headed for divorce only engage one another 65 times in that same period.

And when one of the partners is met with a turning-away response, those in stable marriages re-bid 20% of the time, whereas partners who are headed for divorce rarely even attempt to re-bid. Instead they disconnect from their partner.

But even amongst those who re-bid, 20% is a very low figure – it suggests that, even in a stable relationship, a turning away bid has the effect of closing down communication between people.

Turning away from bids also increases conflict. If a bidder is repeatedly ignored, they're likely to become angry and critical of the respondent. As a result, the emotional temperature goes up and small incidents flare up into big issues. A small dismissal today can lead to relationship meltdown next year. From little acorns . . .

Why we turn away

Stonewalling is a deliberate attempt to turn away. Much more often, though, we're just being thoughtless. So solution no. 1: be thoughtful.

We may argue that we're buying space and time from the demands of others. But turning away is not a skilful way to do it. We'll get a far better response if we accept the bid and then explain to the other person that we feel the need for space.

Three ways to keep from turning away:
1. Observe yourself for a day and find out how many bids you ignore – accidentally or deliberately. Most of us turn away rather more than we think (though we are much better at judging how many times others turn away from us). Once you've learnt to spot your turning-away behaviour, you'll almost certainly reduce it.

2. Are you turning away to avoid a row? It's often the case. We don't want to attack (in effect, to turn against) and so we avoid or deny the situation by turning away instead. Unfortunately, the impact is not so very different. You might try discussing the

issue by understanding more about their underlying concerns. Or simply say, 'I know this is big on your mind but I'm worried it's going to lead to an argument now. Can we discuss it another time?' For more, see chapter 1 – Fight club.

3. Fill the silence. A good proportion of our bids away come from when we can't be bothered to make the effort. A genuine 'uh-huh' will usually be enough to do the trick.

So what am I bid?

Learning the language of bids gives us a magic tool to take control of relationships. When things start feeling shaky we don't need to panic. Instead we recognise what might inadvertently have gone wrong and we increase the dose of towards bids. With a little mindfulness and attention, we change our patterns and the relationship gets back on track, usually without the other person even noticing.

This way we can always have the winning bid.

PY Look out for the bids that people make. Soap operas, for example, often crank up the conflict by including lots of 'turning-away' and 'turning-against' bids. The exchanges between close friends, on the other hand, demonstrate how 'towards bids' create warmth and affection in lasting relationships. Small talk is usually made up of a series of towards bids. What do you notice?

Keep a notebook with three sections, with one for each kind of bid. Write down examples as you hear them. You should be able to get up to 100 of each within a week. This is a swift way to become fluent in the language of bidding.

RY Think of someone who you see quite a lot and with whom you want to improve your relationship.

Day 0:
Write down your feelings about this person and your relationship with them.

Day 1:
Count how many times you make a bid that is away from or against.

Day 2:
Cut the number of against bids by half.

Day 3:
Cut the number of away bids by half (whilst maintaining the lower number of against bids).

Day 4+
Keep cutting the number of away/against bids in half, alternating each day, until you reach a ratio of 5:1 for towards bids:away/against bids. Maintain this ratio for a week.

One month later:
Write down your feelings about the other person and about the relationship. Only when you have done this, compare today's views with what you wrote a month ago.

Bid for attention

Trust me

How much do people trust you? Not as much as you think according to research between pairs of graduates and their professors.

Each person was asked how trustworthy they considered themselves and how trustworthy they thought the other half of the pair (their student or their professor) would rate them. People consistently assumed that their own perception of how trustworthy they are would be shared by the other half of the pair. And consistently it was not. We are, it appears, trusted rather less than we realise.

It has become an almost exhausted cliché to say that trust lies at the heart of a good relationship. Yet, for all it's well-worn repetition, it is not far off the truth.

Whether in teams or with individuals, if we want to have great relationships with our clients, our colleagues, our friends, our family and, perhaps most of all, our lover, then we need to get smarter at building trust.

Familiarity breeds trust

The more we experience something, the more comfortable we become with it and the more we end up liking it. Songs that grow on us, fashion choices that turn out not to be so regrettable after all, unlovable neighbours with whom we find we have more in common than we thought. It's the premise for many a romantic plotline, from *Pride and Prejudice* to *When Harry Met Sally*. The mismatched couple start off loathing each other but by spending time together, they turn animosity to acceptance, then friendship and sometimes love.

If we want someone to trust us it pays to spend time with them, whether signing up for the same project, travelling together or just hanging out. Of course they need to want to as well.

One ambitious executive was surprised to spot his boss's boss getting off a bus outside the office. He decided to use this information to get ahead. He changed his journey into work each morning so that he could share the bus and so hopefully rub shoulders with the great power. Every day he would get up extremely early and travel across town to get on this bus. Sometimes he wouldn't see the boss at all. But sometimes he did and would try to catch his eye. The boss, however, studiously ignored him, raising his newspaper to block the view and rushing off the bus when it arrived at the office. It was months later that the eager executive found out that the big boss was having a big affair which he was trying to keep a big secret. His lover was at the end of this bus route. Striking up conversation with an ambitious executive was the last thing the boss wanted.

As well as familiarity, proximity helps us connect. In the 1950s, a group of psychologists studied friendship groups in an apartment block. Unsurprisingly, neighbours were most likely to be chums, whilst those on different floors were less likely to be described as friends. Those with the biggest number of friends, however, were the residents who lived near ground-floor staircases and mailboxes. Quite simply they came into contact with more people more often. It may sound obvious, but if we want a lot of friends, we should put ourselves somewhere where a lot of people are likely to meet us.

The other good news about familiarity is that when we do things together we build up a store of positive experiences. We can then draw on this bank account of good times when things get tough. Psychologists call this 'positive sentiment override' because the positive memories outweigh the current negative experience. Like saving pennies for a relationship rainy day and then spending your way out of trouble.

Does familiarity breed contempt?

To ensure that predictability doesn't slide into complacency, it helps if we make an effort to keep things fresh.

In an experiment where people were shown posters with a message about stopping foreign aid up to 200 times, they were persuaded most by moderate exposure. After the 200th time of seeing the same poster they began reacting negatively to its message.

Another study looked at two groups of people one of which had recently seen an improvement in their circumstances (eg, moving to a better apartment, receiving an unexpected financial bonus) and the other had recently taken up a new activity.

Whilst both groups experienced a happiness boost, those who had a new hobby, and so experienced continued novelty, found the uplift was greater and lasted longer.

Trust takes two

'I don't trust you.'
'But I haven't done anything wrong.'

In this short dialogue, it sounds like one side is being unreasonable but, in fact, they are probably both being perfectly reasonable. The problem is that each party is referring to a different kind of trust. Trust is not one concept but two interweaving strands, like the two strands of DNA, integral and interdependent. To build trusting relationships, one strand is not enough; we need to deliver on both.

Sensible trust is the rational strand. It's about what we do and what gets done – the visible and practical elements of the relationship. Here actions speak louder than words. It's about doing the right thing.

To build sensible trust we need to be:

1. Responsive
2. Reliable
3. Credible

This is what the response 'but I haven't done anything wrong' is saying. I haven't broken your sensible trust, I've kept my word. The other strand is sensitive trust. This is the emotional part of trust – the sensitive and human elements of the relationship. It's about doing it in the right way.

Sensitive trust also consists of three attributes:

1. Social nous
2. Empathy
3. Intimacy

This is what the person who feels they can't trust is saying: I can't rely on how you will behave, I don't believe that you will look after my emotional needs.

Two strands that form the twine of trust. When we get them both right we build remarkably robust relationships.

Captain Sensible

Sensible trust may sound quite boring. It isn't. In many ways it's the bedrock of trusting relationships. It's also easier to get right. Most of us are reasonably good at building sensible trust when we make the effort. For those who want to get better, here are some tips:

1. Responsive – I'm ready and willing
- Answer the phone when they call, reply to messages swiftly, let them know when you're away or unavailable. Early love can founder when she's expecting to hear back from him in minutes and he's thinking days. Of course, it can pay to play hard to get in the short term but that won't build trust. Even less so with self-important clients.

- Keep them updated. New insights, the latest score, what not to miss on TV, the best place for bargains online, everyone likes to be on the inside track. Actively giving people the relevant scoop shows how prescient we are and how keen to respond to their needs.

- Ask for their knowledge and use it. Whether it's improving on one of their recipes or showing how you've analysed their customer data to reveal a new market trend, most people are delighted to share their knowledge if they think we'll do something useful (for them) with it.

2. Reliable – I do what I say

- Commit and deliver. The Jim Carrey film, *Liar, Liar* is based on a father who lets down his son by making promises he can't keep (and is forced to tell the truth until he learns the error of his ways). It's not just with children that we build trust by making a commitment and sticking to it. The flaky friend or the supplier who always arrives late (and with the wrong samples) quickly erodes trust. A simple alternative is to make small commitments that we know we can meet and stick to them. This will form a pattern and build our reputation for being reliable.

- Diligence. No mistakes, typos, unforced errors, inconsistent 'facts', faulty maths. We get little appreciation when we're error free but oh boy do they notice when we aren't. Like personal hygiene. Wash behind your ears.

- Make an impact. Cook a delicious supper, win a piece of new business, get the builder to repair the roof. Great talk is fine, but we earn our 'trust' spurs by delivering results.

3. Credible – I know what I'm talking about

- Anticipate the future. This is easier than it sounds when we know what we're talking about. A doctor who explains the process and also what we're likely to feel at each stage earns our trust when their predictions prove to be accurate (we may have the runs but at least she warned us). We trust them a lot more the next time they make a prediction.

  A business consultant at a Mind Gym workout explained how she would show a prospective client a graph predicting what would happen to the client's business if they were to employ him. After a sharp improvement, there would be a slight decline. It would then be up to the client whether to continue working with the consultant and reverse the decline or let it continue. Whereas normally, when things take a turn for the worse, the consultant gets fired, this consultant found it always led to more business, because he had accurately predicted that it would happen and so built the client's trust.

- Wear expertise lightly. Snobs are those who feel that they are socially above someone but below someone else. Those who are at the top of the game rarely look down on people, they don't need to. And so with expertise. Those who know their game will merely drop in the odd reference or piece of analysis to make their point.

- Ask specific questions. Knowing what to ask is the surest sign that we both know what we're talking about: during winter do you keep your chrysanthemums in soil or sand? Provided, of course, that our questions are directly related to what they have told us.

Sensible trust is there for the giving.

Swift trust

Trust me quick

We tend to assume that trust takes time to build. It needn't.

Roderick Kramer found that the key to developing trust swiftly is to focus on the goals we are all trying to achieve – rather than concentrating on developing a relationship with the people we are working with, ie, sensible trust rather than sensitive trust.

This may seem counter-intuitive. However, we start to trust someone when we consider them competent and believe that they will deliver on what they say. And so we are better off getting on with the task to build a solid base of sensible

> trust, as opposed to going through what can be a contrived process of bonding.
>
> Leave the team-building exercises until you've already got some successes to bond over.

The sensitive type

For most of us, building sensitive trust is harder. This is because it's tricky to spot when we're getting it right, or wrong. Somehow the moment just passes. Apparently slight questions – how do you find being a working mum? – are code for something else – I'm struggling, can you help? Catch the hidden message and we're invited in to build sensitive trust. Miss it and we're back on the outside.

1. Social nous

Are you one of us? The way to be included is to hone our social nous. What this means is spotting the social norms and adapting to fit in.

A workout participant in an Internet search company shared how, when she started, she was surprised by how many smiley faces and other symbols appeared in emails. Equally, she recognised that in order to get on and be seen as one of the team she would need to use them too. Now she sprinkles them like Gordon Ramsay's expletives.

When a colleague promises, 'I'll do it by Friday' does that mean: I'll do most of it by Friday? Friday becomes Wednesday, becomes the following Friday? It'll be on your desk when you get in on Friday morning?

When we talk or write we pitch what we say based on our assumptions about our audience. For example, *The Economist* is pitched in a different way from *Nuts*. Neither is right or wrong, but each is aiming to speak to its reader in a voice that that will connect. Social nous is about understanding the nuances of our audience so we pitch correctly.

We have joined up as a daytime member at a gym that's set up for mothers (or poker night or a new church, or any other group of people with a shared interest). What do we look out for to fit in?

First up, what do people talk about? Baby bottles or Beyoncé? The Olympics or cup cakes? The price of oil or the price of olive oil? And what shouldn't you say beyond, 'Goodness your baby's ugly'?

We'd also want to know what behaviours are acceptable and what's taboo. Is it ok to breastfeed in public? Or bring your husband along? How scruffy can you look (it may be a gym but there are still standards, my dear)?

Social nous requires acute antennae, to pick up the clues on how this person or group behaves, and deft footwork, to adapt to match their style.

Is this disingenuous? It doesn't have to be. Just because we put on a t-shirt or turn up bang on time doesn't mean we're betraying our true identity, only that we've observed what matters around here and responded respectfully.

2. Empathy
Research on customers' buying behaviour shows that they are likely to spend considerably more time with people whom they believe have their best interests at heart. Hardly surprising. Equally, our most determined efforts to build trust can come to nothing when we put our interests before theirs.

Chapter C – Cool to be kind, explores how to strengthen our empathy muscle. It plays a vital part in building sensitive trust.

3 Intimacy

Love maps
In the long-running TV quiz show *Mr and Mrs* each half of the couple took it in turn to be tested on how well they knew their partner's preferences such as their favourite jam or the first album or CD they bought.

Professor Gottman (referred to by his peers as the 'Mozart of Marriage') used the same principle to develop what he called 'love maps'. These love maps are that part of our brain where we store all the important information about our significant other – a kind of mental notebook where we record their likes and dislikes, beliefs, values, goals and worries. And not just the big stuff: our love map reminds us of our husband's favourite breakfast cereal and the name of our lover's cat.

Couples with detailed love maps are strongly connected. They're aware of each other's thoughts, feelings and motivations, what surprise treat to bring home, when to leave the other person alone and how to calm them down. They understand each other, and they each feel the warm glow of being 'known' by the other person. As a result their relationships are resilient and can weather conflict without collateral damage.

Love maps, and their workplace cousins, are created when we pay close attention to the details of the other person. We spot the photographs on their desk and remember what they picked out from the Sunday papers.

To check your present love map, answer the questions at the end of this chapter under 'I try', with your partner.

There's also one for work: key client, your deputy, the boss. Worth doing for all of them to see who you know best and where the gaps are.

Love maps are only a part of the story. They estimate how intimate our relationships are but not necessarily what to do about them.

Tentative invitations
The challenge with creating intimacy is getting it right. The lover's lunge or the social equivalent, overshare (when we share more personal information than the other person wanted to hear) can lead to enormous embarrassment. Rather than take the risk, many of us decide to steer clear.

This means we're missing out. In a psychology study, three main effects of self-disclosure were identified:

- People disclose more to people they like (relatively obvious).
- Those who do disclose intimate secrets tend to be liked more than those who don't (less obvious).
- People prefer those to whom they have made personal disclosures (not at all obvious).

The route to intimacy starts with tentative steps. We offer some relatively minor piece of personal information. The other person can either help build intimacy, respond by asking for more detail, share their own personal example, or they may change the subject. The trick lies in accepting all responses as equally valid. We haven't been rejected if they change the subject, we've simply identified where a boundary is, at least for now.

Name and inquire

Another route to intimacy and building sensitive trust is to talk about the issue that we're all thinking about but none of us is talking about – the elephant in the room.

A technique to help do this is called 'name and inquire'. We state what we see happening and inquire by sharing from our perspective what we think is going on, for example, 'I get the impression you aren't happy with...' , or 'It may just be me but it seems that this issue is causing more pain than any of us are letting on...'

There's the story from David Maister's research into trusted advisors, of a top lawyer whose client was suing his own mother. The counsel met his client outside the court a few moments before the first hearing. The client seemed especially nervous, twitching, unable to hold his look and playing obsessively with his fingers. The lawyer stopped seeing a client and started to see a man struggling with his conscience, a son's love for his mother, and the desire to do the right thing.

He decided to go beyond his legal remit and call it as he saw it. He confessed to his client that he, the lawyer, found it hard to imagine how it must feel to go into court against one's own mother. He wondered aloud if many sons could go through with it.

The client stopped and looked at the lawyer. And then the client did a remarkable thing. Despite months of preparation, he decided then and there to drop the lawsuit and settle the matter with his mother's lawyer immediately, outside the court. The lawyer lost his fees for a big trial but he gained much more.

A month or so later, the client sent completely unrelated work to the litigator's firm and eventually handed over all his business and family legal needs. The result of having established sensitive trust.

Lean on me

Action book heroes tend to be craggy loners, striding out solo into the world, reliant on nobody. Meanwhile the needy folk are at home hiding behind the sofa and feeling anxious, presumably. Well, it turns out that may not be an accurate picture. Welcome to the 'dependency paradox'.

Californian psychologist Brooke Feeney won The Mind Gym prize for Fresh Thinking about Thinking, with her study of 115 couples over six months. The results showed that the greater the support they provided for each other, the more independent they both were. Safe in the knowledge that their partner would give them the back up they needed, individuals became braver and more willing to go it alone.

'Just as a person driving a car without an insurance policy may be reluctant to drive long distances or to take unnecessary risks,' she explains, 'so too, are individuals reluctant to take independent excursions away from a partner who does not provide good "coverage" in an emergency.'

It appears that the easiest way to stand on our own two feet is to lean on someone else.

Crowd dynamics

The story of the remarkable turnaround of Unilever in Holland hinges on the need to build trust, not just between individuals but also within teams. In one exercise, the senior managers climbed to the top of Mt Corrian on the Isle of Skye. The group formed a circle around the peak, alternately facing inwards to the mountain and outwards. At the critical moment, everyone leaned forward and the only thing that kept people from falling over was the equal and opposite reaction from the person on either side.

This type of activity is not uncommon in outward bound team-building activities and sometimes even in families (especially large ones).

Team or group bonding requires not only trust between individuals but also across the whole population.

People do weird things
In Brockworth in Gloucestershire, UK, they chase a 7lb lump of cheese down a hill. In Tetbury, UK, they run up the hill – with a 60lb sack of wool on their backs. In Devon they carry burning barrels of tar through the streets, and in Staffordshire grown men walk ten miles wearing reindeer horns.

And while the act of running up or down a hill, behind a cheese or in front of sack of wool undoubtedly has its own inherent charms, there is something more to these quirky get–togethers. They are all rituals.

At the heart of organisational culture is ritual. New arrivals at Innocent drinks are given a mug with their name and photo on. Bloomberg have stand-up meetings. AA engineers get together for roadside chats. Walmart's stores in Japan have a staff song that their employees sing as they go about their jobs in store. It translates as something like 'we are here to help/ how can we help you?' and they sing it as they stack the shelves, collect trolleys etc.

Sororities and fraternities have initiation rituals. Boy Scouts and Girl Guides are packed with mottoes, hand signals and ceremonies. Tribes from the Mohawk Indians (whose winter ceremony included a dream-guessing game), to the Masons and even the Magic Circle, have their own phrases, chants, handshakes or dances that signify membership and have been passed on through generations. Even contemporary informal clans, such as groups of online gamers, develop their own lexicon and protocol whose primary purpose is to strengthen the bonds between those who belong.

In teams we create our own rituals: the morning scrum, the summer party, the slang, how we welcome new colleagues or say goodbye to those leaving. Powerful teams tend to be full of unwritten and often unmentioned lore, which can make them hard to join but great when we belong.

Family life too. The joke that comes out every year at Christmas along with the plastic Christmas tree (it's grown since last year); who sits at the different places around the kitchen table; where we go for holiday.

Sometimes rituals evolve of their own accord, but we can just as easily create them ourselves. At a school where teachers complained that they rarely saw their colleagues, a 'hello and goodbye' ritual was introduced. Everyone agreed to greet, and say goodbye to, each other every day (but not in the same conversation). As a result, the teachers became more aware of themselves as part of a team as well as individual teachers.

And so, slowly, we build our own unique 'World of WE' (as opposed to you and me), with its own distinctive way of doing things. Creating rituals, in-jokes, symbols and stories is a powerful way to build trust in groups. The stuff that gives us a warm glow of familiarity, that tells us we belong.

Esprit

Team relationships go through phases. The most commonly recognised one in the business world is 'formin', normin', performin''. A more up-to-date model was named after Procter & Gamble manager George O. Charrier who invented Cog's ladder (his initials in reverse).

This describes the stages of team dynamics that a team needs to go through to achieve *esprit de corps* (or 'team spirit').

Polite. We are getting to know each other and so we go out of our way to avoid conflict and confrontation. In conversation we stay on neutral ground, discussing innocuous subjects such as the weather or the journey to work.

Why are we here? The team members each question their own role and the role of others. The team's objectives, vision and values are robustly challenged at this point.

Bid for power. It may sound like a negative stage but this is a natural and healthy step. Roles emerge and a pecking order develops as processes are outlined and each individual's contribution to the team is clarified. There may well be conflict. It's a tricky step and some teams get stuck here.

Constructive. Things are going swimmingly. The group is harmonious, the team members are performing their different roles to complement each other and everybody is working towards the same, successful outcome.

Team spirit. There's an 'all for one and one for all' mentality and a high level of interdependence within the team. The three musketeers.

Many things can move a team up and down the rungs of Cog's ladder. For example, when a new member joins, the team will often move down the ladder back to the polite stage until they get to know the new arrival and understand their role within the team.

A neat way to progress up the ladder is to ask the team to assess together where they are at and what they believe is needed to move up to the next rung. This works partly because the people in the team are the ones most likely to know the answer, partly because a solution developed and agreed by the team is much more likely to stick than one imposed from the outside, and partly because simply by having the conversation the team will progress.

A project team in an oil company use the terms frequently 18 months after they were introduced.

Whatever kind of relationship we want, trust is a must. With vigilance and the right tools there is no reason why we can't get it and keep it. There's also good reason to give it. As Samuel Johnson advised, 'It is happier to be sometimes cheated than not to trust'.

SPY Find out what kind of trust you build by taking the trust detector at The Mind Gym Online. Use your free password on the inside cover to join.

Look at a team that works well. A family, for example, or a group of friends, a work team; a group of musicians, a sports team or any other high-performing group you know. See how many of their rituals you can spot.

TRY Build your love map with your partner. Each have a go at writing down the answers to each of these questions and then compare to see who's love map is fullest. Surprised?

Name two of my closest friends.
What's my favourite music genre?
What is my ideal way to spend an evening?
What was one of my best childhood experiences?
Which people do I most admire in the world? Name two.
What is my idea of luxury?
What is my biggest fear?
What's my pet hate?
What would I put in Room 101?
What's the hardest hurdle I've overcome in life?
Name one person I find it hard to get on with and why.
How would I like people to describe me?
What would be the ideal gift to give me?
What is my favourite place to escape to?
What are two of my ambitions / life-time career goals?
What would my ideal job be?
Describe in detail my day, either today or yesterday.
What do I consider to be my weak spots?
Name two of my greatest career achievements.
What self improvements do I want to make?
Who do I look up to as inspirational in my career? Why?

And a version for work:

Current work goals and objectives.
How they feel about their career.
Next likely career steps.
Who they admire at work.
What they'd be doing if they weren't doing this.
Most recent best day at work.

Most recent worst day at work.
Projects they are currently working on.
Current work load.
Current stresses or worries.

 The love map builder, along with a way to test how well your friends and colleagues know you, is available at The Mind Gym online. Sign up with your free membership number on the inside cover.

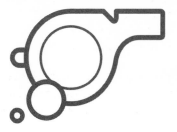

Tough love

The difference between good and bad relationships is not whether there is conflict – all relationships have conflict – but how we deal with it. This section arms us with the best countermeasures for relationship warfare.

I – Fight club, reveals five ways to deal with conflict and how to choose the right one(s).

When conflict goes toxic people and relationships become venomous. J – Draw the poison, gives us the antidotes.

Chapter K – Deal or no deal, helps us find ways to negotiate a solution that leaves both parties satisfied.

Covert conflict is especially pernicious. Follow the blog in chapter L – I smell trouble, for rapid response tactics when they really are out to get you.

Chapter M – The hardest word. Discover how to apologise so they accept it, and forgive when that's the last thing you feel like doing.

Most relationships go through periods of trench warfare, peace negotiations and *détente*. But boardrooms and bedrooms don't have to become battlegrounds. This section provides the blueprint for how to run your own peace mission.

① Fight club

Can you think of someone you always end up arguing with? Or someone with whom you can't face it, so you let them have their way?

Most of us get into patterns. Whether it's an individual (Dad), a subject (politics), a situation (in traffic) or time (of the month), we hear the argument brewing and we respond just like we did before. No matter if last time we felt bruised, angry, dissatisfied or weak; and the time before that too. We still adopt our typical response and carry on much as before.

Now is the time to change. Conflict is a vital and nourishing part of any relationship. Without it we wouldn't get to know each other properly, many of the greatest inventions, songs and dynasties would not exist and our minds would be a lot narrower. Conflict is very good for us but only if we know how to handle it in the right way.

Thirty years ago, two industrial psychologists, Kenneth Thomas and Ralph Kilmann, studied conflict in a large manufacturing company. They found that there were five ways in which people there dealt with conflict.

Thirty years and plenty more research later, it appears that we all use these same five modes. It is also clear that being mentally agile, adopting the right mode in the right way at the right time, lies at the heart of handling conflict effectively.

The Julia Roberts guide to conflict

Julia Roberts has covered a wide range of roles in her cinematic career and, for quite a few, the way her character deals with conflict is fundamental to the plot. So, here are the five conflict handling modes as illustrated by Ms Roberts.

1. Compete: Erin Brockovich

In this film, Ms Roberts plays single mum and true-life character Erin Brockovich fighting for the rights of a small community against the polluting antics of a big Californian water company. From her boss to her part-time lover to the downright nasty lawyers on the other side, everyone either stands in her way or lets her down. But there's no stopping this formidable woman. Assertive, unco-operative and totally unwilling to compromise, she plays to win and doesn't give up until victory is hers.

Compete is used when we want to win. We give high importance to meeting our needs and low importance to meeting the needs of the other person.

These are the occasions that we most naturally think of as conflict. We are determined to get our way come what may.

2. Accommodate: America's Sweethearts

In a very different role Ms Roberts plays a PA to her dominating older sister – a Hollywood A-lister. Co-operative and accommodating she's willing to put her own feelings aside to help her sister reunite with her estranged husband for one last public appearance. Happy to lose the battle to win the war, she continuously puts her own interests aside to give the others what they want.

Accommodate is when we attach low importance to meeting our own needs and high importance to meeting the needs of the other person. It is the opposite of competitive.

When we accommodate we may feel that we have been weak or walked all over, although we are just as likely to feel that we made a wise choice about which battles to fight.

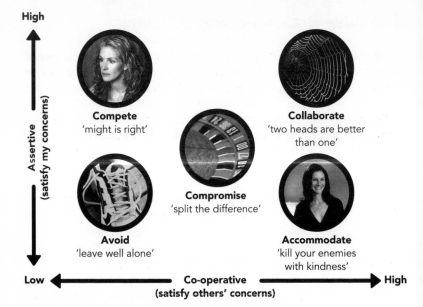

High

Assertive
(satisfy my concerns)

Compete
'might is right'

Collaborate
'two heads are better
than one'

Compromise
'split the difference'

Avoid
'leave well alone'

Accommodate
'kill your enemies
with kindness'

Low ◄─────── Co-operative ─────────► High
(satisfy others' concerns)

3. Avoid: The Runaway Bride

Unable to face up to that all-important conversation, Ms Roberts's character repeatedly accepts proposals and then ducks out, jilting a series of fiancés at the altar. At one stage she even leaps on a FedEx van to escape. One guest asks, 'Where's she going?' to get the reply, 'I don't know but she'll be there by 9 am.'

Avoid is when we give low importance to both our needs and theirs. Unlike 'accommodate' we don't give in, we run away. This can mean physically leaving the room but more often we change the subject or offer a delaying tactic.

4. Compromise: Ocean's Eleven

Playing Danny Ocean's estranged wife, Tess, she can only stand by and watch as he plans the biggest heist in history. As the story unfolds around her she continually compromises – not really taking a position on either side and often leaving people feeling dissatisfied with her behaviour and with the outcome.

When we compromise, we give a little and expect the other person to do the same. Ok, you can have the walnut shelves if I can keep the juke box. Here we are slightly assertive and slightly co-operative.

Fight club

5. Collaborate: Charlotte's Web

In this animated story Julia voices Charlotte the spider who organises the animals to work together to save the day. Extremely assertive and also highly co-operative, she brings all their different interests together to ensure a result that suits everyone.

We give high importance to meeting our interests and also to meeting yours. We work on coming up with a solution that makes us both feel satisfied.

Flexibility is everything

Although Ms Roberts's characters each have a dominant conflict type they also switch modes in response to changes in the situation.

Erin Brockovich takes a brief respite from competitiveness to be co-operative when her relationship with the biker-next-door is on the line. In *America's Sweethearts*, Julia's character finds love and professional respect when she reverses a lifetime of capitulation to demand recognition from her sister. In fact, in each of the films, it's when a conflict forces Julia's character to switch modes that she achieves self-realisation and a positive breakthrough.

That's why this chapter is so important: research clearly shows being able to switch between modes when dealing with conflict increases our work success. It's likely to make our home life a lot sweeter too.

Keep on rowing

'The best way to keep children at home is to make the home atmosphere pleasant, and let the air out of the tyres.'
Dorothy Parker

Can there be anything worse than the rows between parents and teenagers? Yes, it seems – not having rows.

According to a study by Tabitha Holmes at State University New York, conflict can strengthen parent-adolescent relationships. For whilst parents may see conflicts as destructive, teenagers say that rows bring them closer to their parents and help them to understand their parents' point of view. They're

---

also aware that a good row forces them to think through and articulate their own opinions and feelings – something that teenagers say they only do when forced to defend their position.

'If your teenager is rowing with you, it's actually a mark of respect,' says Holmes. 'It shows they value you enough to tell you their genuine feelings and thoughts.' The time to start worrying is when your children don't fight with you. Are they afraid, or just not bothered about sharing their views with you?

Which mode is best?

Sue is a generally confident and highly respected team leader in a graphic design company. Steve is a sparkling creative who works in her team. Recently, though the quality of his work remains good, Steve has been missing deadlines and working more slowly than other members of the team.

In Steve's appraisal Sue raised the matter. Steve replied: 'My missing deadlines are your fault – you overload me, you don't brief me properly and you don't give me enough warning. If I had more time the quality of my work would improve.' Sue listened to his complaint but it didn't change her opinion.

The conflict is built on two apparently contradictory views:
• Sue thinks Steve misses deadlines and is slow.
• Steve thinks Sue overloads him and is bad at briefing.

Drawing from the Julia Roberts school, Sue has five options:

1. Compete
'Steve, the facts are there. You have the same number of clients as your colleagues and you are delivering less work. You have missed four out of the last five deadlines, which lets down our clients and is clearly unacceptable.'

Sue may listen to what Steve has to say but she won't give ground. TV's Supernanny uses competition. She may get down on eye level to talk to the child, she may use a soft low voice and pile on the

positive encouragement: but in the end her position is clear. Even if she has to take a child back to bed 98 times, if that's what she wants to achieve, she will achieve it.

On the up side
Competition gets things done. If Sue is convinced that only one outcome will do, this will get the result. And it's unequivocal – if Steve was hoping that he could charm his way round Sue, this position says loud and clear: 'Don't even think about it.'

The compete mode is useful when we're sure of our facts, clear about our position and want to move quickly.

On the down side
There's only one winner and being on the receiving end can be pretty crushing.

Sue might find herself with a demotivated Steve, paying lip-service and completing his designs so they're just good enough, but conserving his design energies for a new gaming website that he's building in the evenings.

Repeatedly competing will make Sue seem unco-operative and argumentative. People will start to back off, either avoiding her altogether or simply avoid telling her the truth.

2. Accommodate
'Ok. I can see that you've got a lot on and without a clear brief it's easy for your time to get taken up doing the wrong thing. What can I do that would give you the clarity you need?'

Sue may want to give Steve the benefit of the doubt so that next time, if he still isn't delivering on time he really won't have an excuse. She may also think that this is a battle worth losing in order to win the war for award-wining designs. Or she just feels that she can't be bothered.

When we're faced with the dinner-party bore, whose dogmatic views we disagree with, sometimes we might slog it out but other times – well, do we really care that they believe crop circles are landing pads for alien spacecraft? If a polite nod of support is going to move us on to pudding in peace then it can be worth it.

On the upside

In Sue's case it means that she keeps the peace and avoids the appraisal stalling on this single issue. She may also hope that by taking responsibility herself, she'll prompt Steve into taking some responsibility too.

Accommodating is the friendly option. It's useful when there's little at stake. So, our visiting colleague from the Stuttgart office insists that we can't possibly drink wine with steak. Well, I'm happy with beer – unless I've a sommelier's reputation to protect it's hardly worth fighting over.

If what's at stake is relatively trivial or the issue is terrifically important to the other person, or we just want to make them feel good, we may be wise to give in.

On the downside
Weakness.

Steve may read Sue's accommodating behaviour as feeble – it might even undermine her leadership of the team. Steve may think he's got one over her and continue as normal, and others may follow suit if they begin to see Sue as a soft touch.

She's also missed an opportunity to resolve the situation as Steve will think he's done nothing wrong.

3. Avoid
'Moving swiftly on . . .'

'I hear what you say. Now let's talk about the creativity of your designs . . .'

If Sue takes this stance she'll have moved the conversation on to the next part of the appraisal. There are good reasons why she might decide to do this. It could buy her more time to gather evidence, or it might be necessary to take the heat out of the situation.

On the upside
Avoidance prevents minor issues turning into major ones. It also reduces the tension and allows time to heal, or, just maybe, the issue will blow over.

If Steve is suffering from a personal tragedy, Sue might well avoid the issue altogether and focus instead on how to support him.

On the downside
Are we sweeping it under the carpet?

If the issue doesn't resolve itself naturally, then we're not doing anything to help it along. It might fester and lead to an explosive confrontation. If we get a reputation as someone who avoids dealing with conflict, people may find it hard to talk to us about things that matter to them. It may also result in important decisions being made without ever being discussed or agreed.

Conditional avoidance
In Sue's situation she could strengthen her position by making the covert avoidance more overt, highlighting the fact that she is going to leave the subject for now, but specifying exactly when they will revisit it.

4. Compromise
'I'm willing to change the way I brief you and I'm also willing to commit to a minimum number of days warning for any deadlines. In return, I expect you to produce designs at the same rate as the rest of the team. Do we have a deal?'

Sue gives a little to gain a little.

On the upside
Compromise is a quick and easy tactic, useful when time is tight and we need a solution quickly. It shows that we've taken the other person's views on board and that we're willing to adapt our position to reach an agreement. Ideally, it encourages the other party to do the same.

On the downside
This mode of operation can turn into a habit of 'game playing' that exhausts the other party and makes them suspect that they are being exploited. If compromise isn't really appropriate to the issue, it might lead to an unsatisfactory outcome with everyone feeling hard done by.

Style tips

To use this technique well, we need to be a confident negotiator. When compromising we have to consider in advance exactly what we're prepared to give away and what we need to keep. It's in this balancing act that the skill of compromise resides. For more on negotiating see chapter K – Deal or no deal.

5. Collaborate

'We need to get to an outcome where you're delivering at the same pace and quality as the rest of the team. Clearly there are reasons why you think that isn't possible at the moment. Let's discuss how best to do this and then develop a plan to improve the situation.'

On the upside

The solution is more likely to be creative as the problem is examined, prodded and probed until the best answer is developed. Even better, there is agreement and so we feel good about it.

On the downside

Success is far from guaranteed. Fine, if time isn't an issue, not so good if we're against the clock. In the wrong situation, collaboration could lead to frustration and, in Steve's case, even more missed deadlines.

Collaboration can also be a way of sidestepping personal responsibility. We should check our motivation before we reach for this mode.

Love match

How should we respond to the other person's style?

In 'love' relationships there are three predominant types of responses: the 'conflict explosives', who have a broadly competitive style, the 'empathisers' who want to talk about how they feel, and the 'avoiders'.

Professor Gottman found that if the two styles were the same, the relationship would work. A couple of avoiders, for instance, could ignore a conflict for years, but still feel

---

satisfied with the relationship. If you know a couple who are always rowing but have been together for ages, the chances are that they are both 'conflict explosives'.

The difficulty comes where there's a mismatch between the two styles. Then the fireworks could signal the finale.

Paper, scissors, stone

'I had a colleague who I'd marked down as an undiluted pessimist', explained an avowedly optimistic participant in The Mind Gym's Conflict Handling workout. 'Until one day, when I was feeling very down and letting everyone know it, and to my complete surprise he tried to cheer me up with a very uncharacteristic and ebullient optimism. I realised that he is not necessarily particularly optimistic or pessimistic, just contrary. He'd argue with his own shadow.

'What this workout has shown me is that his preferred conflict mode is compete. As he is always going to be assertive (giving high importance to his needs), in order to get the most from him I need either to accommodate, in which case there is no argument, or if I really care about this issue, collaborate. Competing or avoiding are likely only to prolong the pain.'

It's not just our conflict-handling mode that matters. Theirs does too.

Turn the page to find an indication of what's likely to happen when we respond to people who display each of the different conflict modes.

Other person ▶ My response ▼	Compete	Accommodate
Compete	Fireworks. This is going to be a big battle and even the winner, if there is one, may find the victory unsatisfying. If they're a bully or seriously misguided or the issue really matters, it may be worth it. Otherwise try something else.	You appear to get your way but don't be deceived. They may not be as convinced as you imagine. Watch out for completely dominating them and creating someone too scared to tell you the truth.
Accommodate	It will be easier now but beware problems down the road. If they are always competing, anticipate an argument where you know you are right, research all the facts and switch to 'compete'. They'll respect you more from here on.	Sounds like the issue doesn't much matter to either of you. Make a decision and move on.
Avoid	A good way out when the answer will become clear later in any case. If this pattern persists, you are likely to drift apart. Chose a topic to have a full discussion about.	What's to avoid? They want to help. Let them.
Compromise	A great way to see if there is movement. Get them to share all their thoughts and then ask whether they are interested in reaching a compromise.	Generous and often wise to ensure that the accommodator still leaves with something. By showing you've made sacrifices they're less likely to feel aggrieved.
Collaborate	Well worth trying. Ask: what would need to happen for you to change your view? Any response other than 'nothing' shows movement and there's something to work with.	Make them feel important and show how their views matter.

Avoid	Compromise	Collaborate
They start avoiding you because they can't face the argument or don't think it matters. Ask them questions and listen to their views to get them involved or you'll be on your own.	They are making a sacrifice and expect you to do the same. Sometimes it isn't worth fighting to the bitter end – take the olive branch and be grateful. If you don't, expect them to turn to 'compete'.	The other person wants your needs to be met. That's a great start. If you're not in a rush, indulge in a conversation to see if there's a way through. If you need speed or are determined about the outcome, it still pays to acknowledge their effort.
Engage them by asking for their views and showing how keen you are to help. Or just let it pass.	If there is something you want, say so. Those who don't ask, don't get.	If it matters, share what you really think. If not, tell them not to waste their time.
Nothing cooking.	If you feel it's all or nothing this could be the way to go. Equally, if you want a resolution, see how far they're willing to move.	There is a magic solution and your ideas may be just what's needed to discover it. Listen to what they're asking and share your thoughts. The outcome is unlikely to be as bad as you fear.
Be upfront with what you're willing to give way on and ask if that appeals. Watch out that their apparent avoidance isn't just a clever negotiating tactic. Know when to walk away.	Time to do a deal. Ask what their intrerests are and where yours overlap.	Before you offer to meet them half way, explore the issue together with a full discussion about what you both want and how you could both get it.
A neat way to engage a person who's scared of speaking out. Show how safe the conversation is, if necessary put in extra safeguards.	Explain that there's no rush: better to reach a solution that everyone believes in and will stick to than come up with something that won't last.	Aim for agreement on what a successful outcome would look like first. If you get stuck, come up with a comprehensive list of options and evaluation criteria to asses them.

Power games

The research shows that, unsurprisingly, we accommodate with people of greater power. One situation where the power dynamic is apparent and important is between pilots. The story goes that an experienced captain was going through the pre-flight drill when he asked his co-pilot to flick a particular switch. The co-pilot thought this was a bad idea but, given the elevated status of his boss, he accommodated and flicked the switch. As a result the landing gear retracted leaving the plane floundering belly down on the runway.

More than fight or flight

In conflict with subordinates, we're more likely to use collaboration. Most people have a strong need to be liked and a collaborative style is seen as a way of staying popular as well as keeping the team in agreement with the outcome. Participants in Mind Gym workouts often describe bosses who compete but dress it up as collaboration: what do you think? Well, I think we should so let's get on with it. This mixed message is more disheartening than a straightforward 'say it and stick to it'.

With our peers we are more likely to compromise. Because we're on equal footing in terms of status, co-operative deal making and exchanging of favours is likely to happen.

Time to change

When it comes to conflict, the choices are more than fight or flight ('compete' or 'avoid').

The opportunity lies in spotting what we tend to do and, if it isn't getting us the result we want, changing. You may have already spotted your predominant mode(s) at work, at home and in other places too. If not, or you want to be sure, there's a questionnaire to identifiy your preferred model(s) at The Mind Gym online when you register using your free membership code on the inside cover of this book.

Putting together a strategy

Once we're aware of our conflict preferences we are better equipped to deal with problem situations when they arise. We can become mindful, making conscious decisions about how we approach the conflicts we are getting into and, indeed, whether we should be getting into them at all.

One workout participant, whose preferred conflict mode was competing said, 'I now understand why I get some of the reactions I do from my friends. I'm a passionate person and feel strongly about things, so when I hear something I disagree with I come right out and say so. I now realise that's not always the right thing to do.' Another participant who most frequently used a collaborating style said, 'I've been told that I can sometimes be seen as a weak leader at work. My team believe that some decisions I should simply make myself instead of always trying to reach a consensus. Ironically, I may end up more popular as a result.'

PY Look around you for someone who uses the competitive style. It might be your mother, your boss, or the bus driver. Watch how their conflicts get resolved. Does the competitive style work for them, or are there occasions when a different approach might get a better result?

RY Think about someone with whom you regularly come into conflict. Identify your respective styles. Now ask yourself: is it the content of the argument or the styles you use that intensify the bad feeling? Try using a different style next time and see if it brings the argument to a speedier conclusion.

(J) Draw the poison

A massive argument, a blazing row, but what was it all about?

When it comes to arguments, big things often come in small packages. The most trivial difference (where to put the saucepan) turns into accusation (you don't do anything around the house), personal affront (or care about me) and, in extreme, to action (I'm out of this relationship, my mother always said you were a selfish b******d). All in seconds.

You don't have to attend every argument you're invited to

What's your poison?

Whether we're on the receiving end of the venom, or we're the one dishing it out, the trick to stopping arguments escalating is to separate form from content. And that's what this chapter is about – identifying the poisons we regularly reach for and recognising those favoured by people around us. Whilst this knowledge may not be enough to stop tempers flaring, it will help us prevent the spark turning into a fire.

Here's a brief toxology of six pernicious argument poisons, identified in terms of their symptoms (so that we can see them coming), the antidotes (in case we feel tempted to use them ourselves) and some remedies (to help us out when someone uses the poison against us).

Poison 1: I know you

Symptoms
'You're being pedantic', 'You're over-reacting', 'You're being ridiculous/unreasonable', 'You're angry/unhappy/insecure/flaky'.

Just reading those comments probably sets your teeth on edge. Here is someone taking the high ground and assuming superior knowledge of our feelings. And, oh boy, is that irritating. If we weren't annoyed before, being told we're angry is sure to push us over the edge.

Worse still is being told what we should do:

'You need to listen to other people'; 'You ought to get your facts straight before you go making claims like that', 'I suggest you stop shouting'.

Antidote
Unless the other person has shared their feelings, don't go there. In assuming we know what others are experiencing we run the risk of putting them on the defensive – and there's a good chance we'll get it wrong.

After all, there can be a variety of interpretations for someone's behaviour. A man is screaming; is he upset, angry, physically hurt, or overwhelmed with joy? Until he tells us, we don't know for sure.

The key to this antidote is to separate the observable facts from our interpretation of them. So, keep your voice in neutral, tell the other person what you are observing. Give them a chance to correct any mistakes in the facts or our interpretation. For example:

'This conversation is getting louder – how are you feeling?'

Compare that to: 'You're shouting' or 'I know you're angry'. The word 'shouting' is a strongly nuanced word, suggesting the other person is out of control. Using 'I know' suggests we can read the other person's mind. It's likely to send the argument into a kind of pernicious pantomime bickering: 'Oh no I am not', 'Oh yes you are...'

If someone is repeatedly making the same point we could say:

'I have heard the same thing three times and I'm not getting it. Can you explain what you mean in a different way?' rather than, 'You keep repeating yourself'. 'Repeated' comes loaded with negative connotations and inevitably makes the other person feel patronised.

Our aim is to get the other person to confirm that we've read their feelings correctly: 'You bet I'm angry.' / 'You have no idea.' Then we're in a position to empathise: 'I too would be angry in your situation'; 'I completely understand why you don't feel listened to'. In this way we get on side with the person, rather than encouraging them to feel hostile towards us.

Here are some simple phrases that can turn the 'I know best' attitude to 'I am responsible'.

I know best	I have a different experience
You are very muddled	I haven't understood
You obviously don't understand	Have I been clear?
You're wrong	I have a different recollection
You don't love me	I don't feel loved
You aren't listening to me	I don't feel listened to
You're over-reacting	I imagine you feel strongly about this
You're wrong about X	When I experienced X
I didn't say that	I may not have been clear, what I meant to say was...

You're very touchy/neurotic/flaky	It's my understanding that...
	I imagine that this is a sensitive subject
You're being aggressive	I am feeling uncomfortable with the tone
	of this conversation

Remedy

Assume the best intentions. That may sound tough when someone is telling you they know better, but try to consider why the other person is saying these things. What's the most generous explanation? Are they frightened rather than angry, careless rather than malicious, stressed rather than rude?

If it's someone you know well, remind yourself that they're acting out of character. But why? Turn detective-cum-armchair psychiatrist and try to work out what's eating them. A few words of support or a hug may be all that's needed to stop the poison spreading.

Alternatively, you could always concur. If someone tells you you're angry, agree: 'Yes, I am angry. I feel that my effort has been wasted.' Then pause. Allow the other person to respond. You'll probably find you've taken the wind out of their sails. At the very least showing your vulnerability will have changed the tone of the conversation.

Best wishes

A Mind Gym workout participant described the relationship he was having with his newly pregnant girlfriend. She was suffering from morning sickness and when she wasn't vomiting she was getting annoyed with him.

Here he had two choices: to react back (after all she is being totally unreasonable, shouting at him for doing things she asked him to do only moments earlier) or to employ what psychologists call 'Positive sentiment override'. That is, that you recognise that the person who's upset with us is still the person we love – they're just making it tough for us right now.

Positive sentiment override requires us to look for the positive explanation of their behaviour: 'they're tired, who wouldn't be', rather than 'they're being difficult'. When we love, admire or respect them, this can become a natural habit and a very healthy one for robust relationships.

Poison 2: Universalisation

Symptoms

Under the influence of this particular venom not only can we mind-read, we are also all knowing. Without pausing for breath we generalise from the specific to the universal. So, not only are you not listening but you never listen. Not only are you late with your report but you are always late. And whilst we are on the subject, nothing ever gets done on time around here. Nothing. Ever.

Really? It's untrue, of course. There are always exceptions. Even the most tardy employee will meet a deadline occasionally. And they'll probably point that out: 'Actually, my presentation was on time last week.' This provokes the other person, the temperature rises and, bingo, we're on our way to a full-blown row.

Under the influence of this poison certain words elbow their way to the front: always, never, every, forever, anything, anyone, everyone, typical. They are usually combined with 'you' and they sound like this:

- You always know best.
- You never take my advice.
- You never give any thought to me (the children/the cat/ the future).
- Nothing ever gets done properly.
- Typical of you to forget something.
- Every time it ends in disaster.
- This always happens.
- You never listen to anyone else's view (double whammy: 'never' and 'anyone').

Glad to be grey

People who are absolutist thinkers pride themselves on

'knowing what I think'. They have clear rules that they apply every time they encounter a similar situation. They see things in black and white. Grey, in their opinion, is for flaky wimps. What they don't realise is that it's the people who see things in shades of grey who are much more likely to be open to new ideas, solve problems and have strong relationships. It appears, too, that absolutism is inversely correlated with wisdom.

In a study by Alistair Ostell and Susan Oakland, 80 head teachers were classified as 'absolutist' or 'non-absolutist' in the way they handled two work problems. When the teachers were interviewed results showed that the absolutist head teachers perceived themselves as less effective at managing their emotions and handling problems, and experienced their jobs as less pleasant, than the open-minded and more flexible non-absolutist heads. They also had poorer mental and physical health. The non-absolutist heads – those who saw things in shade of grey rather than black and white – also reported finding problem solving easier and experienced better health.

Antidotes

In a court of law the jury comes to a decision based on the evidence of the case in question. Previous convictions are not taken into consideration. In this way the jury is encouraged to come to an unbiased judgement about the specific offence. It's a discipline we can usefully employ when we're trying to avoid applying this particular poison.

When ascribing a cause to someone's behaviour, keep to the specifics. Don't go wide screen. If your partner is late home tonight, be angry about tonight. Resist the urge to bundle it up with all the other times they've been late and forgetful, summarising it as: 'You never do anything that you say you will.' They'll just get defensive.

Keep yourself focused on the details by using these antidote phrases:

On this occasion
It tends to be

With this client
Right now
During the full moon
When I'm tired

With this particular poison, the secret lies in controlling the borders. Small is definitely beautiful.

Remedy

Don't rise to the bait. Recognise the sweeping statements for what they are – the hyperbole of anger. Ignore the inflammatory comments – picture them as arrows, see them falling short of their target, dropping harmlessly to the ground a couple of feet in front of you. Then move the conversation back to the matter at hand:

'There may well be wider implications. For the moment, can we focus on resolving this particular issue?'

'I understand. On this particular occasion, what do you think we should do next?'

Getting enough satisfaction

Passion, love, commitment. Whilst these may not disappear, recent research suggests that they tend to diminish in importance as a relationship continues. Instead, what we look for is satisfaction. Indeed, low satisfaction is an important predictor of relationship breakdown.

So, here's how to get satisfaction:

1. We support each other. And not only does this affect relationship satisfaction, it's also been shown to affect general health levels.

2. We avoid the negative loop. That is, we don't let small disagreements escalate into full-scale rows. One of the signatures of a dissatisfied couple is their fondness for the negative loop.

3. We don't do the demand-withdrawal dance. Another signature of the dissatisfied couple – one of them makes

---

a demand by starting a tricky conversation; the other one withdraws by reaching for the volume switch on the TV.

4. We put a positive spin on character flaws. The rest of the world may think you're bossy, but in my eyes you'll always be a strong leader. Taking a positive view (described by psychologists as 'cognitive distortions' or 'unrealistic beliefs') is associated with relationship satisfaction.

5. We give the benefit of the doubt. When looking for the reasons behind our partner's behaviour, we attribute the best motives, rather than the worst. For example, she missed the start of the film because the train was late, not because she's thoughtless and selfish.

6. We are each other's dream partner. We didn't make a compromise; we aren't second best, we're not holding out for Brad Pitt or Angelina Jolie. We've got exactly what we want in each other.

7. It's getting better all the time. Satisfied couples feel that their relations are constantly improving and getting better with age.

The good news is that our satisfaction is biased towards whether we feel that the relationship has improved recently. And so when we make an effort to change these things we start to feel improvements relatively quickly, provided that we don't lapse into old ways.

Poison 3: Labelling

'A mental midget with the IQ of a fence post.' Tom Waits

Symptoms
Name-calling, character assassination, mud-slinging; it goes deep. Attacking what I say or do is one thing, but it takes a real restraint to keep cool when someone launches an attack on my identity.

You're lazy, cunning, cruel, insensitive, stupid, you've lost your touch.

That's the full-on version. There are other variations, more cunning and subtle. The accusation can be made by association: 'Only a fool would think like that', 'A child could do better'. Or, we can be invited to work out the insult for ourselves: 'Is this the first report you've ever written?' And let's not forget this particularly nasty insinuation: 'What happened to your sense of humour?'

To boost the venom, others may be brought in to hammer home the message. 'Everyone thinks you're out of your depth', 'All our friends believe you're a fool'. Or, if that's too factual for your attacker, they might try hypothesising: 'I bet if you asked your family...', 'Any sane person would agree...'

Antidotes

When we feel ourselves reaching for a phial of this particular poison, we need to engage in a swift mental turnaround and redefine those negative characteristics as positive ones. So, instead of lazy, consider her unmotivated. Instead of denigrating his obstinacy, admire his determination. Don't worry that she's passive, be pleased that she's calm and relaxed.

And don't wait until things get tense; take pre-emptive action. Start off by reinforcing the positive aspects of the other person's character to get yourself in a positive mindset:

- I appreciate how much you care about this
- You have been incredibly generous with your time
- I really admire your persistence/patience/application
- You deserve more appreciation than you've had

But, you may ask, what if my partner truly is passive? Well, is anybody 'truly' anything? Character judgements are always going to be subjective. Opting for a positive interpretation will not only avoid the argument turning toxic, it will also help to weatherproof your relationship. Making positive attributions is one of the signs of satisfaction that indicate a healthy, resilient relationship (see previous box).

Remedy

In the heat of the moment, we all say things we don't mean. The challenge is to remember that's true of the person who is yelling at us, right here, right now. Not just when they apologise later.

Indeed, the more forcefully they hurl the abuse, the less likely they are to mean it.

So, imagine yourself wrapped in a protective shield. Nothing can get through it. Watch the insults bounce off it. For the poker players amongst you, take the option to 'stick' – you don't have to raise the stakes to stay in the game.

'It is often better not to see an insult than to avenge it.' Seneca

That said, the other person obviously wants to be heard, so offer the odd token acknowledgement: 'uh-huh' 'ok'. Keep it neutral and then steer the conversation back to the core issue. Use a question, 'Whose advice would you rate on this subject?', or a statement, 'I am unclear how you would like me to rate the options.'

Who, me?

Some psychotherapists suggest that when we find a particular fault in someone else it is, in fact, a fault we are aware of in ourselves. So when someone accuses us of something, imagine they are in fact describing themselves. Feel sympathy rather than anger. Similarly, when we reach for the insults ourselves, pause and consider – why has this matter agitated us so much? Who am I really criticising?

Poison 4: Toxic words

Symptoms

'Sticks and stones will break my bones but words will never hurt me,' we are told. Maybe so, but they can certainly turbo-charge an argument. Particularly these two words: NO and BUT. We don't even have to say them, we can roll our eyes, turn away, snort in derision, laugh dismissively, or just storm out and slam the door behind us. They all get the NO message across loud and clear.

NO brings the barriers down at the same time as it raises the temperature. And BUT is just NO in smarter clothes. They are powerful poisons.

Antidote

When things start to get heated, lock the word 'NO' away in a box and bury it in a deep hole. Think of yourself in the role of a mediator rather than a prosecutor and deliberately opt for moderate language. Aim to build and open up the conversation.

The quickest and easiest way is to use the words 'Yes and', rather than 'No but'. When we hear an idea that we don't like it's easy to shut it down straight away with a swift NO. 'Yes and' forces us to take a constructive attitude.

For example:

'Yes, the client might be wrong and we should get all the facts before we respond.'

'Yes, it is an original idea and we should check whether more budget could be available to fund it.'

Build the idea still further by suggesting three things you like about the suggestion. Then address the negatives by suggesting three things you wish were different about it. To the person on the receiving end that will sound very different from 'three things I don't like'.

For example, you might suggest I sell my car and buy a motorbike. I like that idea because it would make my commuting cheaper, a motorbike would be easier to park, and it would be quicker in city traffic. What I wish was different is that I could carry luggage, keep out of the rain, and that my friends wouldn't suggest I was having a midlife crisis.

It's a powerful strategy on many fronts. Our antagonist feels listened to; we show that we're open to finding a solution, and we let the other side know what matters to us, making it easier for them to suggest acceptable alternatives. We may even find ourselves modifying our own position as we explore the pros and cons.

Remedy

When all you're hearing is variations of NO and BUT the discussion has ground to a halt. To get it moving again reach for questions and suggestions.

For example: 'What would make you rethink your view on this?' causes our antagonist to pause. They may answer 'nothing', in which case we can bring things to a polite close. More likely, though, they will offer an olive branch, 'If the boss came down here now and said she was sorry'. Whatever their response we have a chance to discover what lies at the heart of their anger and move towards a solution.

Making suggestions will also move the discussion on:

'We can call the client directly, we can set up a conference call with the whole team, we can keep quiet and hope the issue blows over. What other options are there?'

But keep the alternatives genuine. Throwing in an option that is clearly unacceptable is just as toxic as any aggravating phrase. 'So, shall we get on the train or stay on the platform for the rest of the day?' That's just plain sarcasm.

We can work it out?

Divorce is generally a messy business. With both sides fiercely fighting their corner, agreements can be a long time coming. Which is why many marriage guidance organisations suggest mediation.

Using an impartial third party to negotiate, mediation helps couples to deal positively with the practicalities of relationship breakup, without having to resort to court hearings.

Mediation works along these key principles:

- Win/win: Problem solving is collaborative, aiming for a solution that's acceptable to all.
- Future focus: Whilst it doesn't try to reconcile warring parties, the emphasis is on rebuilding relationships in some shape or form, rather than placing blame.
- Acknowledging feelings: by allowing people to let go of their anger and upset they will be able to move on to pleasanter matters.

> • By working with the individuals rather than against them, mediation is recognised as one of the fastest and most cost-effective ways to settle a dispute.

Poison 5: It's not me

'Don't look now but there's one too many in this room and I think it's you.' Groucho Marx

Symptoms
When we're attacked we obviously want to protect ourselves. But taken too far, self-defence can turn into a self-righteous tantrum. It'll probably sound something like this:

- I'm not trying to be difficult, but...
- I'm NOT disagreeing... I'm not shouting...
- It's not my fault
- I told you so
- I can't take any more of this

Antidote
Forget the blame game. Turn your attention elsewhere. When you feel defensive and you hear yourself overusing the word 'I', deliberately focus on finding a solution to the disagreement rather than identifying the cause. Remember, this problem is probably bigger than the both of you.

Remedy
If you suspect you're likely to meet with this particular poison, avoid aggravating the other person's defensiveness by steering clear of the word 'you'. If they're agitated they'll hear an implicit criticism every time you use it.

Use 'I' instead, and talk from your own personal experience. Keep your statements positive: 'I am trying to find the best solution', 'I do appreciate that there is a wide range of opinion'. In this way you'll avoid making provocative accusations.

If, however, it's too late and you're already in the thick of things, empathise. You may feel the other person is being self-pitying and boorish but they may simply be looking for acknowledgement. 'I know it's not your fault', 'I can see why you feel that you've had enough'. Try offering partial acceptance of their position: 'You are often proved right'. Or just a gentle smile (take care with this one, it's easy to look condescending). Staying calm is the most effective way to a quick apology. As Mr Kipling advised: If you can keep your head when all about are losing theirs and blaming it on you...

Poison 6: 'Can I just'

When we're angry, we get impatient. We want to say our piece, and we don't want to hear what the other person has to say. So we interrupt and talk over them. In response, they shout over us. We yell back over them, they bellow over us. The volume goes up but neither of us actually hears a word that's said.

Antidote
However desperate we are to have our say, we're almost always better off letting the other person finish their speech. If you feel you're itching to interrupt, try these remedies:

- Swallow or take a deep breath to avoid speaking.
- Nod to show you are listening.
- Take notes to show you are listening (and to distract yourself from what you're feeling.)
- Keep eye contact (if they think you're not listening that will raise the heat further).

Remedy
- If they interrupt you once: stop. Let them have their say before you start again.
- If they continue to interrupt, ask them: 'What's the best way for me to respond so that you can hear my point of view?' or, 'Can I share my thoughts without interruption?' (Note the wording there: 'without interruption' not − 'without you interrupting me'.)

Doctor in the house?

Now we've got a packed medicine chest with which to ward off any conflict toxins. As we become more skilled at recognising the signs and applying the appropriate remedy, we'll find the exchange of views may be both full and frank but rarely fierce and ferocious.

What a relief!

Deal or no deal

The Mind Gym's 'Negotiation' workout starts with an exercise about an orange. Not any old orange but a magic orange.

Three people are each given their own brief but not allowed to see the other briefs. The first person takes on the role of the farmer whose sole harvest is one magic orange a year. The livelihood of the whole village depends on how much money he gets for his orange. Last year he received £10,000 which was just enough to keep everyone alive and healthy. He needs at least as much again this year.

The second character plays a famous zoologist, who has discovered one of the last remaining couples in a rare breed of gorilla. The only way for them to mate successfully is to give them the juice from the magic orange. He has raised £10,000 for this purpose, though the funds are desperately short and he has been told to do his best to get the juice for £5,000.

The third character is a world-renowned botanist, who specialises in rare plants with medicinal powers and is equally keen to get hold of the magic orange. She has found a plant with remarkable healing powers for cancer sufferers but the only way to keep it alive is to grate the orange rind into a powder and feed it into the roots. She has a bequest of £20,000 from an elderly patron at her American university but is keen to keep as much as possible for a field trip to the Andes.

And off they go, each preparing for a battle in which either the gorilla doesn't mate or the healing plant with the power to cure certain cancers doesn't grow or the village people suffer.

The advantage that we have is that we can see all three briefs and, if you've read them carefully, you will have spotted the way through. The zoologist wants the juice of the orange. The botanist wants the rind.

The canny farmer will interview them one by one, find out what their real needs are and get them each to make a sealed bid with their best offer. He will then sell the orange to both of them, potentially netting £30,000. Equally, either the zoologist or the botanist could talk with each other and discover that they could make a joint bid, paying £5,000 each, and then split the juice and the rind.

But they rarely do. What happens is that because it's a negotiation we get competitive. Sometimes this works and sometimes it's very expensive.

Two schools

In economics there's Monetarist and Keynesian; in architecture classical and modernist; in politics socialist and capitalist. Negotiation is much the same with two apparently very different schools of thought:

• Collaborative – Win/win
• Competitive – Start with 'no'

Neither is right or wrong and both have a part to play in our deal-making toolkit. And they have more in common than either will readily admit.

Collaborative
The core assumption with getting to 'yes', also called 'win/win', is that we can have our cake and eat it. How? By growing the cake. This means that even when it looks like it's impossible for us both to get what we want – you want to go out, I want to stay in – we keep searching for an outcome that gives us both (pretty much) what we want: we invite friends over.

And eat it

Collaborative negotiation tends to be the better option when there is a high level of trust and where it is important to reach an agreement. With our life partner, business partner, long-term client, mum or son, we probably want to start with a collaborative approach. Given how quickly roles change so our suppliers can become clients, investors become employees, people who work for us get promoted to become our boss, it pays to start collaborative with most people where we might want a long and harmonious relationship. They are partners not the enemy.

When win-win is well done, everyone leaves feeling good and relationships are stronger than they were before.

The risk lies in appearing soft, accommodating, weak and malleable – quick to oblige the other party and slow to deliver. What can start off with the intention to collaborate quickly becomes the road to compromise or failure, especially if the other party is keen to compete.

Competitive

At the other end of the negotiation spectrum is the competitive approach. Sounds aggressive but it doesn't have to be.

In these negotiations the goal is victory. We are less worried about creating a bigger reward for everyone, and more concerned with getting the most for ourselves. A competitive negotiator sees the other party as an antagonist. However, this does not mean treating them badly or getting aggressive, far from it. It does mean that we disclose as little as possible, whilst encouraging the other party to say as much as they can.

It's perfect for the bazaar, for emergencies and when buying a second-hand car. We don't want a relationship, just a result.

When well done, competitive negotiation delivers results cleanly and comprehensively and builds our reputation for strength and resolution. When overdone, it can appear hard, aggressive, uncompromising and unreasonable and can put people off dealing with us at all.

Sneaky advantage

There is no right or wrong approach. Most of us will use both styles every day. There are four tactics that lie at the heart of all successful negotiation. And four more that give us a sneaky advantage when we opt for the competitive approach.

Negotiator bias

Research reveals that most of us go into a deal with what is called the negotiator's bias. We see ourselves as fair and honest and our opponents as scheming and competitive. When disagreements arise, each party tends to view their own behaviour as innocent, while viewing the other as intentionally harmful, hostile or aggressive.

So bearing our biases in mind, how do we make sure our emotions don't run away with us? Getting off to a good start helps. In another study, pairs of negotiators who were instructed to schmooze for 10 minutes before starting discussions were seen to have higher rates of agreement and to reach more creative deals than those who get straight down to business. It seems that the idle chit-chat over the tea and biscuits isn't wasted.

---

1. What really matters

The trick lies in not listening too literally to what people say (their position) but in finding out what they really care about (their interest).

Your position is that you want to go out, but your interest is that you want to see some friends; my position is that I don't want to go out, but my interest is not to go out in the rain, so friends coming over for supper suits us both; or waiting until the weather changes.

The rule of five

The rule of five 'whys' says we need to ask 'why?' five times to get to the real interest.

'I want to go to Ibiza.'
'Why?'
'Because I want to lie on a sunny beach.'
'Why?'
'Because I need to relax.'
'Why?'
'Because I'm working too hard.'
'Why?'
'Because my boss is dumping on me.'
'Why?'
'Because I can't say "no" to her without losing my chance of promotion.'

The underlying need is to find a way to say 'no' to the boss and still get promoted. A long way from Beneras beach.

More tricky is to know which 'why' question to ask next:

'I want the orange.'
'Why?'
'So the gorillas can mate.'

Here we have at least a couple of options: why do you want the gorillas to mate? And why will the orange help them mate? The first option will lead us on a bit of a wild gorilla chase, the second will uncover the real need and so enable us to negotiate the best result. It's hard to know which 'why' to go with and so best to remain nimble. Try one and, if that doesn't lead anywhere, we can always switch tack.

The five whys are equally useful when applied to our own thinking. We may have talked ourselves into a corner, defending a position we don't really hold in order to appear consistent – I must have it repaired today – when our true interests are somewhat different – it must be repaired properly so that it doesn't break down again and I'll accept a rental in the meantime.

You're arguing forcefully but, deep down, you're not quite sure why – this is when to ask yourself the five 'whys'.

2. Talk my language

One exasperated corporate client vented his frustration: 'We've been going through an IPO. It's no secret it's been in the business press most days for the last six months. I get a letter or an email from a supplier who wants to meet me pretty much every day. Do you know how may mentioned the IPO? I'll tell you. None. Not one eager supplier mentioned the single most important thing going on in my business.'

If we were to hold an auction on what people would pay to cut their journey time to work (or on the school run), we might be surprised by the variety of bids, even across groups with similar wealth. The reason is that different people will give a different value to shortening their journey to work. Some will pay handsomely for a little more time with their young children, others will find those few moments between one life and the other a relaxing part of the day and some will want any excuse to get away from home at any cost, in fact they'd bid to make the journey longer.

When we're negotiating we tend to see things from our perspective. As a result, we describe the issues in ways that make sense to us, rather than in ways that appeal to the other person. It always pays to talk about the value and the outcomes from the perspective of the person we're negotiating with.

3. Build a powerful alternative

The Harvard Negotiation Project talks about: Best Alternative To a Negotiated Agreement (BATNA). This is the best possible outcome if we don't reach an agreement.

When the Russian government is negotiating with Western oil companies, the BATNA for the Russian government is that they get the full benefits from the oil for themselves, and for the oil companies that Russia is less likely to get foreign investment in future. It's clear who has the upper hand.

Compare Margaret Thatcher and the coal miners in 1980 and 1984. In 1980 the UK government's BATNA was power cuts across the country. By 1984, when stockpiles had been created at the power stations rather than the coal mines, the governments BATNA was an unpleasant and divisive strike, something they felt they could live with.

When we are negotiating it pays to build up our BATNA so we can walk away. We do this by increasing the options, say a selection of suppliers pitching for the same project, or a choice of different apartments to rent.

If it's appropriate we can let the other person know that we have other options but there's usually no need to. The BATNA is simply a piece in the negotiation jigsaw and the better the BATNA the better our negotiating position. Reminding ourselves that we have other options may also reduce our anxiety.

4. No pain, no gain

The more the other party feels that they will lose out if they don't reach an agreement, the more likely they are to settle. To strengthen our position we may well encourage them to see how weak their BATNA is. Gently.

So, if we don't reach a deal, what will happen?
Will anyone back at Head Office care (who, how much)?

Or drop it in: 'I suppose that if we don't reach a settlement it isn't exactly the end of the world.'

On the other side, we may well talk up the benefits of reaching agreement.

'How will you feel if we close the deal?'
'What might others/the rest of your team/ your partner then do/think?'
'What longer-term consequences might there be? Will you get promoted?'

Win-lose

Call my bluff

Here are six tell-tale signs that the other person is not being entirely straight:

Ask direct questions which can be answered by 'yes' or 'no'. If you get a long-winded response then start to get suspicious.

Little in life is perfect. If an explanation, set of benefits or case study about a past success sounds too good to be true then it probably is.

Ask questions about detail. An HR professional negotiating a starting salary was suspicious about the new starter who claimed to have worked for a well-known advertising agency. 'Remind me, what number Charlotte Street are their offices?' he asked. The candidate, who had only temped there for a week as one of many short-term jobs, couldn't remember.

As Vic Reeves quipped, '88.2% of statistics are made up on the spot.' Ask where the data comes from, what assumptions have been made and what further information is available from this or other sources.

Expert bluffers may look you in the eye or may look away. They are, however, likely to put their fingers on their face more than usual, scratching their nose, rubbing their eyes or touching their mouth.

When someone is over-friendly and gives you more compliments than you deserve (and that's not always an easy thing to judge), remain alert for the other alarm bells.

And here are four more tactics that are especially helpful for competitive negotiation.

5. Need for speed

'Last few days – sale must end Sunday.' Goodness knows why it 'must' end, is a new tax being introduced? Is the warehouse going

to go up in flames? But we don't think like that. As customers we are far more likely to think, 'better get this bargain while it is still there'. A car salesperson's well-worn technique is to tell you that they are just short of their monthly target and, so they can hit their numbers, they'll give you a special deal. If you buy today. Have you been had?

Research demonstrates that negotiators who feel that they need to act urgently tend to put themselves in more difficult positions.

When the Vietnamese were negotiating with the US over a settlement to the Vietnam war, the first thing the Vietnamese did was rent a property near the negotiations for two years. They were not going to rush.

6. Knowledge = power

The key to gaining knowledge is to use questions – lots of them.

Open questions are best. These begin Who, What, When, Where, Why, How and they are great for eliciting lots of information. Closed questions, that start with, for example, 'do you?', 'is it correct that?', 'am I right in thinking?', 'did?', are best avoided. We get a 'yes' or 'no' and that's often it.

Leading questions are worse still, because they reveal our position and tell us precious little about the other person. Avoid, for example, 'Don't you think this is the right thing to go for?' or 'What do you like about our excellent product?'

This may seem startlingly obvious. If so, start tracking the number of open questions you ask compared with closed/leading/other kinds of question. Most of us overestimate the proportion of open questions that we use.

And what happens if the other side starts to question you? Simply turn it to your information-gathering advantage by reversing it back on to the questioner: 'I'm not entirely sure, what's your opinion?'

The goal of this tactic is depth – we want to get as deep into their concerns as possible. And we want to demonstrate empathy.

7. Start with 'no'

The tactic behind 'start with no' is more subtle than it sounds. The aim is to open with an offer that the other person is going to turn down. Positively invite them to say no: 'Could you produce a full draft by this afternoon?' Or 'Would you pick the children up from school every day next week?'

The idea is to desensitise ourselves to hearing the word 'No'. When we're worried about being turned down we will often compromise or accommodate rather than face refusal. To overcome this, give yourself permission to hear 'no'. Don't intimidate the other person though. Make it clear that you're simply starting negotiations – 'Do say no to this, I want to be as clear as possible' so that the other party does not worry about turning you down.

In one episode of *The Apprentice* we are invited into Donald Trump's inner sanctum to watch the big man at work. The brief clip goes something like this:

Trump: So you're saying you can do this piece of work for three hundred and fifty thousand dollars.
Supplier: That's right.
Trump: I need some movement on price. Could you do it for two hundred and fifty thousand dollars?
Supplier: No, that's a little too low.
Trump: Would you have a problem at two hundred and sixty thousand dollars?
Supplier: No, I could do it for two hundred and sixty-five thousand dollars.
Trump: Great, you've got a deal.

Having heard no, our next step is to discover why the request is not feasible. That will provide us with an insight into the criteria that our opposite number is using to evaluate their decisions. We can move forward to a logical discussion, rather than an emotional one.

Throughout all this we're not giving away anything about ourselves; simply gathering information about the other person's interests and positions.

Decision-making traps

To negotiate skilfully we need to have all our wits about us. But when there's a lot a stake we often fall into thinking traps that compromise our decision-making skills. Here are four of the most common ones.

Anchoring – We give disproportionate weight to the first information we receive. Ask a canny waiter to recommend a bottle of wine and they will point to an expensive wine and warn, 'Don't buy this one, it's very over-priced'. They will then point to another bottle, more expensive than you intended but cheaper than the first, and advise, 'This one's extremely good value'. Overcome this trap by looking at each piece of information separately, or setting down your parameters in advance.

Sunk-cost – We make a decision to justify past choices, even if the past choice no longer seems valid. For example, we've got planning permission to build the house extension so we feel we should do it, otherwise all that time and money will be wasted. Whereas the collapse in property may now make this a dumb investment.

Confirming evidence – We unconsciously seek out and focus on information that supports our existing viewpoint while avoiding and playing down information that contradicts it.

Status quo – Given the chance we often opt to leave things as they are. The top brass at Intel got out of this trap by firing themselves. They walked across the road to the coffee shop and re-hired themselves. When they returned to HQ, they looked at the business challenges as the new owners with a fresh set of eyes.

8. Appear un-threatening

Would you rather negotiate with a business student or a theology student? What assumptions would you make? And how would those expectations influence your behaviour?

A study by de Dreu and colleagues put these questions to the test. Not only did participants expect the business students to be more competitive and opportunistic and the theology students to be more ethical and co-operative – but they themselves behaved in the same way: co-operating with the theologian and making competitive choices with the business student.

Some negotiation coaches even suggest that appearing a little bumbling can be an advantage. In the same way as TV detective Columbo would adopt an absentminded air, they encourage negotiators to 'accidentally' leave something behind or to knock something on the floor – almost encouraging the other party to patronise them.

It's a tricky call – unless you're a skilled actor there's a fine line between seeming self-effacing and coming over as Mr Bean. The ideal is to demonstrate competence in the delivery of the goods or services we are offering, but to stay low key in the negotiation itself.

The research also shows that a key to a successful deal lies less in the technical details or a favourable price and more in the negotiator's ability to reign in their emotions. Not only do angry outbursts lead to fewer joint gains and an unwillingness to work with each other again but combative participants are less likely to get a good deal for themselves than those who maintain positive regard for the other party. It seems that we have nothing to gain and everything to lose by expressing high emotions during a deal.

A briefcase

A man was looking through a window at a briefcase that was marked eighty dollars. The shop owner came out and offered to sell the case at eighty dollars. The man turned it down. A number of price reductions then followed with the potential customer standing firm – he had a perfectly good briefcase after all. 'All right,' said the shop owner. 'fifty-five dollars.' Again the man said no. The shopkeeper came back with his final offer – sixty dollars. 'Hang on' said the man, 'you said fifty-five dollars before.' 'Did I?' replied the shop owner, 'I shouldn't have done that, I've made a mistake. I'm sorry, but

I must honour the deal, so you can have the case for fifty-five dollars, just don't tell anyone else.'

A few moments later the man walked away, happy to have achieved not only a brand new briefcase but also a smart bargain. The shopkeeper was even more delighted – by appearing slightly bungling, he had sold a briefcase at a price he was happy with.

And when it's all over?

Jack Welch, turnaround CEO of General Electric, advises always to leave something on the table for the other party. A Harvard Business School professor, Howard Raiffa, agrees. In his research experiments he found that sellers who had been instructed to be benevolent to their buyers got a better outcome that those who'd been told to be tough.

While it is in our interests to leave the other party feeling good, we would be well advised to play down our own positive feelings. Research shows that – independent of the outcome – negotiators felt less satisfied when they believed their opponents were happy with the final outcome. Even more alarming, another study found that negotiators who told the other party they felt good about the outcome ended up making fewer gains in subsequent negotiations with them. So, a word to the wise: don't break out the champagne until they have left the room.

Y When you next see two people negotiating (fictional or in real life) – try to spot who is taking which negotiation approach: competitive or collaborative? Do they stay with that style throughout the negotiation, or do they move between styles? What tactics are they using? If you were in their place, would you handle things in the same way, or would you have gone for a different technique?

I smell trouble

First post

 21ST FEBRUARY, POSTED BY STU_PENDOUS

Hi there world, virgin blogger here. I've never written a blog before but my girlfriend (yes, geeks have girlfriends too) keeps telling me that writing things down can be very therapeutic, so I thought I'd give it a whirl.

So what's bugging me? Well, it's work, weirdly. I say weirdly because normally I love what I do. I design software, heading up a team that develops web applications. We dream the ideas up with our creative team – they do the pretty look and feel, and we make it work. It can be a bit stressful at times, but I enjoy it and I like to think I'm pretty good at what I do. I even picked up an award recently.

Anyway, I'm getting some really bad vibes from some of the guys on the creative side. I can't put my finger on what it is – conversations seem like hard work, it all feels a bit tense. Perhaps I am just being paranoid, but the last couple of weeks have been a real slog. I can't work out whether it's just me being a bit tired, or whether there's something more to it.

Comments (5)

23RD FEBRUARY, POSTED BY EPICUREAN_LIFE

Saw you were out there and thought I'd say hi. Made me laugh about the girlfriend; I'm a geek of sorts too: a psychologist – well, at least I'm studying to be one at university. I'm in my final year. Up to my ears in Kant (that's a psychologist's joke, by the way).

Anyway, enough about me; let's talk about you. Tell me more about the bad vibes.

23RD FEBRUARY, POSTED BY STU_PENDOUS

Hi EL, good to hear from you. I was starting to think I was talking to the void.

Work: so glad you asked. Things are not great, actually. Still bad vibes a go-go. Nothing specific, you understand – just little things. I can't work out if any of it's real, or if I'm just imagining it.

23RD FEBRUARY, POSTED BY EPICUREAN_LIFE

Hard to say, since we've only met virtually. It could just be a few bad days in the office. Is there some reason why your colleagues might be more stressed than usual? Or are you under pressure, or perhaps just tired and in need of a holiday? I know I'm only a student, but I still know what it's like with deadlines. It's easy to feel suspicious or irritable when you're stressed – seems like the whole world is having a go at you, when in fact they're probably not even thinking about you. My advice, for what it's worth, is to chill out a bit and see if it passes.

And remember: just because you are paranoid doesn't mean people aren't out to get you!

Sorry. Another hilarious (not) psychologist's joke.

23RD FEBRUARY, POSTED BY STU_PENDOUS

Point taken.

P.S. Here's one back: man goes to see his psychiatrist. He says,

'Doctor, people tell me I'm a wheelbarrow.' The psychiatrist replies, 'Don't let people push you around.'

23RD FEBRUARY, POSTED BY EPICUREAN_LIFE

Touché. Only technically a psychologist is not the same as a psychiatrist, but I'll let that one pass. After all, I couldn't tell the difference between a RAM and a goat if my life depended on it.

SOS

28TH FEBRUARY, POSTED BY STU_PENDOUS

Aargh. EL, are you out there there? Can I climb onto your virtual couch?

Comments (5)

28TH FEBRUARY, POSTED BY EPICUREAN_LIFE

Hi Stu, I've got you on Google blog alert. Be my guest. The cushions are all nice and plumped up (actually it's got last night's pizza and a couple of beer cans on it, but you don't need to know that).

28TH FEBRUARY, POSTED BY STU_PENDOUS

Thanks. Okay, I did what you said, tried to take things easy – and nothing's changed. If anything it's got worse. There's definitely something going on. I'm pretty sure I am not being paranoid. It's just little things – a couple of people are making less eye contact with me. Not exactly avoiding me, but kind of distracted whenever I try to talk to them.

The worst thing is this: at lunchtime, a group of us usually wander out together to get something to eat. But the last few days, they've shot off without waiting for me. Maybe they're just in a hurry – but it's freaking me out anyhow. It's like there's something going on that they're not telling me about.

Anyway, what do you reckon?

P.S. The pizza thing – that's gross, by the way.

28TH FEBRUARY, POSTED BY EPICUREAN_LIFE

Hmm (he said, stroking his metaphorical beard). I can't say what's really going on at work, because I'm not there. But I think I have a fairly clear idea of what's going on in your head.

In some ways it doesn't matter how real the problem is: if it's upsetting you, you need to address it. Best case scenario, it turns out to be your imagination, and you all have a laugh about it in the pub. Worst case, you're right – but at least that way you can lance the boil before it takes over your life.

Personally, I think you've got a bad case of office politics. We psychologists have a name for this – well, a few actually: 'covert conflict' or 'indirect aggression'. But it all boils down to the same thing: a headache for you. You can sense the tension, feel work friendships slipping through your fingers – but can't work out why. You get a strong feeling that you have upset someone, but no one will tell you what you're actually supposed to have done. You walk into a room, and everyone stops talking – or changes the subject. Was it you they were discussing? Perhaps. But you'd be the last to know.

It's not unlike being bullied at school. Is there anyone at all you can trust? It might be a good idea to have a quiet word to see if you can shed some light on the issue.

28TH FEBRUARY, POSTED BY STU_PENDOUS

There are one or two people who might be able to help. Trouble is, I don't want to stir things up if this really is all in my head. My girlfriend's not much help, either: she just thinks I'm being over-sensitive, which is a bit rich coming from her. She's met my work lot a few times, and thinks they're a nice bunch – can't understand what the problem is.

But you're right – I'll grasp the nettle. I might try talking to Tony. He's a bit of an outsider, but he keeps his ear to the ground.

28TH FEBRUARY, POSTED BY EPICUREAN_LIFE

Great. Meanwhile, I'll look up some studies on covert conflict. I think my flatmate's got something on the subject. His girlfriend's certainly an expert – you should have seen the look she gave me the other day after I'd finished in the bathroom. Okay, so I'd used up her precious Aveda shampoo – but at least I didn't borrow her toothbrush (well actually I did, but she doesn't know that, does she?).

The plot thickens

1ST MARCH, POSTED BY STU_PENDOUS

You remember you said I had to look for something concrete? Well here it is – more like a ton of bricks than concrete: I was just about to approach dull Tony for my chat, when Dave arrived at my desk. In front of my entire team, he gave me a really hard time about a project we're working on. Just dismissed the work out of hand – didn't want to hear what I had to say – started pointing out all the rough edges which, quite frankly, are irrelevant at this point. It's only a first prototype (he knows that very well), but he started criticising tiny details anyway. Then he said something about being 'disappointed' that my team wasn't further ahead in the project.

Let me tell you, I was furious. I could feel myself going red, and everyone in the office was looking at each other, like they knew this had been coming for ages. EL: I was right. They all hate me.

Did your flatmate turn up anything useful?

Comments (7)

1ST MARCH, POSTED BY EPICUREAN_LIFE

Ouch.

Still, at least you now know that there really is something up. Now it's just a question of finding out what – and why. I'm still trying to get by the Ice Maiden, but as soon as I do, I'll hit you with the science. Meanwhile, here's a couple of thoughts.

1. This kind of thing is common in offices (that's in many ways why I'm still a student). Work is the place where we are all supposed to be grown-up and professional. And so the obvious, which is to have it all out in the open, maybe have a bit of a shouting match, and clear the air, doesn't happen. Tension builds. It broods, broils, festers. And then it starts to escape in little toxic blasts, a bit like a volcano. People have a go at you in a roundabout way. They're angry at object A (eg, you), so they have a go at object B (your work).

2. You are a man, and men learn the finer points of this game slightly later in life than women. This is because at school, the girls learn these games early. They scheme, they bitch, they plot – but on the surface it's all smiles. Young boys on the other hand, just punch each other's lights out to solve a problem, and then go back to normal. Trouble is, you can't really punch someone in an office, can you?

Just for the record, though: is this Dave bigger than you?

1ST MARCH, POSTED BY STU_PENDOUS

6ft4 with his stupid sticky-up hairdo.

That's all very clever, but what about some practical suggestions?

1ST MARCH, POSTED BY EPICUREAN_LIFE

Ooh. If I weren't an (almost) qualified professional, I'd say you were taking your frustration out on me. Luckily, taking offence is not my thing.

In answer to your question, Dave's behaviour is actually a bit of a gift. Now you've got an excuse to tackle the problem head on. After all, he's had a go at you, so it's not like he can feign innocence if you challenge him.

There's no need to have a big showdown – just ask whether there's a problem. This is a lot like the situation a mate of mine found himself in recently. Having always got on really well with his (female) boss, she suddenly and inexplicably went all frosty with him. So he waited until the end of a meeting when they were alone, and just asked the question: had he done something wrong? She said no, not at all; in fact she seemed quite surprised that he had thought so – and the relationship immediately became much warmer. All he needed to do was clear the air.

It's tempting to withdraw and avoid the other person if you're feeling mistreated, but I don't think that's a particularly good tactic.

You should have a direct chat with Dave, and find out what's really going on.

1ST MARCH POSTED BY STU_PENDOUS

Easier said than done. All my instincts are telling me to withdraw. I'm not a confrontational person at the best of times, and I hate the idea of having a public row. Or worse, crawling to him.

1ST MARCH, POSTED BY EPICUREAN_LIFE

That's my point, though. Don't go crawling to him; keep your head, and don't let him see that his aggression is intimidating you. Just be really calm and reasonable. No one can argue with calm and reasonable.

Otherwise, how are you ever going to make this stop? It's messing with your head already. Sooner or later it's going to start affecting your work. And then where will you be?

1ST MARCH POSTED BY STU_PENDOUS

Alright, alright, point taken.

I've got a project meeting with Dave tomorrow. I'll try to find a way to ask him what's going on.

1ST MARCH POSTED BY EPICUREAN_LIFE

Break a leg!

Call to arms

3RD MARCH, POSTED BY STU_PENDOUS

Okay, the time for talking is over. This is out-and-out warfare.

I've been taken off our major project. It's been given to one of the other development teams. Some guff about 'trying out a new work flow system'. This is the first I've heard of it. We don't do things behind closed doors at this company, that's what I liked about this place, we discuss decisions. Nobody discussed this one with me.

Comments (7)

4TH MARCH, POSTED BY EPICUREAN_LIFE

Hmm. I had a feeling something like that might happen.

You most definitely have a bad case of office politics. If we don't do something quick, it could be terminal.

Seriously, though. I'm not surprised you're angry. Being removed from a team or taken off a project is a typical tactic, designed to destabilise you, knock your confidence and generally make you feel irrelevant.

It's these little passive acts of aggression – not copying someone into an email with the latest news, conspicuously leaving them off the invitation list for a party – that reduces a person's opportunity to express an opinion and so excludes them. It gets worse if others start to join in. Maybe your mates lunching without you a few weeks ago was significant after all: it may be that Dave is lobbying others to create a negative opinion of you (not that I'm trying to make you more paranoid or anything; just might be a possibility).

I'd say your next step is to see if you can track the cause of the conflict. Think back: has there been a conversation or negotiation that didn't go as well as usual? It doesn't have to be a big number – the things that spark off tensions are often outside of our awareness. It could be a phrase that got someone's back up, a joke taken the wrong way. It might have seemed trivial to you at the time, but it could have triggered resentment and jealousy.

4TH MARCH, POSTED BY STU_PENDOUS

Resentment and jealousy, you say? Are you telling me this is my fault?

4TH MARCH, POSTED BY EPICUREAN_LIFE

Of course I'm not. I'm just wondering whether you might have inadvertently poked some kind of hornet's nest. You know, stirred something up without realising it. There's no point in being defensive with me: think, man.

4TH MARCH, POSTED BY STU_PENDOUS

Sorry. Just feeling quite a bit raw right now.

I won't lie: my girlfriend does say I can be a bit full on sometimes. But I don't see what's wrong with that. That's just me. And besides, I'm just trying to let people know that I'm good at what I do. Is that wrong?

4TH MARCH, POSTED BY EPICUREAN_LIFE

It's fine to want people to spot your talent – but not if you're rubbing their noses in it. Show not tell, I always say: don't brag, just get on with doing a good job, and the credit will be yours by right.

Think about it. Could you have unwittingly trodden on Dave's size 12s? What about that award you won. It was one of the first things you mentioned on this blog, so it clearly means a lot to you. Did you by any teensy chance maybe show off about it a bit?

4TH MARCH, POSTED BY STU_PENDOUS

I'm trying to think. That award was a big industry thing, quite prestigious, really. And now you mention it, Dave did seem a bit put out when he heard about it. I don't know why – his team

designed the original idea, but we changed it a lot as it went through development. You don't think he expected some sort of credit do you? It was really quite a different concept by the end of the project. Do you think that could have something to do with it?

4TH MARCH, POSTED BY EPICUREAN_LIFE

Hmm, now let me think…

Er, YES! And I've got a lots of evidence to support my view...

Two researchers, Pat Heim and Susan Murphy, have written about this (I finally got past the Ice Queen. I got my girlfriend to lure her out for a bonding chat, and raided my flatmate's files. Interesting on a number of levels, not all of which I wish to share). Anyway, they talked about something called the power-dead-even rule, which they think lies at the root of covert conflict. It goes like this: we all have an idea of where we fit in a social structure. Our status, and that of everyone else, is in balance. If something changes that – someone's rewarded, promoted or favoured in some way – then people take action to redress the balance. In organisations, that tends to happen through covert conflict and indirect aggression – becoming distant, critiquing work, leaving you out of meetings / emails – in fact, exactly the kind of thing that's been happening to you.

I am convinced that this is what you're seeing with Dave. Maybe he feels you've 'risen above your station' in some way – either because he thinks you're being cocky, or because the awards you've been winning have raised your status relative to his – and so your relationship is out of balance. He needs to redress the balance, take you down a few pegs.

He might not even realise the reasons why he's doing it. Often, people don't know what's behind their feelings of irritation; so don't expect Dave to come out with it if you ask him what's wrong. I'm afraid it's your job to do the detective work.

The recognition thing

8TH MARCH, POSTED BY STU_PENDOUS

Ok.

I've been thinking about what you said and I think you might have a point there. Dave has always been a bit touchy about credits on work, but I've always ignored it. He can get a bit grumpy if he isn't given enough recognition, that kind of thing. But I don't think that justifies him trying to edge me out. In fact, that makes me even angrier – it's so petty.

Comments (3)

8TH MARCH, POSTED BY EPICUREAN_LIFE

Well hello stranger. I was beginning to think you'd had enough after my last mini lecture.

Whatever; it sounds like you've got to the heart of it. A bit of a breakthrough, if you like.

Question is: what now?

If working with Dave wasn't an issue, I'd suggest moving on from the relationship – some games just aren't worth the candle, as the old saying goes. But you like your job, and you're good at it. Why should you leave?

You need to fix your relationship with Dave. It's not going to be easy, but it should be perfectly possible provided you proceed with caution.

First, a few words of warning. Avoid meeting fire with fire. Now you know what's going on, it's going to be very tempting to hit back by badmouthing Dave. Not a good idea. Not only will it raise the temperature further but, as someone who doesn't usually play this sort of game, you'll probably be terrible at it. Also, all the people who were (however secretly) on your side will just think you're as bad as Dave and deserve what's coming. And you don't want to lose their support.

Secondly, use your loaf. It's not enough to 'keep your friends close and your enemies closer'; you must also take pains to ensure that other people in the company, particularly those in senior positions, are aware of the work you're doing. That way they'll have something to offset the negative information they might hear about you. Copy the relevant people into emails so that credit can't be pinched, and when appropriate, ask people to give their opinion in front of others. This puts antagonists on the spot – they've either got to come clean, or alternatively they'll show themselves up as having one public and one private story, which immediately reduces their credibility.

(Of course, it's all about balance – don't suddenly bombard your boss's inbox or openly confront people at the company meeting, keep it low key.)

While all this is going on at work, give yourself a boost elsewhere. Go home and see your mum, spend more time with your girlfriend – whatever it takes to make you feel loved and confident. Maintain standards at work too, to keep your confidence up.

 8TH MARCH, POSTED BY STU_PENDOUS

That's good advice, thanks. You've encouraged me to step back a bit, to try to see things from the Dave's perspective, which is good.

Also, when I think about it, I wonder whether part of the problem is the culture of the company. We're very friendly but it's also a very competitive place – you need to make sure you get seen to be doing a good job. I tend to focus on making sure that people know that I'm doing good work with my team. And to be honest I don't often think about the effort that other people have put in.

One of the designers did once say (after a few drinks in the pub) that I treated her like the 'oily rag'. She made out it was just a joke, but perhaps she was really trying to tell me something. After all, I do tend to ignore them a bit. I certainly don't say much about their contribution when I present the finished work. Maybe that's what got up Dave's nose. The award might have been the final straw, perhaps?

8TH MARCH, POSTED BY EPICUREAN_LIFE

Mmm. The oily rag thing is really telling – in some ways I wish you'd mentioned it earlier. Whether you are or not, it shows that people think of you as being a bit high-handed. Maybe you don't take other people's work seriously enough, or maybe you patronise them – or maybe it's a combination of the two.

Trouble is, how do you tell the team leader that's he's taking you for granted. It's no coincidence that this girl was maybe a bit annoyed, and even then had to pretend it was only a joke.

It's very hard when you're in charge of a group of people but not in overall control to get the balance right. You have to make sure you acknowledge everyone's work, whilst at the same time ensuring you get the credit higher up. Think of those interviews they do with the top players after a football or rugby match. They always choose the person who has played really well and ask them how they managed to be so brilliant. And the players invariably say that they're part of a team, and that there are lots of people on the pitch, and that they are simply a small cog in a well-oiled machine, etc, etc... In other words, they deliberately avoid being singled out and play down their own part in the team's success.

I am sure you thoroughly deserved that gong you're so proud of – but you should have thought about all the other people who helped you achieve it – and allowed them to share in your glory. After all, you've said it yourself: you like to be rewarded for your efforts; your colleagues are no different.

I really think this is the root of all your problems.

You probably know what's coming next. Yup: you've got to meet Dave's need for recognition. It'll probably feel like you're indulging him; but it's the best chance you've got of fixing your relationship with him, and moving on.

So (deep breath): is there a way you could acknowledge Dave's contribution and raise his status a bit?

P.S. By the way, it's interesting what you say about the company culture. This may sound odd but do you reckon there's a way

you could frame this experience as being positive? I mean, it's helped you to understand the organisational culture better, and given you a chance to reflect on your relationships at work. And you're seeing your own actions from another perspective. So some good stuff might inadvertently have come out of this not-so-good situation.

Truce?

12TH MARCH, POSTED BY STU_PENDOUS

EL, you'd be proud of me: I spoke to Dave.

Like you said, I didn't make a big deal of it – just said that I felt that we'd had a good working relationship before and that I felt like something had gone awry.

Initially, he denied there was anything wrong – he didn't actually talk to me, mind, he talked to his coffee cup, but I made a big effort and pushed on through. I said it seemed a bit unfair that I'd got so much of the glory from the award, when the original idea had been his. And I was super nice about some of the work he's done recently (it is pretty good, in fact). I suppose I did flatter him a bit, saying he was one of the best creatives in the business and that I really wanted to carry on working with him. And I asked him if he wanted to come in on a high profile project that I've just taken on. That went down really well.

I still can't help feeling like I'm pandering to someone's temper tantrum. But the truth is that since our chat, he's been much more relaxed around me. In fact, everyone's been more relaxed. And yesterday I brought my award into the office. It was my girlfriend's idea, actually. I'd been keeping it on the mantelpiece in the living room, and after I showed her our conversations and told her about my chat with Dave, she suggested I take it in as a kind of gesture. A way of sharing the success, I guess. One of my team seemed quite surprised that I'd brought it in, so I just explained that it wasn't really mine, it belonged to everyone because of all their hard work. The guy actually made me a cup of coffee, can you believe it. And yes, we all had lunch together.

P.S. I think my girlfriend might have had an ulterior motive with the award thing: looking at it objectively, in the cold light of the office, it's a pretty hideous object. I think she just wanted to get the damn thing out of our living room!

Comments (4)

12TH MARCH, POSTED BY EPICUREAN_LIFE

Well hurrah and halleluya. Well done. It takes a lot of self-control to have that sort of conversation – particularly when someone's talking to the china.

And yes, I'm sure you're right about the award and your girlfriend. When it comes to interior decor, men and women are on different planets. Or, to coin a phrase: men are from B&Q, women are from Habitat. But that's a whole other conversation.

12TH MARCH, POSTED BY STU_PENDOUS

I'm back on with the main project at work. Dave said he really needed my input. I can't tell you what a relief it is.

EL, you're a genius. I couldn't have done it without you.

12TH MARCH, POSTED BY EPICUREAN_LIFE

Not really – I've just read the books.

I'm really happy for you. Now: don't screw up again. Just in case you're tempted, I've made you a little list. Think of it as a user's guide to office politics.

1. If you think it's about you, it probably isn't. Don't read too much into a single instance of someone's behaviour.

2. Recognise when you're on the receiving end of covert conflict and understand that it's fairly common.

3. Put on a public face of strength. Find other people, activities and challenges to bolster your self-esteem.

I smell trouble

4. Observe what's happening, and if it's appropriate, confront it with the people involved.

5. Think through what may be causing this. More often than not, it's because someone feels that the power-balance between you is out of kilter. They probably won't have recognised this as an issue themselves. But they will feel irritated by you.

6. Ask yourself whether you feel it's worth investing the energy and time to salvage a relationship.

7. Don't badmouth your antagonist. It won't help reach a resolution, and because you've turned it into a competition, they may win.

8. Guard against gossips and misinformation by managing communication. If you're concerned about people taking credit for your work, copy others into emails or present your ideas publicly. Build positive coalitions of support.

9. Find ways to be resilient – whether that be through seeing the advantages of the situation, using social support, focusing on other activities, and occasionally escaping the situation for a while.

10. When your status is raised, be careful how you communicate with others. Play down success and be generous spirited.

 12TH MARCH, POSTED BY STU_PENDOUS

I shall print it out and keep it in my wallet. And once again, thanks.

(M) The hardest word

'*Sometimes you're the windshield, sometimes you're the bug.*'
Mary Chapin Carpenter

Which is to say, we're going to bump up against each other as we go through life. Sometimes it's our toes that get trodden on, other times we do the treading. It's going to happen.

Occasionally the issues will be far bigger and the hurt much more severe. We may find ourselves having to apologise for something we're ashamed of. We may need to forgive something we consider to be way out of line.

Asking for and granting forgiveness can be a very tough call. It takes courage and it takes skill. Sometimes we try our very best and don't get the response we wanted. But if we're looking to create successful relationships it's worth reflecting on the tricky business of the 'S' word.

The 'S' word

'*My mother could make anybody feel guilty – she used to get letters of apology from people she didn't even know.*'
Joan Rivers

I'm not going to apologise. Why should I? I didn't do anything wrong. Well not in comparison with what he did. Anyway, I might get away with it, he might not even notice. And if I act indignant he might think he's in the wrong and apologise (yeah, right). Anyway, he should say 'sorry' first. He started it. And if I do say 'sorry', what then? 'I knew I was right' he'll sneer with his eyes and how will I feel? I'll feel like I want to climb into a hole. I'll feel that most horrible feeling of all, I'll feel guilty. No, no, no, I'm not going to apologise. Anyway, why should I? I didn't do anything wrong, really.

And so the voice in our head goes on, convincing us not to say 'sorry'. And the longer it goes on the more likely we are to talk ourselves into a position of unfounded righteousness: we were in fact right all along and that there is nothing to apologise for.

There might be another, quieter voice, desperately trying to be heard: go on, just say you're 'sorry'. It doesn't matter. Admit you're wrong. What's there to lose? Don't be so proud.

But this little voice gets drowned out, which is a shame because one thing we know for sure: seeking and giving forgiveness lies at the heart of successful relationships.

'Love means not ever having to say you're sorry' is Ryan O'Neal's final line in *Love Story*. Great cinema, lousy advice. Love usually means saying 'sorry' an awful lot.

The recipe for humble pie

Step 1: Accept responsibility
Apologies start with 'I'. 'I was wrong, I messed up, I shouldn't have, it was my fault...' No blaming the photocopier, or the confusing email, or the recipe book. Or the way you looked at me, or what you told me last week or even what Mary did (the cheek of it). For once, it pays to be entirely egotistical.

I MADE A MISTAKE.

When a bank ran a series of conferences to explain a difficult restructure, the leaders were surprised by how well these difficult messages had been received. Eager to find out why, they asked a group of managers. Top of the list was: 'someone from head office admitting they'd made a mistake'.

When so many people are happy to pass the buck, it makes a big impact when someone is willing to step up and take responsibility.

The wrong kind of sorry

In 2001 a US spy plane entered Chinese airspace without permission and collided with a fighter jet resulting in the death of the Chinese pilot. The White House rapidly issued a statement expressing 'regret' at what had happened.

The Chinese were outraged. In Mandarin Chinese there are numerous way of apologising, each with their own shades of meaning. The White House's apology was translated as being merely *yihan*, an expression of regret that carries no guilt. The Chinese demanded a formal apology – *daoquian* – which communicates a sense of responsibility and expression of remorse. Eventually the tension was diffused when the US Ambassador to China wrote a letter worded in such a way as to translate into an unequivocal apology.

Step 2: Be specific
To make the apology ring true, make it specific. Spell it out in detail – 'this is what I did and this is what made it wrong.'

'I was wrong' is good. 'I was wrong when I told the client we could deliver in 24 hours' is better. 'I was wrong to tell the client we could deliver in 24 hours and I made a mistake telling the team by email rather than coming in to see them' is excellent.

Make it clear, too, whether you are apologising for your behaviour or for the consequences of your actions, or both. 'I'm sorry you're upset' is dangerously ambiguous. The listener may suspect that, whilst you regret that they're upset, you think they're being over-sensitive and it's really their fault. 'I'm sorry I upset you' takes responsibility but still doesn't show that I know what I did wrong. Better still: 'I'm sorry I said that you were turning into your mother, it was unkind, it's not true and I didn't mean it.' (Flowers would be a good idea too, see step 5).

'The thief is sorry he is to be hanged, not that he is a thief' goes an old proverb. If we want forgiveness, we need to be specific about what the forgiveness is for.

If we don't know what it is that we did wrong, then it pays to ask. 'I can see that I've behaved badly to you. What is it that has most upset you?'

A Mind Gym member explained, 'My best girlfriend introduced me to her boyfriend's brother. We got on really well and started going out, discreetly to start with and then more publicly. My best friend was furious, I could tell because she used to call me two or three times a day and the calls stopped. I thought she might be angry because the brothers didn't get on that well; or because, maybe, she secretly fancied "my" brother herself. When I asked her why she initially shrugged it off as nothing, but when I pushed she said she was deeply upset that I hadn't told her immediately. It was only then that I knew what to apologise for in order to regain our friendship.'

Step 3: Help your victim understand what happened

From Forest Gump to the most successful business leaders (according to research by London Business School) we love people who show a flaw. It proves they're human and it allows us to sympathise. And so it pays to explain the sequence of events or emotions that led to our error: why we did what we did. We need to steer clear of self-justification, or the benefits of our apology will be lost for good, but we do well to tell our story as fairly as we dare.

'I felt under pressure to hit this month's figures. In the heat of the moment I made a snap decision. It was the wrong one.'

'I didn't feel listened to and I wanted to get your attention, although this was clearly the wrong way to do it.'

'I felt nervous about telling anyone, especially after what happened last time, but I should have known that I could trust you.'

People find it reasonably easy to forgive if the consequences were unintentional and not too severe – 'I thought it would be best to let everyone know as soon as possible, which was why I sent the email, I hadn't appreciated how much upset it would cause.'

But I'm not sorry

An insincere apology is a sure fire way to make things worse. In research experiments, subjects on the receiving end of sham apologies showed increases in blood pressure, heart rate, sweat and aggression. In other words they got even more worked up. The recipients of false apologies were also far less likely to respond with forgiveness.

'A stiff apology is a second insult... The injured party does not want to be compensated because he has been wronged; he wants to be healed because he has been hurt.' G.K. Chesterton

If we can't say it like we mean it, better not to say it at all.

Step 4: Explain why it won't happen again
'It'll never happen again, I promise you.' If we've got previous form, a simple promise may not be enough.

We can give credibility to our conviction in several ways:

- A simple strategy. 'I'll produce a checklist for everything we need to take when we go away for the weekend, including contact lenses, and pin it on the inside of the cupboard.'

- Describe what you'll do if you see the same problem arising again. 'Next time, I'll ask the client what is pushing their deadlines and see if there's a way of relieving the pressure at their end.'

- Explain your prevention measures. 'Next time I feel unfairly accused, I'll breathe really deeply and count to five before I say anything and, when I do speak, I'll keep my volume at normal levels.'

- Give the other person some control over the situation. 'Let's agree that if you hear me getting defensive, you give me the look and take over the conversation with the client.'

- Ask them what we can do to give them assurance that there won't be a repeat. If they say 'nothing, only time', then leave it at that. Although it may not sound like it, this is a conditional promise of forgiveness. That's progress.

The aim of these strategies is to rebuild trust – we want the wronged person to feel confident in us again. So as well showing that we've given some thought to preventing another injury, we need to make sure that the other person feels acknowledged and respected.

Step 5: Make amends/reparations
Actions speak louder than words. What works best to recompense the wronged person?

Conspicuously punishing ourselves will rarely do the trick – it just appears showy and is of little value. Unless by working through the night for the next week we're going to reverse the situation, we shouldn't expect the other person to be impressed by self-denying acts of masochism (except in teen movies).

Think instead of reparations that focus on making the situation better for the other person. Consider what can be done to tidy the mess: do you need to clarify with the boss who really did the work, or repair the neighbour's trellis? Alternatively, offer a little comfort to compensate for the inconvenience: 'I'll pay for everyone in the team to take their partner out for dinner as compensation for working late again.'

Top 5
1. Restore the damage: dress to dry cleaners, explanatory email to upset client.
2. Relieve their pain: do the ironing, cover for their meeting with a sales rep.
3. Trinket: flowers, chocolates, The *Sex and the City*/*James Bond* DVD box set.
4. Treat: VIP pass to Glastonbury/Glyndebourne/Gleneagles.
5. A pre-emptive strike: here's the analysis that will give you the edge at the next executive meeting.

Step 6: Give it time

Once we've done our apologising, we may feel an overwhelming desire to put the issue to rest. We've probably spent a lot of mental and emotional energy preparing to say sorry and now we're keen to move on and put it behind us. But what about the other person? For them, the process has only just started. They're probably still feeling aggrieved and will need time to assess our apology.

A full repair takes time, patience and consistency. We can't expect immediate forgiveness. All we can do is hang on in there and keep to our promise that it won't happen again.

When not to say sorry

On the naughty step

If we want to maintain the relationship it pays to be generous with our apologies. We may not feel that we were even largely responsible but, so what, for the sake of the partnership, friendship or working relationship, we're generally better off taking it on the chin.

Equally, there are times when it may pay to hold back. Here are a few:

• The behaviour is repeated. Maybe they are bullying, unaware or just insensitive.

• The issue is more important than the relationship. No need to be sorry for being tough on a poor performing member of your team, or the contractor who has failed to deliver what they promised.

• It's clear we aren't to blame – someone drives into the back of our car, for example, or causes us to miss a project deadline by requesting last-minute alterations.

• We can't say it genuinely.

• There's an issue of legal responsibility.

The hardest word

- The other person lost their temper and we kept ours (though we may still apologise for what we did that contributed)

- The other person's behaviour is beyond the rules of what is widely considered acceptable (clearly violence against you, for example). In these situations it is important to get out and seek professional help.

In these situations we can show empathy with an expression of regret, but stop short of making an apology that might give the impression we're taking the blame. 'I regret that your project won't meet the deadline, but incorporating the new material will take a few days.'

It's not the quantity

The word 'sorry' is uttered 368 million times each day in the UK according to a survey carried out by an insurance company, (not always the first people to say sorry themselves). This means the average Brit will say 'sorry' 1.9 million times in their lifetime.

The British are famous for using the word 'sorry' for just about everything, from indicating that they can't hear ('I'm sorry?') to apologising when someone pushes a supermarket trolley over their blameless foot ('Oh, I'm so sorry').

But whilst their fondness for expressions of regret may have the British apologising to inanimate objects, it doesn't make them any better than anyone else when it comes to genuinely making amends. It's quality not quantity.

Forgive and you shall receive

Sometimes it's us in the victim position. We've been slighted or hurt; our prospects have been damaged or our life inconvenienced. Someone has screwed up and we're suffering the fallout.

We're probably furious and deeply upset and the last thing we feel like doing is forgiving.

The greatest national example of forgiveness in recent times comes from South Africa. Led by Archbishop Tutu, the Truth and Reconciliation Commission encouraged people to share and admit to past atrocities and, by so doing, be forgiven. No war crimes trials or revenge punishments, however shocking the behaviour had been. It was an unprecedented act of forgiveness by an oppressed group of their oppressors. It was risky and, in many people's eyes, unnecessary. And yet it provided an extraordinary national catharsis and a peaceful transition from white, apartheid rule to democratic government.

If the vast majority of Black South Africans can forgive at this level, what's stopping us, every day? There are three common reasons:

Fear
We want a protective cloak against future wrongdoing. We're worried that if we forgive too easily we'll seem weak and the transgressions will be repeated again and again. On this, we're generally deluded. The other person will soon grow tired of seeking our forgiveness if we withhold it unreasonably and their views of us will sour fast. They are more likely to repeat the wrong because they care less about what we think, than hold back because we haven't yet forgiven them.

Loss of control
We think it's in our best interests to hold back from forgiving, imagining that this gives us an extra bargaining chip in the negotiations of life. However, forgiving can give us the moral authority to exert more control rather than less.

Righteous indignation
We believe that they were wrong. That what they did was unacceptable by the rules of society, morality or our own specific standards. They have transgressed and they should not be forgiven, at least not easily. We may well be right, the question is, 'does being "right" help?' Sometimes the principled stance is the right one – there are certain behaviours that are simply not acceptable and so the relationship must end. Even then we may at some later stage choose to accept their apology and forgive them. Equally, we should recognise that if we don't forgive, the relationship is very unlikely to prosper.

The personal benefits of forgiveness for us (forget about them, they're in the doghouse) are immense.

When we feel angry and hard done by, we tend to replay the hurtful event over and over in our heads. Like prodding a bruise, we keep the pain going by revisiting it. We might increase the irritation by comparing ourselves to the person who hurt us – 'It's all very well for them . . .' These routines are exhausting and unproductive – forgiveness frees us from these behaviours.

Forgiveness also reduces guilt. Not just the transgressor's but in many cases the victim's too. People who have been wronged often beat themselves up for having 'allowed' the situation to occur in the first place. Forgiveness draws a line under the past and helps us get rid of those bad feelings.

In several medical studies forgiveness is positively linked to lower blood pressure, better sleep quality and fewer somatic complaints (eg, migraine, headaches, heartburn, nausea).

Forgiveness is also the first step towards rebuilding a relationship. It signifies that both individuals involved have stopped experiencing negative emotions and are willing to move on. Granting forgiveness allows reconciliation to begin.

With a few extreme exceptions, we're better off forgiving, even if you don't think it will have a beneficial effect on our relationship with the other person; it will.

Here are 10 common reasons we give not to forgive. And 10 ways to change our mind:

	Reasons not to forgive	And how to change your mind
1	It's not fair.	It's not about fairness; it's about me. When I have forgiven, I'll be better off.
2	They need to do more to apologise and make up for their wrong doing.	Tell them what they need to do to earn my forgiveness.
3	I believe in justice.	I am merciful/generous/kind/loving.

	Reasons not to forgive	And how to change your mind
4	I would never have behaved like that.	I really appreciated being forgiven when I got things wrong/behaved badly.
5	I'll lose the power I have over them.	The power will disappear fast and their sorrow may well turn into a personal grudge. Forgive promptly for maximum return.
6	It is weak to forgive, I'll lose face.	It's heroic and strong to forgive: Mandela, Gandhi, Mother Teresa.
7	They wouldn't have forgiven me if I had done that.	Do I want to be like them?
8	Past behaviour is a good predictor of future behaviour; they'll do it again.	Make them commit not to repeat the wrong as a condition of forgiveness.
9	I need to protect myself.	I can protect myself in other, better ways.
10	It hurts to forgive them when they have behaved so badly.	It will hurt more to maintain the grudge and keep revisiting the negative emotions.

Forgiveness improves with age

Those over 45 are more likely to forgive and those that do forgive have better mental and physical health, according to a US study by psychologist Loren Toussaint.

The study also revealed:
- 60% said that they have forgiven themselves for past mistakes.
- 52% have forgiven others (women appeared slightly more forgiving 54%:49%).
- 43% have actively sought forgiveness for harm they have done.

The path to forgiveness

Admit you're angry

You are furious and you want to stop being furious. But you don't seem to be able to get rid of your anger – indeed, your thoughts keep bringing the painful event back in high definition sound and colour. Perhaps you also feel annoyed with yourself for feeling angry.

Happy anniversary

Many people believe they shouldn't get angry, but it is a natural and essential part of the process of forgiveness. To rid ourselves of feelings, we have to acknowledge them.

We can let them out physically by crying, punching a cushion or howling at the moon. We can write them out, run them out, paint them out, or bash them out on the piano. But just trying to think them away won't work – and ignoring them will simply cause them to fester. Better to front up to your fury and free yourself to move on.

Phone a friend

Forgiveness, particularly if we've been badly bruised, takes guts. It helps if we get some support. Tell a friend that you've decided to take this step; ask them to acknowledge your commitment to forgive, and use them for encouragement if your resolve weakens.

Mark the forgiving

Forgiveness doesn't necessarily mean reconciliation or even making contact, but it might be a good idea to mark the act in some way. A reconciliation hug, a meal together, an offer of help, or some other symbol that says 'We've put that behind us now.' If you are no longer in contact with the person, some kind of private act to mark the fact that you're moving forward may be useful.

Cut some slack

Some people find themselves in a constant state of irritation and resentment. The world and everyone in it winds them up. If you reckon just about everyone owes you an apology, from the driver who almost pulled out in front of your car to the sour-faced woman behind the cheese counter in the supermarket, you may want to make things easier on yourself by finding less that needs forgiving.

Take phrases like 'This is unacceptable...', 'Everyone knows you shouldn't...', 'How can anyone allow...?', 'What an idiot...' and temper them. For example:

- Make them personal: 'I don't like it when...'
- Give them fuzzy edges: 'It is usually the case that...'
- Delight in otherness: 'I love the fact that we're all different and so I should accept it when...'
- Acknowledge exceptions: 'Ted always looks a mess but he's so funny that I can forgive him...'
- Dismiss as unimportant: 'So what? It doesn't matter.'

If we often find others' behaviour disappointing, it's as likely to be because we have high standards as because we have stumbled amongst a world of nincompoops. Whilst having high standards may have benefits in other ways, it also leads to excess faultfinding. For example, if I am extremely punctual and believe it's rude to turn up late for a meeting, however informal, I will take offence when you arrive ten minutes late. If, instead, I view punctuality as a guideline rather than a rule with, say, 15 minutes grace on either side, I'll find myself demanding an apology less often.

As we are inclined to break our own rules from time to time, and usually more often than we realise, having softer edges to our rules will make life easier on ourselves as well as on those around us.

Confucius said that before you seek revenge, first dig two graves. Forgiveness means you don't need to dig any at all.

Here we go again...

Sometimes our best efforts to forgive and forget are thwarted. The person just keeps on doing the same thing, again and again. There's a pattern emerging and we have a sinking feeling that no amount of forgiveness is going to break it.

If we're really convinced we've tried our best to no avail, it's time to make a choice. We could reconcile ourselves to the situation and either live with our frustrations or keep on forgiving; we could give the other person the benefit of the doubt yet again and trust that hope will finally triumph over experience; we could try to think of a way in which we could help them break their pattern; alternatively we could cut our losses and get the hell out of there – leave the job, ditch the unfaithful lover, ignore the back-stabbing friend, and move on.

Undskyld, Verontschuldig me, Je regrette, Entschuldigung, Sygnomi, Me desculpo, lo siento, Ursäkta, Mi dispiace.

As far as linguists can tell, there's no language without a word for 'sorry'. And so it must be doing something right. In the search for better relationships it's a useful gadget to have at our disposal. Used skilfully it saves time, heartache and broken crockery.

PY Look at a celebrity, politician or public figure who has chosen (or been forced) to make a big apology. What did they do or say to help the victims forgive them?

When BA chief Willy Walsh apologised for the disruption of the new Terminal 5 opening at Heathrow airport, he accepted full personal responsibility and explained some of what had happened:

'A number of issues led to the events we saw yesterday. There were problems in the car parks, airport areas, computer glitches and the baggage system ... I am not pointing the finger at BAA. Both British Airways and BAA made mistakes, but I am taking responsibility for the mistakes we made ... The buck stops with me.'

RY Think about a time when you felt wronged that is still bothering you. Are you ready to forgive?
1. Make a list of all the benefits of letting go.
2. Take your anger out on an inanimate object, say by bashing a pillow.
3. Work out the worst outcome from forgiving and decide what other protective measures you can put in place.
4. Talk with someone who knows and cares about you and ask advice.
5. Give it a go.

A different relationship

When Mikhail Gorbachev, former President of the Soviet Union, was asked to identify the turning point in the Cold War, he replied, 'Reykjavik'. The summit in Iceland led to a conversation with Ronald Reagan which moved beyond the usual weapons control agenda to a discussion of each other's values and assumptions. It was a moment of truth. A moment that redefined the relationship and ended the Cold War.

When we want to end our own cold wars, we need our own team of advisors. This section introduces you to them.

We start with N – Out of a rut: what to do when we're caught in a repeat pattern that's dragging the relationship down. When it feels impossible to be positive, let alone come up with the solution, tuck into chapter O – Tough talk and uncover the magic of dialogue. For dealing with those people who are particularly irritating, take a look at P – Tricky people. And for guidance on what to do when it ain't worth it any more Q – Graceful exit.

And finally (though not strictly in this section), New beginnings: how to make sure that whatever you've found helpful in this book doesn't go the way of most New Year's resolutions.

(N) Out of a rut

Your partner/lover/flatmate arrives home late one evening. Everything about their manner screams 'I've had a very, very bad day'. You listen sympathetically whilst they get it off their chest and then offer a restorative drink.

They don't want one. You make some well thought out suggestions as to how they might resolve the situation. Your ideas are all dismissed as impossible, ill informed, or just plain wrong. You suggest food. They're not hungry. How about a light-hearted movie? How could they possibly laugh at a time like this? Finally, you suggest that things might seem better after an early night. Bad move. Don't you realise that they are going to be up half the night sorting out this mess? In fact don't you understand anything? Obviously not.

And with that they decide to go out for a walk – taking the opportunity to slam the door angrily on their way. Now it's you who needs a drink. You're feeling dejected, annoyed and hard done by.

As you sip your sedative, you ask yourself, 'How did that happen – again?' Something similar happened yesterday when you tried to help your friend who's going through a divorce – and last week when you struggled to cheer up your brother after his book was rejected by yet another publisher. In fact, it's always happening. The subject changes but the routine is depressingly familiar – you start out wanting to help and end up feeling rejected and hard done by.

Are you being unlucky or is it something you're doing? Almost certainly it's the latter. Which is good news because it means you can change it.

Groundhog Day

In the film *Groundhog Day* Phil Connors (played by Bill Murray) repeats the same day again and again. Even when he commits suicide it makes no difference, he still wakes up the next morning and has to live through the same day in which he realises it's a repeat but all the others are living it as if for the first time. The only way out, he finally discovers, is to love someone else more than himself.

Most of us have Groundhog Day arguments, or at least patterns of behaviour that repeat themselves, whatever we try to do to stop them.

Most frustrating is the fact that we often don't realise we're back in the old routine until it's too late; until he storms out, or she slams the phone down, or we find ourselves skulking out of the boss's office feeling angry and foolish. Again.

So why do we repeat these dreary and painful routines? There are two main reasons:

First, we don't recognise what's going on. There was a series of advertisements for a fizzy orange drink where a monster would appear to the viewer but remain invisible to the other people on the screen. As some hapless person drank the orangeade, the monster would slap them on either side of their head, leaving the drinker baffled. The slogan ran: you've been tangoed. These Groundhog Day arguments are similar, they come from nowhere and leave us feeling knocked about but none the wiser.

The second reason why we repeat the same old unhelpful patterns is that, in a slightly perverse way, they provide us with a stimulus we need: they're familiar, they confirm our world view (no one appreciates me; see, I knew it would end like this) and they give us an emotional 'hit' (albeit a negative one), which proves we still matter.

'When I told my father that I was pregnant, all he said was, "Well your bum certainly looks bigger,"' recalled a still seething Mind Gym member. This insensitive response was probably driven by the father's need to prove to himself that, even with the arrival of a new generation, his daughter still minded what he thought. On a subconscious level he wasn't sure that he could get a positive emotional response but he knew he could get a negative one. And so he did.

The American psychotherapist Eric Berne wrote a seminal book about these Groundhog Day moments called *Games People Play*.

Berne called these toxic routines 'transactions' or 'games'. Having carried out extensive research, he concluded that we play these games in an attempt to get attention (which he called 'strokes') from the other person. We're also looking to confirm our role in the relationship. That role might be a negative, painful one but it's the one we feel comfortable with, it's the one that confirms our beliefs about ourselves and the other person. When we find a game that delivers the goods, we keep on playing it, over and over.

This isn't what's going on at the surface, of course. These motivations are well hidden in our subconscious. To a casual observer we may be having a rather dull disagreement about how to load the dishwasher. Indeed that's probably what we think we are doing. It's only when that banal argument leaves us feeling utterly wretched that we get an inkling that we're playing for much higher stakes.

The roles of the game

Great relationships are based on security. These toxic transactions start when we feel a lack of security. At this stage we tend to adopt 'positions' or 'roles'. This is a temporary response to the situation, like an actor playing a part, and no more a reflection of our true character than Dustin Hoffman's performance in *Rain Man* suggests he's autistic. The difference is that we don't tend to be aware that we're doing it.

There are three roles we tend to adopt, each looking for security in a different way:

What's your game?

- The **Persecutor** is asking the other person to 'agree with me'. He or she will, at that moment, see him or herself as 'correct' or in some way superior and will persist in trying to get you to agree.
- The **Rescuer** is saying 'value me', or , 'appreciate how I can help'. They see their role as providing valuable support or rescue. They want you to follow their advice.
- The **Victim** is saying 'protect me'. He or she believes they are in worse-off situation or in some way below the other person. They look for a Persecutor to mistreat them, or a Rescuer to confirm that they can't cope.

What happens in the 'game' is that we take on one role (say 'rescuer') and the other person takes on a different role (say 'victim') and then, at some stage, we switch and take on one of the other roles. Say, you switch to persecutor and I, as a result, switch to victim. The game is completed only once the switch has taken place.

Steven Karpman described this as 'The Drama Triangle', which can be drawn like this:

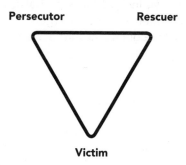

In all psychological games one person takes on one of these roles and the other person another, different role. The game's denouement occurs when one person swaps role, forcing the other into a different role.

Stupid

We're in a sleekly designed urban apartment at the end of a long day. Charlie offers Tim a glass of red wine and as he does so, he accidentally spills it on the new carpet. Charlie freezes at the shock of what's just happened.

'So are you just going to stand there staring at it?' demands Tim, slipping seamlessly into the persecutor role.

'Ok, ok, I'll clear it up,' says Charlie, swiftly slipping into 'victim'.

"I should think so too,' says Tim, tutting loudly. Charlie returns from the kitchen with a cloth but it's not over.

"Not that cloth, you idiot, can't you see it's filthy? You'll ruin the carpet." Charlie, now thoroughly ensconced in the victim role, murmurs an apology, gets a different cloth and starts attacking the stain.

'You're rubbing it!' yells Tim. 'Don't you know you should be dabbing it?' And with that he shoves Charlie out of the way and takes over, complaining that he'll have to sort it out 'as usual'. 'And I suppose you're just going to stand there watching,' he sneers over his shoulder to Charlie.

And that's when the switch happens. Charlie's had enough: 'It's only a tiny stain for heaven's sake. This is just typical of you – obsessing over trivia. Don't you have anything better to worry about, you pathetic little man', and marches out.

Now Charlie's playing persecutor and a very effective one. Tim, sitting on the floor with a cloth in his hand, suddenly feels small, stupid and very unhappy. He's become the victim. Game over.

This is unlikely to be a one off. Tim and Charlie probably play out variations on this theme repeatedly. Tim berates Charlie for being stupid until Charlie turns on him. Or, to use Berne's language: Tim plays persecutor until Charlie the victim moves into being Charlie the persecutor and Tim becomes the victim.

If the game is repeated, that's evidence that it works. It's painful, yes; but it's effective. Indeed a game may be so efficient at delivering the desired negative hit that we find ourselves playing it out with other people in our lives too; continually taking one of three roles: Victim, Rescuer or Persecutor and then switching so that we've 'got them'. Of course, we're often totally unaware that this is what we're doing.

If you want to play poker, find someone with a deck of cards
We can play these games anywhere. All we need is a playmate who wants to play in the same game.

The fact that these games are particularly common in our intimate relationships may be an indication of how good a match we have chosen in our partner. We've found someone who meets our needs – negative as well as positive. So, in the same way as a well-organised person might be the ideal partner for someone who's prone to losing stuff and forgetting things – a partner who tends to believe that others are incompetent (a Persecutor) will be the perfect playmate for someone who tends to believe they don't come up to scratch (a Victim). Or, the Victim might hook up with someone who believes that other people always need help (a Rescuer). In either partnership the two playmates truly 'complement each other'.

Once we've found someone who will take on the appropriate role, there is a whole variety of ways in which we can play out these little dramas. The one with Tim and Charlie is called 'stupid'. In the scene that opened this chapter – the person who'd had a bad day, and the partner who was keen to help – the game was 'Why don't you, yes but...' ('Why don't you have an early night?' 'Yes but that's a bad suggestion because I have to work through the night').

Eric Berne lists lots of different games – each with its own snappy title including: 'If It Weren't for You', 'Kick Me', 'See How Hard I've Tried', 'Wooden Leg' and the expressively named: 'Now I've Got You, You Son of Bitch'.

Sometimes we might not go as far as switching roles. We might just pass the time role-playing Victim and Rescuer with each other. This kind of routine might get tedious, but it's unlikely to be painful. You might call it 'Game Lite'. To get the true payoff we have to move to the new position. Every good story needs something to change if the dénouement is going to feel satisfying. In our psychological games it's that final switch of roles that brings the story to a painfully satisfying conclusion.

Off games

So now we know that we're likely to be playing these pernicious games – how do we stop them messing up our relationships? Well, first of all, we ought to take heart. Game playing isn't very nice but it's normal – pretty much everyone plays games at one time or another. Knowing that we're in a game at least gives us a way to understand what's going on. It may also reduce the antagonism we feel towards the other person. After all, they're caught up in a game too.

1. Break the gaming habit

If our games are going on at the unconscious level, we need to bring them into consciousness. Once we can identify them, we can begin to take control of them, and maybe even stop them before they begin. Psychotherapists describe this process with the phrase: Name it, Claim it, Tame it. By observing what's going on, we reduce its impact.

So next time you find yourself asking 'How did I end up feeling so bad?' play the scene back and plot your positions on the drama triangle. Which role did you start in? Where did you end up? And what about your playmate? Can you think of other relationships in your life where you play these roles?

Now share the knowledge

Talk to the other person about the game. Share your observations. ('This is what I think is going on? Does that sound right to you?') Between you identify when you tend to play this game and what sparks it off. Then create a strategy to help you avoid it next time – maybe an alert that wakes you up to the fact that you're slipping into the game. You could agree on a word or a signal that indicates: 'We're doing that thing again, aren't we? Let's stop shall we? (We're doing that thing' NOT 'You're doing that thing' – remember it takes two to dance the toxic tango). Get skilled at alerting yourself in this way and you'll find it easier to sidestep the games. You'll also defuse the tension.

2. Stop the game before it starts

Something lured you into the game – what was the hook? Or, if you were the one who did the hooking, what bait did you use? If we can spot what got us into the game, we have a chance of getting out. Because although the game may feel irresistible, it's not. We may not be able to control what the other person does but we do have control over our own behaviour.

How to turn down the invitation
Below you'll find a list of some of the most popular hooks that are used in games, from each of the three positions (V/P/R). Next to them are suggestions for responses that will help you to stop the game developing. However, just because we've turned down the bait once doesn't mean it won't be offered again in another form. The other person wants to play, and the more we turn them down, the more determined they'll become. After all, you've had such fun together before: 'Come on, you know you enjoy this game...' It takes a lot of will as well as skill to avoid getting hooked. So be prepared to hang on in there.

Persecutor

Hook	What to avoid	How to stop the game
You idiot, look what you've done (again).	I'm sorry, I didn't mean to. (V) I'll put it right straight away. (R)	I have made a mistake. I'm sorry. What would you like done to put it right? It's easily sorted. I'll do A, B and C.
What are you doing it like that for?	I'm only trying to help you. (R) I'm sorry, is this wrong? (V)	How do you think it should be done?
If it wasn't for you I'd be free to...	I know I get in the way. (V) Poor you, that must be awful... (R)	What do you want to do...?

Rescuer

Hook	What to avoid	How to stop the game
You look like you're in a bad way.	You're so right. (V) Mind your own business. (P)	I've got this tricky problem and I'd like your advice. Thanks for your concern but I'm feeling ok.
I think you'd find it easier if...	Yes, I thought I was doing it wrong... (V) What makes you think you know better...? (P)	Thanks. I'll come and ask you if I get stuck...
Here, let me do that for you...	Thanks, I am terrible at doing these things... (V) I doubt very much if you'll do it better than me. (P)	I'm doing ok right now but thanks for the offer. I'd like to do it myself but I'd like to hear your advice.

Victim

Hook	What to avoid	How to stop the game
It's all a disaster.	How can I help? (R) Well you should have seen it coming. (P) Call that a disaster, you should hear what I'm going through... (P)	Oh dear, what are you going to do about it? Tell me what happened.
What do I do now?	One idea would be... (R) Don't ask me – I don't know any more than you. (V) Work it out yourself, after all that's what you're paid for. (P)	What options have you got? What do you think would be the best approach?
I'm stuck...	Let me do it for you. (R) Have you thought about... (R) Well don't look at me. (P) I'm not surprised, you'll never get it. (P)	What could you do to get unstuck? What haven't you tried? What other ways could you approach this?

Putting the bait back in the box
Perhaps you've realised that you're the one doing the hooking. And as you know from experience that it leads to a game that ends with both of you feeling bad, you'd like to stop doing it. So, next time you feel yourself slipping into that role and reaching for the bait, ask yourself, 'What do I really want right now?' If you're playing a game, you want attention, but is there a less toxic way of getting it?

For example, perhaps you've noticed a tendency for acting hard done by when you feel tired after a long day. You know your partner always tries to help but it never feels good enough, and you always end up feeling angry and unappreciated. Perhaps what you really want is simply a hug? Or a five-minute uninterrupted audience so you can have a good moan and then forget it and move on? Or perhaps being left alone in silence for a fifteen minutes 'wind-down' would do the trick? Identify what it is you really want and see if you can negotiate a positive way to get it from the other person. You'll save time, energy, and quite possibly your relationship.

3. Leaving the game half way through
Switching to a new position is the final move in these psychological games. Once you've made the switch, there's nothing much you can do: you're in the painful position and the game is over. Up until that point, though, you're still in with a chance – you can get out. It's hard, and the other person isn't going to like it – but it can be done.

If you feel you're in the middle of a game, press the pause button. Then tune in to yourself. Become aware of what you are about to say and realise that it is totally the wrong thing to say. It will only continue the game. Using all the will and skill you can muster, choose an alternative response. The grid above should give you some ideas. When you find one that works – remember it. You're going to need it again.

4. I didn't get out in time
Ouch. You're probably feeling very bruised. But don't give up – tomorrow's another day and experience makes avoiding the games easier. In the meantime, reduce the pain by recognising that episode for what it is – you've been had, simple as that. Try laughing to yourself about it.

'Ok, so I was caught again. I got hooked into the old "If it wasn't for you" routine again – but that's quite funny in a way and there's no point in feeling hard done by now I know what's happened.'

I SPY   Identify a game that you play in your life – it could be with a partner, a friend, a work colleague. You are looking for something that is played regularly. Identify the hook. Identify the positions you both start in? Where do you end up?

I TRY   Give the game a title (keep it light-hearted). Now create a signal that goes with that title. Next time you feel yourself starting out on the game, use the signal to make you both aware that you've started playing.

(O) Tough talk

He wants a baby; she doesn't.

I think I'm pretty good at my job; my manager's always finding faults.

I need to focus on my career; you want me to spend more time at home.

I find you controlling; you find me incompetent.

He wants to commit; she wants to be free.

In some relationship dilemmas there's a solution that meets everyone's needs (see chapter K – Deal or no deal). Others, like the ones above, are trickier. The stakes are high, the consequences are far reaching and the topic is emotionally charged. The answer isn't simply to generate more options. It's more fundamental than that. And the big problems that cause real relationship damage tend to be in this camp.

One study found that when couples talk about problems in their relationship, 69% of the time the discussion is about an ongoing issue that has been a problem for many years. 31% of the time the issue is related to a specific situation.

But are they? The resolution lies in having the right kind of conversations, which psychologists call 'dialogue'.

Dialogue is a state a people get into when they are really listening to each other and actively seeking to resolve an issue, even if they can't immediately solve it. To do this we need to understand each other's perspectives and build upon what each other says. But listening isn't easy, particularly if the other person is aggressive or a little reluctant to share.

Here's a situation that resolves what looked like an impasse. The bits written in italics explain the principles behind the conversation.

Dramatis Personae

Susie – a working mother (she spends three days per week working and two days looking after her children)

Tom – a working father, married to Susie

Jane – a registered childminder who has been looking after Susie and Tom's children for the last eight months

Scene one
Tom and Susie are getting ready for bed.

Susie: We need to fire Jane and get a new childminder. I really don't think things are working with her at all. It's a pity because it was working at the start, but I can't believe the stupidity of some of the things she's done recently.

Tom: Like what?

Susie: Well, the thing that's really getting to me is that she's avoiding talking to me. When I got home from work the other day, all she said was, 'The children have had their tea and are ready for their bath.' And then left with the quietest of 'goodbyes'. She couldn't have got out of the door any faster.

Tom: Maybe she had somewhere to go?

Susie: No, it's really not working. Some of the things she has done have been unbelievable. She put bleach in the washing machine and then put the children's clothes into the next wash without rinsing the machine. She spilt coffee all over the carpet on the stairs and didn't clean it up properly. I went into the boys' room the other day and the furniture had been rearranged, but she put one of the beds right against a radiator which could easily lead to a burnt hand. I'm at my wit's end, constantly checking up and asking her to do things differently.

Tom: What do you think we should do?

Susie: Well I think you should ring her up and tell her not to come back. I don't really want to talk to her any more.

When we feel in some way slighted or wronged it's very easy either to avoid the situation or to attack it. See chapter 1 – Fight club. When we're in a situation where we feel we want to make some sort of resolution dialogue is called for. We can decide whether we want to do that by asking ourselves the following.

Tom: I suppose the question is what do we really want? I don't think either of us want the hassle of finding a new person when she gets on well with the children and has done a great job for us in the past. Shall we see if we can work it out?

The crucial question here is: What do you really want? For you and the other parties involved. This helps us to understand what we should be aiming for. It may seem difficult, distant or in some instances downright impossible, but it's worth checking your motivations and desires to uncover what the ideal is. Typically the goal should be getting what you want and having a positive relationship at the end. People often feel to get what they want the relationship has to suffer, but this doesn't need to be the case. These sorts of conversations are often avoided because of fear of the confrontation, reluctance to look weak, and the uncertainty about the outcome.

Susie: It would be a pain finding someone new. And the children do love her. I suppose it's worth one last try. Ok. I'll give it a go. Shall I ask her whether she can stay a little later tomorrow so we can talk to her? I think it's important we're both there.

Tom: Fine. We should definitely both be there.

Susie: What shall we say?

Tom: I'm not sure what we should say, but I think I know how we should say it. She'll have her own story, which will be right and proper in her mind. If we go in saying that she's out and out wrong, then we won't get very far. In fact it'll probably turn nasty pretty quickly. We need to listen, talk about how we're feeling and what we're thinking and see if there is some sort of resolution.

> Tom is describing the difference between debate and dialogue. Debate assumes there is a right answer and you have it, it can be combative and about finding flaws in other people's arguments. Dialogue assumes that many people have pieces to the answer and together can craft a solution, it's more collaborative, and focuses on exploring common ground and discovering new options.

Susie: Well, you'll need to lead the conversation tomorrow and help me out if I start to get angry.

Tom: Ok. Can I suggest something though? If we go into the conversation tomorrow expecting to get angry, we probably will and that won't get us very far. When we talk tomorrow it's important that we're generous-spirited in the conversation. She is bound to say stuff that will irritate us, but we need to interpret what she says in the best possible way and give her the benefit of the doubt. If she says that she thought moving the furniture was fun for the boys, we should agree. It probably was. What we want her to do is have fun with the boys and avoid any unnecessary accidents. We also need to understand her situation. It can't be easy spending all your time in someone else's home and looking after their children. Do you think you can do those things tomorrow – give her the benefit of the doubt and see things from her perspective?

Susie: It's going to be difficult, because I'm still really irritated. But, I'll do my best.

Dialogue improves your health

Research shows health improvements from improved communication and having courageous conversations. Research was carried out with patients with life-threatening diseases.

Feeling brave?

Some were given teaching in communication skills and supported in having tough conversations with people. A control group received no such training. The results showed that of the group who were taught improved communication skills, only 9% succumbed to their disease, compared to 30% of the control group who died.

Research by Kiecolt-Glaser & Glaser also showed that people who routinely failed at engaging in dialogue had much weaker immune systems than those who were good at it.

Scene two

Around a kitchen table cluttered with children's toys, finger paintings and three cups of tea, Susie and Tom are sitting side by side. On the other side of a table sits Jane, with her arms crossed.

Tom: How was your day?

Jane: It was ok. We went to the park this afternoon and it rained a bit. We got a little wet.

Susie: Did you go to the café in the park – that's where we usually go when it rains?

Jane: Yes, of course.

Tom: Jane, Susie asked you to come and talk to us now because we can all feel that there's not a good atmosphere between us at the moment. When you first started working for us we agreed that the most important thing is that we keep talking. It feels like we've stopped doing that – talking. I know that it's been a bit tricky recently, but we'd be really keen to clear the air.

So, let's start talking and listening again. We'd both really like to hear what you're thinking and feeling and we'd like to share our story. I'm sure there are things that we've done that have upset you and there are things that have upset us. We're both confident that with the right conversation we can sort this out.

> *'And they're off', as they say in racing. The context has been set and the conversation has begun. All of us will have felt our hearts race as we open these sorts of conversations. The critical thing is that it's happening. Tom is also trying to make the conversation one where Jane feels like she can talk openly – making it a safe environment.*

Jane: Yes, I think it's important we talk. Definitely. I'm not sure if that will help though. I really like your children. They're great fun, spirited and sparky, but I find everything else pretty tough at the moment.

Susie: We definitely want to change things. We think you've looked after the children really well over the last few months, but I think we'd all say that something has to change if it is going to continue. We've had some really good times, like the trip to the zoo we did a couple of months ago. I'd love it if we could work this out, and I really mean that, but if we can't it's probably better for both of us to part company. I know that would make Tom, the children and me very sad though.

Tom: Susie, why don't you tell us a little bit about what you think is going wrong at the moment.

Susie: Ok. I feel there's been an atmosphere recently. It feels like it's stemmed from the fact that I've been asking you to do quite a few things differently. I was upset that you had put bleach in our washing machine, spilt coffee on the stairs and changed the furniture round in the boys' room.

Jane: I agree about the atmosphere. To be honest, I've been wondering recently whether this is the right job for me.

Tom: Is it your job as a childminder in general or working with us specifically?

Beyond black and white

Nelson Mandela had been released from Robben Island Prison but no one knew what would happen next in South Africa. Would there be a revolution? Or a slow dilution of the more extreme apartheid laws?

In an initiative to find a peaceful way through, a dialogue was set up bringing leaders from opposite sides of the political, ideological and economic spectrum together. It started as a single event but turned into a series of significant conversations named after the retreat where they were held: the Mont Fleur process.

It would have been easy and tempting for this diverse group to argue about their differences; however the dialogue was very specifically focused on South Africa's future, not its past.

Together they developed over 70 possible scenarios for the country's future, ranging from out and out civil war through to crashing the South African economy. These they grouped together and honed down until they had four remaining. The scenarios were given names – Ostrich (which represented a white government ignoring the winds of change), Lame Duck (where a black government was elected but did not have economic control), Icarus (where a black government was elected and redistributed wealth so quickly that the South African economy crashed), and finally Flight of the Flamingos (where a slow and steady change in power led to a new South Africa).

The group then wrote the scenarios up and published them in a leading weekend newspaper. The scenarios were read and discussed, and became a shorthand for discussing South Africa's future. President de Klerk said, 'I am no ostrich.' One of the leaders of the ANC's opposition successfully persuaded his colleagues to reverse their economic policy in order to avoid the Icarus scenario.

In this way, dialogue played an important role in the peaceful resolution of an apparently intractable problem.

Jane: I'm not sure. Probably a bit of both.

In these delicate conversations people can often either attack or retreat. If they attack they will start to accuse the other party, becoming aggressive. This is mainly because they want to control the direction of the conversation or are trying to persuade others to share their point of view. If dialogue is needed this approach is unlikely to work.

The alternative is withdrawal. Normally this is to avoid the discomfort that's involved in these sorts of conversations or to protect oneself. Here, Jane is withdrawing a little. When someone withdraws we need to dig a little deeper. We can do this by asking for more detail, or by prompting the next statement. Prompting involves making it easier for someone to say something by suggesting it.

Tom: I understand that Susie has asked you to do quite a few thing differently recently. I can imagine that must be slightly demoralising.

Tom is making a suggestion there, he's prompting the next response and asking Jane for her story.

Jane: Yes it is. I find it difficult to be fairly constantly told what I'm doing wrong. For example, the other day when I was going out you asked me three times whether I had the right stuff in the children's bags, and then checked them yourself anyway. I find the rule about not having anyone else in the house whilst you're out over the top – I have friends who look after children, and it would be good to see them here during the day, rather than always having to go out. I get told everything from the temperature I put on a wash, when I should and shouldn't use fabric softener, or questions about coffee stains on the carpet – which I don't think was me, by the way. It all amounts to feeling pretty worn down.

I am qualified and I know how to look after children and sometimes it feels like you don't recognise that fact. I feel like I'm not trusted and not doing a good job. And that's hard. I shouldn't have put bleach in the washing machine, or moved the furniture in the boys' bedroom, and I understand that you have very high standards, and I like that. But I feel we should keep these things in perspective, particularly when I'm doing lots of other things really well.

This will have been tough for Susie to listen to. She now has three options. She could retreat and effectively opt out of the conversation. If she's tempted to do this, she needs to ask herself how else Jane's words could be interpreted so that she could feel more positive. In this instance she could focus on Jane recognising her motive being around her high standards.

She could go on the attack and accuse Jane of generally being careless. The question she needs to ask herself if this happens is what is the aim of the conversation – what does she want to get out of this?

Susie: I can understand why you feel this way. I understand that the frequent requests and reprimands are frustrating, particularly because you're well qualified. I know I do have high standards and I want the best for my family. I take great care with everything I do at home, so when I think something has been done without much care, I get really frustrated.

Susie has done a couple of things well here. The first is that she paraphrased what Jane has said, demonstrating that she's listening. The second is that she's being tentative in her descriptions. It would be easy for her to say something like, 'I can't stand careless people, and you're being careless,' but again that won't get the conversation very far, as Jane is bound to react badly.

Jane: I do really understand that. And I want to make the best of it. I really like looking after your children and working with you both.

Tom: Ok, so what do we do about this?

Tom is moving the conversation towards coming up with some plan of action. Often in these situations the answer isn't obvious. It's unlikely that Susie will stop making requests of Jane. And it's equally unlikely that Jane will stop making what Susie sees as careless mistakes. Instead they can talk about what they do when those things happen. So they have to find a way of keeping the dialogue going.

Susie: Well, for a start, why don't we say that you can have your friends here during the day, if they are looking after other children?

Our original thought was not to have people over who we didn't know, but if it's to see friends who look after other children, that seems to make sense.

Jane: That'd be great. I'll also make an effort to be even more careful, and if you pull me up on something, I'll do my best to see it as you being careful about your home as opposed to criticising my professional competence.

Susie: And I'll make an effort to be less pernickety. Would it be better for me to save the feedback up and talk once a week, or do it there and then?

Jane: Probably there and then. But if you see something good, it'd be nice to hear that too.

Tom: Great. I'm really pleased we've sorted that out.

Susie: Me too.

Recap: 6 tips for dialogue

- **Focus on what you want for yourself and the other person**
  There's a temptation to believe that to solve the problem the relationship has to suffer. This doesn't have to be the case. Ask yourself what the ideal is for you, the other person and the relationship.

- **Get yourself in the right frame of mind**
  Dialogue needs an attitude of empathy, openness and honesty. It can be tempting to play down the situation, but the gravity of the situation needs to be shared, along with the desire to find a resolution.

- **Share your story and ask for theirs**
  In any situation there are facts and there is the surrounding story. In dialogue we need to share the facts, tell our story and listen to theirs. We also need to understand that their story is as valid as our own.

- **Control your own retreats and attacks**
  Like a battle, there is a temptation for both parties to retreat and attack over the course of the conversation. Remaining even

minded can be very hard, particularly if you feel wronged or attacked yourself. If you feel yourself going into retreat or attack ask yourself how you'd behave if you really wanted the situation resolved or how you could see why the other person might be saying what they are saying.

- **Help bring them back from retreats and attacks**

  It's been emotional

  The other person may very well also go into retreat or attack mode. If they retreat, dig deeper by asking questions, checking whether you understand the situation by paraphrasing or remarking on their reaction, eg, 'I get the impression you're not very comfortable with this – can you share what you're thinking or feeling?'

  If they attack, then acknowledge their concerns and reconfirm what you're trying to achieve.

- **Create a plan of action**
  In some situations a solution may emerge. In others it won't. What is possible, as in the scenario above, is that people can find a way to talk about the situation and what to do if it happens again. It may take some time for all the parties involved to come up with something that works, but the only way a solution may emerge is if the group are able to talk, listen and understand each other.

What if the other party doesn't want to talk or listen?

Then there's a problem. Sadly the answer to this is that it's probably got to get worse before it's likely to get better. Both parties need to believe that it's not worth knocking chunks out of each other any more and that dialogue is the best option left.

In national conflicts, you often hear calls for dialogue – whether it be between the Chinese and the Dalai Lama or the Spanish government and the Basque separatists. Unless the parties involved believe that dialogue may lead to resolution the fighting will continue. Thankfully we have more control over our personal relationships than in the complexity of national struggles, but they can feel just as overwhelming. The first step is to persuade the other party that it's time to talk to each other.

I SPY Listen out for when other people attack or retreat and think about how you would react to maintain a dialogue.

Attack: empathise, summarise, acknowledge that what they are saying is valid, remain calm.

Retreat: ask prompting questions, eg, are you finding this difficult? Or state how you'd feel: If I was in your position I think I'd feel frustrated. Is that something you feel?

I TRY If there is a situation where you keep having the same unproductive conversations (or arguments) then dialogue may well be the answer.

Make sure that the appetite is there from both sides to resolve this and prepare how you are going to set up the dialogue.

Don't expect it to work perfectly the first time but if you keep to the principles above, you will increasingly reach resolutions where previously there was only conflict.

(P) Tricky people

Some people are invariably easy-going and generous-minded – a delight and a joy to be around. If everyone was like them, relationships would be straightforward and you wouldn't be bothering with this book. Sadly, it doesn't work like that. There are plenty of people who are... well, complicated. They wind us up, they get our goat, they press all our buttons. Sometimes it is possible to avoid these characters; but more often than not, we're stuck with them.

Developing a healthy relationship with someone you cannot stand is not easy. We can become overwhelmed by feelings of negativity towards the person concerned. We can become obsessed, blocked, troubled. This unhappy situation can distract us from the good things in our lives, and it also takes up far too much precious time and energy. Far more efficient is to learn to identify these types through their, how can we put this politely, 'quirks' – and to develop techniques and ways of neutralising their negative effects.

This chapter aims to identify some of the common characteristics of tricky people (be prepared, you may identify aspects of your own personality too). At the end of each mini-portrait, you will find a list of effective tactics for dealing with this type of person.

The Dumper

Just the essentials

'Hi guys!' Jason, Creative Director at Wannabe Design Studio, thumps the door open with his shoulder, his arms full with quadruple-shot expresso, BlackBerry, laptop, itouch and all the broadsheet newspapers, none of which he will read. 'Wow,' he says, as he dumps the lot on the desk, 'You're all looking pretty relaxed.' This is not intended as a compliment.

'Just a few things I need you to get on to,' he says, pacing the room. He peppers his speech with words like 'vital' and 'critical', before delivering the inevitable: 'needed for tomorrow'. 'So, I'll leave you to get on with it,' he says. And he's as good as his word – for approximately 20 minutes, until he remembers another 'top-priority detail', which is about to become your problem too.

Despite Jason's inept and annoyingly frequent interventions, his team usually manage to get everything done on time. Trouble is, Jason's obnoxiousness is matched only by his ineptitude. Take, for example, the time he accidentally deleted an entire pitch presentation ten minutes before a crucial meeting. Thankfully, some bright spark had a back-up copy, and one was rushed off in record time. The client never noticed a thing. Jason's bacon was saved, but he nevertheless still took it upon himself to give his team a dressing down later that day for not being quick enough off the mark.

Occasionally Jason 'clears the decks' to do some 'blue-sky thinking', which is Jason-speak for getting his team to take on all his work while sits in his office doing . . . well, you can probably fill in that gap yourself.

How to deal with The Dumper:

Get an idea of what's coming
Book a regular planning session and use it to focus The Dumper on future priorities. If you can, get him (or her) to articulate what they're going to need and want. Get someone else to come along to back you up if he changes his mind unreasonably.

Ask them to describe the ideal output
Dumpers often don't think before they take action, so their requests can be vague and generalised. Get them to focus: what do they want, how do they want it, when to they want it, and so on. Force them to give you as much detail as possible. That way you won't all be running around like headless chickens.

Build slack into your schedule
You can't predict what may be coming your way, but you can be pretty sure that it will be coming. Factor in extra time to deal with this nonsense.

Compromise, if necessary
When Greece fell behind schedule building the stadium for the 2004 Olympics, they took a view that a stadium with no roof was better than no stadium at all. With dumpers, sometimes you need to negotiate leaving the roof off.

The Stress Cadet

The final straw

Amelia is having a total 'mare of a day – again. The plans for her press launch are going into meltdown – again. Of course, it would have been a lot easier if the account team had given her a clearer brief, but they never do, do they? And where are the invitations? Perhaps she'll give the designers just one more quick call. Then she absolutely must ring the estate agent. The new house has turned out to be a complete shocker. And Peter's no help. She's convinced he's having another affair. She'll call him in a minute, check if he really is in Geneva. Just as soon as she's emailed the train company to complain about the lack of seats this morning and found someone to tell her why her laptop is running slow. God only knows when she's going to get out to Waitrose to shop for her best friend Rosie's birthday dinner party tonight, which she agreed to organise even though she knew today was going to be busy. 'I really can't take much more,' she tells her team at their fifth 'catch up' meeting of the day. They know just how she feels.

How to deal with The Stress Cadet

Help them to understand they are in control
Stress cadets are perpetually worried that they will fail. Remind them of past triumphs. Make them feel confident in their abilities so that they stop wasting energy on the negative and start taking positive action.

Gently minimise the gravity of the situation
Talk it down. Introduce a little levity – but don't belittle their concerns. Encourage them to visualise the worst case scenario, and then point out just how far away from it they really are.

Focus them on what can be done (as opposed to what can't)
Concentrate their attention on the here and now. Help them think positively about small steps that can realistically achieve results, rather than trying to fix everything at once.

The Jackboot

Monty (real name Martin) believes in the stick-and-carrot approach to motivation. Without the carrot. An ex-military man, Monty runs every project with martial precision. Each colour-coded step is meticulously planned, all risks are assessed, and mitigation for every contingency is outlined. No excuse, then, for anyone to deviate from the 'critical path'. At 9am each day the team are on parade

Pulling power

for 'Inspection' – and God help anyone who isn't word perfect on their task list. Punishment will be swift and usually very loud. Mind you, Monty doesn't always scream and shout – sometimes he sneers instead, or lets rip with a barrage of searing sarcasm (he describes it as 'dry wit'). Monty learnt his leadership style from *Warfare in the Dark Ages* (January's book of the month from the Military History Battle Book Club). Well, if it was good enough for Charlemagne, it's good enough for 'BankOn IT Solutions'. Yes, sir.

How to deal with The Jackboot:

Listen to what they say without interrupting
If they don't get a chance to express themselves, they'll just get frustrated. If they're interrupted, they'll get even more irritated. You don't have to agree or disagree: just listen.

Match the energy – then slow down
You don't need to shout back, just react. If you stay impassive, they'll feel ignored. Speak clearly and strongly, gradually reducing the volume and the pace to calm things down.

Identify something that can be done immediately to make things better
Focus their attention on a current solution, rather than past grievances. Help them see that getting rid of the problem is easier than getting agitated about it.

The Bullshitter

It wasn't me

Darren believes that life is a game and bending the rules a little is all part of playing well. If there's a chance to coast, skive or take advantage, you can be sure that Darren has spotted it. Mysterious things happen when Darren is around. Paperwork goes missing, emails disappear, phone calls are taken without anybody hearing them. Customer deliveries take markedly longer too – almost as if they hadn't been posted on

Monday as Darren swears that they were. If only the postal receipts hadn't inexplicably vanished.

Madeline, Darren's manager, is not a suspicious woman but recently she's found herself double-checking Darren's work – when there's anything to check, of course. Darren's record keeping is famously 'light touch'. She wouldn't go as far as to accuse him of lying, just old-fashioned incompetence with a side order of chicanery.

How to deal with The Bullshitter:

Become a bullfighter:
Look out for the perfect story. If everything fits together too neatly, you're probably hearing a manufactured narrative. A lot of unnecessary detail is another sign, as is a rambling answer to a question when a simple 'yes' or 'no' would have done.

Check with other sources
If you've got a bad feeling about a story, check it out with other people before you confront The Bullshitter.

Keep records
If you suspect this is a habit, keep clear records to support any accusations you may have to make in the future.

Be clear about the consequences of lying
They may think they're just bending the truth for expediency's sake. Give them a reality check. Raise the stakes by getting them to focus on the serious outcomes of lying.

Be very clear about performance measures
Put systems in place to track their performance and make sure they know how this kind of behaviour is dealt with in the organisation or group.

Mr Don't Mind Me

John likes his shoes. Or perhaps it's the floor he's so fond of. Whatever it is that's got his attention it's nowhere near anyone's eye level. When he does finally make eye contact it's with such a

Blending in

look of panic that Gerry, his boss, automatically checks the mirror to see if he's grown fangs.

John likes his scarf too, the thick black one he invariably wears to every meeting. It's into this scarf that John confides his whispered answers when Gerry asks him a question. Not that John gets asked many questions. Everyone knows that he has a head full of good ideas, but getting them out takes more skill and patience than most of his colleagues possess.

It's not that John's aloof, in fact, he quite likes people; he just can't work out how to keep all of them happy, all of the time. In discussions he goes out of his way to make sure that he agrees with all parties – even when they hold opposing views. You'd think they'd be pleased, but for some reason they still seem frustrated by him.

How to deal with Mr (or Ms) Don't Mind Me:

Make it safe to get involved
Give each person in the room a chance to outline their position uninterrupted. Don't Mind Me will have to get involved, but won't feel too exposed.

Find the communication mechanism that works for them
It may be that Don't Mind Me is useless at verbal communication; but a master (or mistress) of the pithy email. Work out what works best for them, and use that medium wherever possible.

Give them a role
Ask them to become 'the expert' on a particular topic. Or ask them to argue for the opposing view, or to speak as if they were a customer. Acting 'as if' is a good way of experimenting with different ways of behaving without feeling threatened (for example, suggest they attend the team meeting as if they are the best-informed person in the room).

Reinforce confident behaviour
When they do go for it, make sure they come away feeling good about the experience.

The Control Freak

Betty almost made it yesterday. She got all the way to the lift door before Stacie lunged and snatched the document from its hiding place under Betty's jacket. 'Can I have a quick look at that before it goes out? I might have a couple of comments.' Stacie is Betty's boss – she's editor of *Startle*, a glossy magazine that captures celebrities looking, well, startled. Stacie likes things to be done the right way. That is, her way. To say that she is a control freak would be an understatement. Never, in living memory, has Stacie

All mine

had just a 'few comments' about anything. Seen through Stacie's eyes, her team's lovingly crafted pieces of copy are simply amateurish drafts awaiting the correcting influence of her red pen. By the time she's finished nipping and tucking and ordering rewrites, the magazine is perilously close to missing its deadline – again. Stacie sees herself as a perfectionist – to the magazine's writers she's the literary equivalent of a serial killer.

How to deal with The Control Freak:

Agree their level of input beforehand
Clarify when and where they want be involved, and at what stage they will give feedback. Confirm this in an email if necessary. If they come calling at the wrong time, refer back to the agreed arrangement.

Pre-empt the interference
Take it to them, rather than waiting for them to come looking. This way you get control over at the stage at which they see the work. And you'll dampen down their anxiety.

Frame the discussion
Explain where you are with the work and ask for specific feedback. If you can keep their attention on details, they're less likely to maul the entire thing.

Let go – if you can
Sometimes, it pays to let the Control Freak miss a deadline. So long as it's not your neck on the block.

The Charmer

'Ah – my favourite client,' booms Oscar, cradling the phone and swinging his feet up on the desk. 'Now, I want to hear all your news.' And he really does. He wants to hear all about your children and your garden, how your parents are doing and what you thought of that wonderful little weekend cottage he got you such a good deal on. What he doesn't want to know is how you're managing now he's missed his delivery deadline for the fourth time. 'I'm on the case,' he grins, when you finally bring it up. And, you know, I really think he believes it.

Good-looking Oscar is a triumph of style over content. Charming, witty, attentive, and absolutely rubbish at his job, he believes that how you do something is more important than when you do it – or indeed, if you do it at all. Oscar goes through life creating chaos on a regular basis but somehow he's the one left smiling whilst everyone else comes away feeling like they're a joyless control freak.

All talk...

How to deal with The Charmer:

Avoid small talk
Keep calls and meetings short and to the point. Make it clear before you start that you don't have time to chat and don't let the conversation run on. Set some ground rules: 'no chit-chat', 'no lunch meetings'.

Ask them to set the deadline
Ask them to tell you when they would reasonably be able to deliver. Get them to set 'check-in' meetings to review progress towards the deadline.

Make it public
Ask The Charmer to commit to action in a meeting or a conference call – somewhere they know others have heard. If they let you down, they'll lose face.

Describe the downside
Get them to imagine the consequences of failure to deliver. Don't threaten, just make it sound really, really gloomy.

Ask tough questions
Ask thorough, detailed questions and demand precise answers (Where exactly are you? What does that mean in practice? What are you going to do to get back on schedule?).

The Know It All

Gerald, faithful custodian of truth and accuracy, is never off duty. He's always got an ear open for a fact that needs correcting, or an opinion that lacks rigour. Faced with a sloppy statistic or an incorrectly applied apostrophe, he snaps into action: 'I think you'll find...'

In the office Gerald makes sure he knows all the latest buzzwords and is up to speed with all the new management techniques. He has a diagram for everything and more visions than Joan of Arc. At the end of the day, he'll hand some poor unfortunate who is dying to go home a photocopy of a chapter from a management magazine, 'I think you'll find this useful with the problem you're having...' It's not meant to be crushing, but it is.

None of the diagrams or the articles has any real relevance to the task at hand but then, Gerald doesn't have any really useful guidance to offer. His team call him the Emperor. He loves it, seeing it as a real tribute to his inspiring leadership. The team are of course referring to his clothes – or lack of them.

Nice suit

How to cope with The Know It All:

Make them feel valued
The Know It All wants recognition, so make sure you let them know when their contributions are useful and valuable.

Avoid saying 'no'

If you contradict them directly, they'll probably dig their heels in. The Know It All likes nothing better than a chance to prove just how very right they are.

Encourage them to recognise absolutist thinking

Don't come right out and say it, but do encourage them to consider their position: 'Is that always the case?' Ask for details and encourage them to find counter examples.

Invite contributions from other people by name

Keep a firm hand on meetings and try to prevent others opting out by calling on individuals by name, or taking turns to speak uninterrupted.

Use structured thinking techniques

For example, explore pros and cons in turn. Avoid open-ended discussions that he can dominate.

The Cyborg

Michael has obviously found a facial expression he likes and he's sticking with it. He could be happy, sad, or beside himself with rage – it's hard to say. Inscrutable is probably the best description. His wife calls it his 'screen-saver' look. If he played poker he'd be unbeatable, as a colleague, his Spock–like demeanour makes him difficult to deal with and impossible to read. Conversations with Michael usually drift into an uneasy silence after a minute or two. Suggestions are met with the minimum of comment and even less in

Professionally detached

the way of emotion. Does he like the ideas or loathe them? Who knows?

When one of his team was going through a rough time at home, Michael avoided the issue, telling others he wanted to remain 'professionally detached'. Michael excels at many things, but the more emotional side of life apparently holds no interest for him.

How to deal with The Cyborg:

Don't overwhelm them
Even if you're feeling hyped up, start conversations in neutral and build up to a more emotional delivery.

Uncover their enthusiasm
Everyone likes something. Get them talking about the something they're passionate about.

Ask, without expecting to receive
Don't freeze them out. Continue to ask, in a low-key way, how they feel about something – just don't expect too much.

The Sceptic

'And what makes you think that is the case?' That's Megan's stock response to any statement – usually accompanied by a penetrating stare and a look of mild dissatisfaction. Thorough, rigorous, and somewhat humourless – Megan is waging a one-woman-war against woolly thinking. Her extreme scepticism probably has its

roots in her childhood. Possessed of an inquiring mind and a persistent manner, the young Megan asked a lot of 'why' questions and was woefully disappointed by the flaky answers she received. That business about Father Christmas was the final straw. Now, with a degree in philosophy and a gold medal from the student debating society, she prides herself on her ability to ask challenging questions and speak her mind frankly – often in a very loud voice, in front of exactly the wrong people.

But...why?

How to deal with The Sceptic:

Listen and keep listening
If you can locate the root of their scepticism you can tailor your case to meet their real concerns.

Empathise
You may not share their view, but you can make it clear that you appreciate an inquiring mind.

Give a little
Show that you're not intractable. If you appear willing be to persuaded they may be encouraged to do the same.

Find common ground in their argument and build upon it
When you hit upon something you agree on, frame their agreeing with you as being the reasonable and helpful thing to do.

And finally...

No man – or woman – is an island. We're in the relationship too.

Whatever type of tricky behaviour we're encountering, it's worth keeping the following in mind:

It might be about you
We're not always aware of the impact of our behaviour. It's worth considering whether something we've said or done – something that probably seems inconsequential from our point of view – may be provoking the tricky behaviour.

...Or then again, it might not
We are the centre of our own little universes. As a result, we naturally believe that people think about us far more than they actually do. In fact, they are far more likely to be ruminating about what to have for lunch, or where they left the car keys – nothing to do with us at all. Don't become paranoid. If you think there's a problem, come right out with it.

Most people are well intentioned. Tricky people probably believe that what they're doing is reasonable and rational; otherwise they wouldn't do it. Keep that in mind. Advance with care and don't expect them to realise they're being annoying.

PY Identify a tricky person with whom you'd like to (or need to) have a better relationship. Write a pen portrait of that person.

I TRY   Now create a list of techniques that would help in dealing with that person. Try them out for a while and then revisit your pen portrait. Has your opinion of the person changed? Would you describe them differently now?

Now, feeling brave? Write a pen portrait of yourself.

Ⓠ Graceful exit

Some of us are out the door at the first whiff of gun smoke. Others hang in until the sell-by date is ancient history and the relationship is growing its own mould. Wherever we sit on this spectrum, it's still difficult to know when to stick and when to quit.

In this chapter we explore how to read the signs. And when the sign points to the exit, both how to say 'goodbye' without causing devastating damage, and how to get over it once they've gone.

Should I stay or should I go?

The decision to stick or quit depends largely on how we feel about the relationship. For a rough guide, answer the following questions. As you do, think about a particular relationship where you're considering getting out, with a lover, friend, employer or even a grumpy cousin.

Each of the following questions has two options. Choose the one that best applies to you.

In an atmosphere of tension with this person you would rather:

A. Clear the air
B. Get some fresh air

Your thoughts of this person are often:

C. Sympathetic
D. Critical

An elephant is in the room and neither of you has said a word. You are more likely to:

A. Draw attention to it
B. Overlook the obvious

In this relationship you more often feel:

C. Hopeful
D. Hopeless

When upset with this person, you tend to:

A. Have it out
B. Pretend you aren't bothered

Your general mood with this person tends to be:

C. Positive
D. Disparaging

In this relationship you tend to take:

A. The lead
B. The path of least resistance

You expect the relationship to:

C. Last
D. End

Now add up your totals:

A [　　　　　] Active

B [　　　　　] Passive

C [　　　　　] Constructive

D [　　　　　] Destructive

Graceful exit

Having added up your totals, plot your score on the grid below. Each score relates to an axis, so if you have scored 3 for active and 1 for passive, mark up 3 on the Active axis, then mark up 1 on the Passive axis and so on until you have four dots (or crosses, depending on how you mark).

			Active	4				
	Dodo (Extinction)			3	**Phoenix** (Renewal and repair)			
				2				
				1				
					Constructive			
4	3	2	1					
Destructive				1	2	3	4
				1				
	Cuckoo (Neglect)			2	**Passive**	**Swan** (Loyalty)		
				3				
				4				

Now join the dots and create a shape (probably a rough diamond or possibly a triangle). The quadrant with the greatest coverage gives an idea of your profile.

Phoenix: Renewal

Dodo	Phoenix
Cuckoo	Swan

Keep going with this relationship. There's plenty to work with, most vitally your positive view and your enthusiasm.

The research shows that customer loyalty is greater when the organisation makes up after a bad experience than when the customer has had consistently good service. The same is true in romantic relationships. The fact that we've made it through tough times means that we're more likely to relish what we've got and so make the effort to nourish the relationship.

There is every possibility that this relationship will rise from the ashes. Many of the chapters in this book will be relevant. Try a chapter from the relationship repair kit route (chapters B, C, G, I, J, M, N and O). See Swan opposite. Don't give up.

Dodo: Exit

Dodo	**Phoenix**
Cuckoo	**Swan**

It's not looking good. You have little hope for the relationship and, whether your realise it or not, you're doing your best to end it.

Before walking out the door, it's worth reflecting on whether the relationship is characteristic of those that end:

1   No giving or getting
If you're in a team who are unsupportive or you don't feel like supporting, the chances are the turnover in the team will be reasonably high. Personal relationships are similar, if we feel uncared for, or feel no compunction to care for someone else, we may very well be heading to the point of no return.

2   Big arguments with small triggers
Frequent conversations that start off with something trivial like a towel on the floor and end with character assassinations are worth watching for. It's not the content of the conflict here, but the fact that it escalates into a pitched battle about the other person's personality that's the issue.

3   Turning away
People purposefully ignoring each other is a sure fire way to snuff the life out of a relationship. When the listening and

talking stops it can be difficult to recover. See chapter G – Bid for attention – for more.

4 Beyond repair
All relationships have rocky patches. One of the differentiators between ones that work and ones that don't is whether or not one party attempts to make up with the other. Psychologists call this a repair attempt – it could be anything from a smile, a question or an apology, but it's designed to re-engage and repair the relationship. Greater still is when people feel no need to repair the relationship after a conflict. So, if you've had an argument with a boss, friend or lover and you feel no desire to repair the break, even after some time, it's worth questioning what is happening and whether it's time to move on.

5 No fondness or admiration
John Gottman suggests that the right time to consider leaving a relationship is when there is no fondness or admiration for the other person or organisation left.

If you're experiencing most of or all of the above it's probably time to take this relationship off the endangered list and make it extinct. If not, think about how to turn your energies to a more constructive assessment of what's great about the relationship and how to get the good times back.

Swan: Loyalty

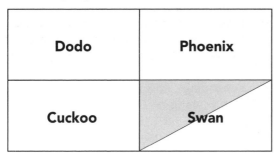

Dodo	Phoenix
Cuckoo	Swan

You are trying to weather the storm and may hope that by keeping quiet the problems will eventually take care of themselves.

This might possibly work for dealing with the occasional bad mood, or temporary relationship glitch (one of you is in the doghouse for not washing up) but if the issues have been around for a while, this isn't going to be enough.

If you want this relationship to last you need to act:

- Talk to the other person. Tell them how you feel and that you want the relationship to succeed.
- Share your concerns that the relationship won't work if nothing changes.
- Ask them how they feel.
- If they also want the relationship to work, ask them how they believe that can happen.
- Agree what you can both do to make it work.

Cuckoo: Neglect

Dodo	Phoenix
Cuckoo	Swan

This relationship is going to end and it's going to be painful unless you act now. Whether by focusing on other interests, spending more time away or forgetting to call you may be hoping it will just go away. It won't and this approach is likely to leave the worst possible feeling afterwards.

Avoid the prolonged, painful death (this isn't an opera). Make a choice. Either pluck up your courage and have it out or tell them it's over and the reason why. The other person will respect you more and you will dilute any lingering guilt.

Serial monogamists beware! All relationships need attention to thrive. Make sure you're not repeating past patterns by letting this relationship seep away.

Exit route

There are four stages of relationship breakdown according to the psychologist Steve Duck.

As you read on, think about a particular relationship you've got that's in decline – a withering romance, an underperforming member of your team, an old friend who you see less and less, a client who is buying less.

1 Is the relationship any good?
We feel generally dissatisfied with the relationship but we're not quite sure why. We may wonder if it's our fault (I knew I shouldn't have criticised her in public), whether we're making enough effort (I should have helped more) or whether we're doing things in the right way (I need to fit in with their way of doing things).

We start to question the value of the relationship: am I over-servicing this client? Is this more effort than it's worth? Is this the right career move for me?

There are two common mistakes at this stage: avoid the issue and take precipitate action.

When we feel general uneasiness then we should pursue our hunch. We should decide what we want from the relationship and answer the question: is it worth fighting for? Avoiding the issue today will mean more pain tomorrow, and less chance that we'll repair the damage. Equally, taking dramatic action at this stage is likely to make things worse. We need more information before we can diagnose the problem, let alone prescribe the remedy.

There is a time for sitting and thinking and this is it.

2 Is the other person the problem?
Here we shift away from a general sense of dissatisfaction to a more focused dissatisfaction with the other person (or organisation).

We may see them as difficult, uncaring or even trying to destroy the relationship but still wonder: am I being fair?

The common mistake is to rush this stage because, once we've decided the other person is at fault, it's easy to start blaming them. Our perceptions are so biased that we see only what confirms our initial view: she didn't reply to my text which proves she doesn't like me; rather than the full set of facts: she did call me out of the blue last week to have a chat.

The trick is to gather information about what is going on without judging it by keeping a journal or a factual blog about what is said and done. Maybe we can spot some patterns and so avoid the triggers that send things off in the wrong direction (see chapter J – Draw the poison).

One way to deal with this stage is to change our expectations of the other person or the organisation – are we asking too much? Should we forgive them for past sins and move on?

Or maybe we simply accept that this is one of their less endearing qualities that we're happy to live with.

At this stage we still believe that the relationship can be rescued. And so if the issue is significant enough to risk destroying the relationship, we brave stage 3.

3 Confrontation – the problem has to be fixed
Now it's time to talk.

We tell the other person about our feelings and problems and discuss them in hope of saving the relationship. This may take the form of 'I can't see where my career is going here' or it can be more direct, 'I don't feel we're having as much fun as we used to and this makes me unhappy'. We will tend to take some responsibility but we also expect them to admit their part.

Ideally, the conversation clears the air, and concentrates on what both parties can do to turn the relationship around. Action follows and, despite some upsets along the way, the relationship starts to improve. The good news is that relationship memories are short and we give undue weight to the most recent events so, once we start the ascent, there's a good chance we'll build enough momentum to keep going.

Alternatively, the conversation reveals how fundamental the differences are. At this stage we may reach for more powerful remedies, such as dialogue (see chapter O – Tough talk) or even mediation. Or we go to stage 4.

4 It's over; I need to build support
At this stage we have decided:

- It's not worth making any more repair attempts.
- We won't accept repair attempts from the other person. We've thought about what they could possibly do to make us change our mind and either they can't or they won't.
- The pain of ending the relationship is less than the pain of continuing.

It's an unhappy time and, typically, we seek out our close friends or family to get their acceptance and support. The risk at this stage is that we overstate the other person's faults (cruel, never listened, selfish, mean), which leads to gossip and eventually they hear some exaggerated form of our narrative on the relationship. They won't like it and we will find it hard to retract.

The most productive conversations tend to focus on (a) how I feel (b) the facts about what happened (c) the responsibilities we both share for the end. Hard to do through the tears but well worth the effort.

For more on how to end it, see the next section.

5 Recovery
This stage starts when the relationship ends. We all need it however much we pretend we don't.

One Mind Gym member says he still has dreams about his boss from ten years ago. Another talked about her tricky break-up and the lengths she went to recover (new hair colour, new friends, and most drastically, new country).

Typically we tell more people about the break-up and start to embellish on the story of the relationship. A fair bit of history is rewritten and, ideally, the story is about why the relationship didn't work as opposed to what was wrong with the other person.

The recovery is also needed for those who are affected by the break-up, eg, children in a marriage or employees in a restructure.

For more on how to make a robust recovery, see below.

Happy endings

Jumping ship?

Yikes, we've decided to end it. What now?

First, imagine that you are on the receiving end. What would you want? When people are asked this question, they typically say they want honesty, respect, and an opportunity to keep their dignity intact. So that's exactly what we should give them.

Here are some tips on how to end a relationship with someone and keep their dignity intact:

Don't rush it
These conversations get the heart racing and, however well prepared we are, we still tend to feel awkward. This awkwardness is infectious and combined with our nerves causes us to speed up, gushing our announcement and then rushing to get out as quickly as possible. This is the least respectful way to behave.

Instead we need to be calm, clear and give it time. Take a few deep breaths before you go in. Make an extra effort to speak slowly and stay for as long as they want.

Do it in person
Text and email are fine for any necessary follow-up (I will leave the keys with the corner shop so you can pick up your stuff while I'm away) but the initial announcement should be eyeball to eyeball, carbon footprint permitting.

Start with the message up front
When sharing bad news it's best to give an unambiguous headline right at the start: I want a trial separation, to resign, to be free (from you). Opening the conversation with lots of questions gives the impression that you feel there's a problem with the relationship and that you want to fix it, not that you want to end it.

Tell your story and share your feelings

Explain what, how and why. You will have your story about the relationship and you should share how you feel. The old cliché of 'it's not you, it's me' is rarely true, and everyone knows it. It's important to take some responsibility, but don't make it all about you – it takes two.

Listen to their story if they want to tell it

Some people at this point will want to leave it at that. Others will want to tell their story and how they feel. The important thing is to be available and listen to their response. There's no need to disagree, to justify your position, to argue, to judge or to sympathise. You've decided that it's best to end the relationship and that's the purpose of the conversation.

Stand firm

The important principle at this stage is to remain consistent, however much begging, screaming, crying or shouting goes on. If you start changing your position then the conversation will turn messy. They deserve clarity and certainty.

Honesty is good too. However, it plays to be cautious on levels of disclosure. It's just about ok to admit you were bored but definitely unwise to say that you found them boring. By and large best to keep to a few, central facts and let them do the talking.

Create distance

This doesn't mean move to Vanuatu (tempting though the South Pacific might be). It means give the person both psychological and physical distance. They will need space to recover from the break-up and so will you. Seeing them every week for the next few months is unlikely to help the healing process.

There may be a time for friendship but it's not now.

I'm over it

We've all been there: coming out of a relationship before we wanted to. Whether we've been made redundant from a dream job or have broken up with someone special, we tend to leave feeling hurt and at a loss.

This section deals with how to recover when the exit wasn't our choice. Not all these tactics are suitable for the ending of all relationships (such as bereavements), so pick the ones you think work best for your situation.

Find yourself before finding someone else
In a recent study, forty people who had recently been in break-ups were asked to describe their reactions to the loss and give detail about what happened at the end of relationship. The study found that women were more likely to confide in good friends to recover. Men were more likely than women to start going out quickly with other people as a means of recovery.

The respondents with more complete accounts about why the relationship ended were also the ones who were more likely to accept that the relationship was over. As a result, they felt more in control of their recovery and so recovered faster.

We respond to break-ups with a variety of feelings including numbness, denial, anger and loss. This is natural and healthy. It may also take time. And that's healthy too; much healthier than rushing it.

As we go through these emotions it's well worth developing a thorough account of why the relationship ended. Don't stop with 'we were incompatible' or 'we had different values' – that's a cop out. If you really want closure, write up the full story from your perspective, then tell the story from their perspective and finally the version from the impartial observer.

The process is cathartic and the understanding a powerful tool to put the past behind us.

Was it really that good?
Recovery is not as simple as being optimistic about the future ('You'll find a new person/job in no time'), though that helps. It's also about creating a more realistic assessment of the past.

In the film *Truly, Madly, Deeply*, Nina (played by Juliet Stevenson) is distraught when her cellist husband (Alan Rickman) dies. He returns as a ghost and she is initially ecstatic, remembering only his wonderful points and their happy times together. As the film progresses, his erratic behaviour starts to irritate her more and more and she recalls what she didn't like about him as well.

What tends to happen when we've been on the receiving end of a break-up is that, after the initial shock and disappointment, we dwell on many of the positive aspects of the past and believe that the future will never be as good. The summer's picnic by the lake was idyllic and we forget that it was one glorious day in four otherwise burdensome years.

Swap the usual double whammy of optimism about the past (she was amazing) and pessimism about the future (I'll never find anyone like her) to pessimism about the past (the time when she locked me out) and optimism about the future (I'm now much clearer about what's important to me).

When the numbness has passed and the remorse or regret is setting in, write down all the stuff that annoyed you about your old work / flame. What didn't work, what was irritating, what did you find difficult to cope with. And then all the things that you want from the future that this relationship didn't provide.

Take responsibility

It takes two

The research shows that the way we describe the reasons for the break-up has a big impact on how distressed we feel about it.

If we say the break-up was because of the other person (he was insensitive or she was dull), or the result of environmental factors (work got in the way), we're likely to feel highly distressed. If, however, we see the break-up as partly our responsibility, 'I was thoughtless', or as a relationship issue, 'We wanted different things', then we're likely to feel more positive.

Remember what's good about you

Being on the receiving end of a break–up, particularly if the break–up wasn't well handled, can leave us questioning ourselves – 'What's wrong with me?' 'What could I have done differently?'

These are good questions. However, it's important to remember all the good and wonderful things about yourself. Just as you've written down what was not good about the relationship, it's worth considering what is good about you. If you find this hard, ask a close friend or look back on relationships that have been successful.

Escape

One way to get over it is to get out of the situation and look for different things to do. A friend of The Mind Gym recalls losing his job. He was struggling to find another one, had a young family to support and cash was running perilously low. He did a simple thing – went to the cinema with his wife. It was a small break from the uphill struggle of finding a new job, but it made all the difference. Those few hours of escape helped him to feel refreshed, revitalised and ready to persevere.

Social support

One Mind Gym member described a tactic to stop re-contacting a recent ex. Rather than calling the ex, she calls a friend whose job it is to dissuade her from making contact. Friends and family can act as experts in distraction and bring a sense of humour and care to the situation.

Remove the reminders

Relationships tend to generate mementoes of happy times: the shell from the beach, the keyring from the London Eye, the first present he bought me. During relationships these act as positive reminders of good times but they are not the things you want around the place after the fact. Put them in a box and put them away. Later, once you feel like the relationship is old news, you can throw them away, burn them (as Rachel and Monica do in an episode of *Friends*, which brings in the strapping firemen and the start of a whole new relationship) or keep the ones that you still value.

The end

The end of a relationship is never going to be easy, but it can be done with respect, dignity and care. In the best circumstances we can be left with a feeling of personal growth and accomplishment. A good goodbye is the start of something better.

SPY Talk to friends and colleagues about how they have left relationships. Look for those who have done it well. What did they do? What worked for them?

TRY For those who have recently had their relationship unilaterally terminated, which of the tactics can you use? How will you use them?

New beginnings

Knowledge is like money in the bank. It's valuable but it is not, by itself, useful. Only when money is converted into something – a house, a train ticket or a toothpick does it become useful. The good news is that, unlike money, knowledge actually appreciates when you spend it, creating new insights and more knowledge (a bit like getting richer by going shopping, if only).

Whatever you have taken from this book is the same. Without action, it is fairly pointless – your relationships will continue much as before. It's all very fine knowing what a conflict toxin is but it requires energy and courage to do something different when one comes along.

Research by Robert Brinkerhoff suggests that after attending a typical training course, only 15% of people are still doing something different a few months later. With books it's even less. And yet you've got this far, which puts you in an elite group already. In return for your persistence (for which many thanks), here are some practical tips on how to turn what you've discovered into better relationships every day.

1. New eyes
There's a children's playground game that goes like this:

Spell out SILK – S, I, L, K.

And again, S, I, L, K. And again, S, I, L, K. And again, S, I, L, K. Now answer this question: What do cows drink?

Most people say 'milk'. Cows, of course, drink water.

What's happening here is that as something becomes familiar we start to get into a habit. We give an instant response that is often the wrong response. And then we're back in the old patterns that didn't work last time and almost certainly will lead our relationship astray again.

This is especially true with people. One Mind Gym member recalls that his father suddenly quit smoking, having previously been on 40 a day. No one in the family noticed for two weeks, until he told them. Another member told of when she lost 16 pounds in weight and her parents still asked, 'Have you put on weight?' when she went to visit. We get so used to how we see people and the pattern of our response that we keep going as before, oblivious that the situation has changed.

So, what to do to get out of the rut?

First off, look for what's new or, at least, look at the same person with a different set of eyes. What if you fancied them, or were introduced by George Clooney, or you were a nurse and they'd arrived in A&E? See them as others might see them. The less the 'others' are like you, the better.

Secondly, try something new. Actually have a go with a tactic in this book that you liked. It probably won't go perfectly the first time so see this as a test case. Don't be put off if it doesn't get the results you wanted. Instead, think about how you can adapt next time.

Thirdly, don't expect the other person to notice anything new. They won't and it's better they don't. No one wants to feel like they're your homework. Look for satisfaction from yourself, not from anyone else.

2. More options
Your lover tells you that what you have done is 'unacceptable'. Think of 10 different ways you can respond. (1) Say sorry (2) walk away (3) ask why they think that (4) take action to resolve the problem (5)

stay silent (6) tell them what they have done is 'unacceptable' (7) explain why you behaved as you did (8) remind them of when they have behaved in a similar way (9) give examples of when others have behaved just like you (10) totally accept the criticism and ask what you can do to recover the situation. And so on.

There are usually not just 10 but hundreds of ways that we can respond. We get tempted to pick the first one we think of and run with it. Far better to come up with a long list first and only then decide what to do. This is easier with a text or email than in the heat of argument. So, in those circumstances where there isn't time to develop a decent range of options, reflect afterwards on what went well or badly, and come up with a list of options you could draw from if it were to happen again.

We always have a choice and we usually have many more choices than we realise.

3. Dream a little dream
Identify a specific relationship that you want to improve, or even a specific conversation within that relationship.

'How could I get on better with my new boss?' 'I know that there's an unfinished conversation to be had with my husband about how much we spend on the house decorations.' 'My girlfriend and I need to talk about our future – I'm just not sure that I want the same future that she does.'

Make a plan. Where to be, what to say, how to respond. Think it through in as much detail as you can manage.

Now imagine putting the plan into practice. Play the conversation through in your head, or write it down. It might sound like an unnecessary effort, but putting pen to paper or finger to keyboard does both clarify what to say and increase the chances that you will actually do it.

4. Prepare for danger
Spot the danger zone – the conversations, people and circumstances that lead into an unhelpful routine. DIY store on Sunday morning, airports, my big brother, whenever we talk about your work, the conference call.

This is the time to be extra careful. Self-regulation (see chapter B) is going to be harder than usual and a lot, lot more important.

In these situations we have three core options: repair, sanitise or retreat.

Retreat means either avoiding the situation altogether (travel separately, skip the conference call) or go silent (which may end up being interpreted as provocative in a passive aggressive way). This is usually the strategy of last resort.

Sanitise involves keeping things factual. We need to avoid taking the bait, or giving it. Instead we stick strictly to what needs to be said and done.

If we want to repair then we either need to change our behaviour or we need dialogue (see chapter O). The ability to discuss stuff that appears difficult or entrenched becomes especially crucial.

5. Daily nudge

The 15% (in Robert Brinkerhoff's research, mentioned above) who change their behaviour in the long term as a result of a course are supplemented by a further 70% who dabble with new ways but sooner or later revert back. Like the gym members who've stopped going by March (50% of all January sign-ups) or the diet that falls at the first sundae, it's easy to try a few ideas out and then give up.

One way to avoid slipping into this category is to commit now to a relationship check-in. It will take only a few minutes. Answer four questions:

1. What have I done differently in the last day/week/month to improve a relationship?
2. What worked well? How/where can I repeat this behaviour?
3. Which relationship do I most want to improve?
4. What can I do differently to help improve it in the next day/ week/month?

If you're serious, put the check-in in your calendar now, or make it part of your routine on the way into work.

If you remember nothing else

Security is the key

A driving force in all relationships is how secure we feel. When we feel safe we're much more likely to think and behave positively towards everyone else. When that security is compromised we may start to feel anxious and are more likely to become guarded or negative. This negative behaviour is then likely to damage the relationship further. Spot the vicious cycle.

The restructuring of organisations often challenges people's sense of security (Is my job safe?) And this feeling can continue indefinitely. A full nine years after a merger, three times as many executives leave every year as in a company that hasn't been through a merger. Those that do leave and find another job have better health and less stress than those that stay.

As people feel insecure they're much more likely to be anxious or leave a relationship altogether. So, the first thing we can do to improve relationships is help ourselves and others feel secure: I'm ok and you're ok.

This can be done with generous listening, empathy, acting supportively, making the other person the 100% centre of our attention, or any of a host of other tactics covered earlier. However, helping create a secure environment is not simply about being pleasant – it's about being authentic. We need to be ourselves or the relationship will be built on fault lines.

One exercise to help with authenticity is to imagine your home looks something like this:

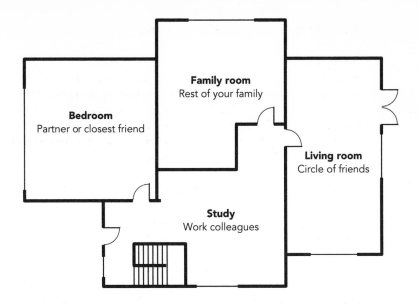

In each room write down at least three words or phrases people in that group would use to describe you to someone who didn't know you. Look at where there similarities are and also the differences. For authenticity, we need to make the walls porous, ie, that people say broadly similar things wherever they come across us.

One Mind Gym member explained that when she did this exercise she was 'supportive' in every room except 'work'. This helped her spot that she was so busy at work that she had failed to be herself. She then adapted to make sure that she could be supportive and as a result feels happier and has better relationships with her colleagues.

Of course, there are going to be times when we challenge people's sense of security unintentionally and other times when we want to (eg, in a negotiation). It's at moments like these that we need to be very aware of the impact. Insecurity is the termite that eats away at relationships. Keep it at bay for happy times.

(Almost) unconditional positive regard
See the best in people. It's far better for our relationships to be occasionally gullible than always distrustful.

Ground-breaking psychologist Carl Rogers came up with the idea of 'unconditional positive regard'. Simply put, this means looking for and seeing the good in people regardless of what they are doing or have done.

But what about those individuals who are genuinely dastardly?

For a precious few, we need to get out fast. Physically abusive relationships are one very clear example. No ifs, no buts, no 'it's my fault'.

In other cases, we can set our boundaries. Many organisations have scheming office politicians who turn the tiniest incident into a heinous act of disloyalty in an attempt to blacken our reputation. In these cases 'unconditional positive regard' would be naïve and hapless. First off, we need to protect ourselves. This may mean being extra careful about what we say to them, avoiding projects or meetings where they are prominent and not commenting about them to other people at all.

Equally, before condemning them outright, we would do well to find out why they're behaving like this. Maybe they feel that they're out of their depth and are trying to cover up. Maybe their mentor behaves like this and they're keen to copy them. Maybe they feel that they've been betrayed and are fighting back. Maybe they're in serious debt and desperately need the promotion to keep their marriage afloat. Finding the reason can unlock a very different kind of relationship, one where we can help and, in so doing, they may help us too. Handle with care, which is different from not handling at all.

The overwhelming majority of people are trying to do the best things for themselves and the people they love. Their intentions can be misguided, their logic faulty and their methods downright repulsive, but if we ask ourselves why and approach the situation positively, we are likely to find a resolution. Start with 'mindless' rather than 'selfish', 'hopeless' rather than 'malicious', 'confused' rather than 'liar'. It's easier to downgrade our assessment when new facts emerge than to upgrade when we've got it wrong.

The law of unintended confusion

There's a (probably apocryphal) internet story about an exchange between President Bush and Condoleezza Rice when she was Secretary of State. Hu Jintao had recently been named General Secretary of the Communist Party in China.

SCENE: The Oval Office

George: Condi! Good to see you. What's happening?
Condi: Sir, I have the report about the new leader of China.
George: Great. Let's hear it.
Condi: Hu is the new leader of China.
George: That's what I want to know.
Condi: That's what I'm telling you.
George: That's what I'm asking you. Who is the new leader of China?
Condi: Yes.
George: I mean the fellow's name.
Condi: Hu.
George: The guy in China.
Condi: Hu.
George: The new leader of China.
Condi: Hu.
George: The Chinese guy?
Condi: Hu is leading China.
George: Now whaddya asking me for?
Condi: I'm telling you Hu is leading China.
George: Well, I'm asking you. Who is leading China?
Condi: That's the man's name.
George: That's whose name?
Condi: Yes.

Difficulties in relationships are rarely the fault of any individual. Usually, they result from a combination of misunderstandings that weren't intended by either party.

When things aren't going smoothly, best to work out what is happening rather than who is at fault. Clarity is a great healer.

Relationships require effort, which is why it pays to be relationship fit. When we're tired not only do we become worse at self-regulation but we also stop making the effort to do the right things for those we love the most.

In-depth research on tennis players who win compared with those who come second, revealed that the difference is not their technique, their strategy or their physical strength but whether they use the brief moment between shots to renew their energy.

Getting married is the beginning, not the end. So is getting promoted. And so is catching the eye of that gorgeous looking person at the bar, hopefully.

In all relationships we need time to recharge. Physical fitness, diet and sleep all play their part. So does dreaming and many of the techniques in this book. One way or another, we need to maintain our energy so we make the effort for those we care most about.

Do sweat the small stuff

If we want to have successful relationships we must tend to the detail. The big gestures on grand occasions are all very nice but our relationship fate is determined less by the anniversary weekend in Venice then by the tick-tock and chit-chat of everyday life. Every little bit matters.

Au revoir

Don't be a stranger. If you want to continue this relationship there is an online gym with tips, insights, exercises and plenty of like-minded people to chat with. The free membership password is on the inside cover of this book. We'd all love to know what has worked for you. Post your stories at The Mind Gym and there'll be plenty of eager readers. Or if you're too shy to blog, find out what insights you can draw from others' adventures.

The beginning of a beautiful relationship?

Bibliography

Antonioni, D. (1998). 'Relationship between the big five personality factors and conflict management styles.' International Journal Of Conflict Management 9(4): 336–355.

Babad, E. Y., J. Inbar, et al. (1982). 'Pygmalion, Galatea, And The Golem – Investigations Of Biased And Unbiased Teachers.' Journal of Educational Psychology 74(4): 459–474.

Baumeister, R. F., A. Stillwell, et al. (1990). 'Victim And Perpetrator Accounts Of Interpersonal Conflict – Autobiographical Narratives About Anger.' Journal Of Personality And Social Psychology 59(5): 994–1005.

Baumeister, R. F. and K. D. Vohs (2004). Handbook of self-regulation : research, theory, and applications. New York, Guilford Press.

Berne, E. (1966). Games people play : the psychology of human relationships. London, The Quality Book Club.

Billig, M. (1989). 'The Argumentative Nature Of Holding Strong Views – A Case-Study.' European Journal Of Social Psychology 19(3): 203–223.

Bjorkqvist, K. (2001). 'Different names, same issue.' Social Development 10(2): 272–274.

Bjorkqvist, K., K. Osterman, et al. (1999). 'Concommitants of physical, verbal, and indirect aggression.' Aggressive Behavior 25(1): 35–35.

Bjorkqvist, K., K. Osterman, et al. (1994). 'Sex-differences in covert aggression among adults.' Aggressive Behavior 20(1): 27–33.

Bluedorn, A. C. (2002). The human organisation of time: temporal realities and experience. Stanford, Calif., Stanford Business Books.

Bowlby, J. (1982). Attachment. London, Hogarth Press.

Boyatzis, R. E. (2006). 'Using tipping points of emotional intelligence and cognitive competencies to predict financial performance of leaders.' Psicothema 18: 124–131.

Brinkerhoff, R. O. and A. M. Apking (2001). High-impact learning : strategies for leveraging business results from training, new perspectives in organizational learning, performance, and change. Reading, Mass.; Oxford, Perseus.

Butler, G. (2000). Overcoming social anxiety and shyness : a self-help guide using cognitive behavioral techniques. London, BCA by arrangement with Robinson.

Camp, J. (2002). Start with no: the negotiating tools the pros don't want you to know. New York, Crown Business.

Carducci, B. J., S. K. Golant, et al. (1999). Shyness : a bold new approach : the latest scientific findings, plus practical steps for finding your comfort zone. New York, HarperCollins Publishers.

Charrier, G. O. (1972). 'COG's Ladder: A Model of Group Growth.' S.A.M Advanced Management Journal 37: 30–37.

Cherulnik, P. D., K. A. Donley, et al. (2001). 'Charisma is contagious: The effect of leaders' charisma on observers' affect.' Journal Of Applied Social Psychology 31(10): 2149–2159.

de Church, L. A. and M. A. Marks (2001). 'Maximizing the benefits of task conflict: The role of conflict management.' International Journal Of Conflict Management 12(1): 4–22.

de Dreu, C. K. W., S. L. Koole, et al. (1999). 'On the seizing and freezing of negotiator inferences: Need for cognitive closure moderates the use of heuristics in negotiation.' Personality and Social Psychology Bulletin 25(3): 348–362.

Dijksterhuis, A. and A. van Knippenberg (1998). 'The relation between perception and behavior, or how to win a game of trivial pursuit.' Journal of Personality and Social Psychology 74(4): 865–877.

Dilts, R. B. (1994). Strategies of genius. Capitola, Calif., Meta Publications.

Drory, A. and I. Ritov (1997). 'Effects of work experience and opponent's power on conflict management styles.' International Journal Of Conflict Management 8(2): 148–161.

Duck, S. (2007). Human relationships. London, SAGE.

Feeney, B. C. (2007). 'The dependency paradox in close relationships: Accepting dependence promotes independence.' Journal of Personality and Social Psychology 92(2): 268–285.

Fincham, F. D. and S. R. H. Beach (1999). 'Conflict in marriage: Implications for working with couples.' Annual Review Of Psychology 50: 47–77.

Fisher, R. and W. Ury (1991). Getting to yes : negotiating an agreement without giving in. London, CenturyBusiness.

Geller, E. S. (2001). Working safe : how to help people actively care for health and safety. Boca Raton, FL, Lewis Publishers.

Glaser, R. and J. K. Kiecolt-Glaser (1994). *Handbook of human stress and immunity.* San Diego; London, Academic Press.

Goffee, R. and G. A. Jones (2006). *Why should anyone be led by you? : what it takes to be an authentic leader.* Boston, Mass., Harvard Business School Press.

Gollwitzer, P. M. (1999). 'Implementation intentions – Strong effects of simple plans.' American Psychologist 54(7): 493–503.

Gollwitzer, P. M. and V. Brandstatter (1997). 'Implementation intentions and effective goal pursuit.' Journal Of Personality And Social Psychology 73(1): 186–199.

Gottman, J., M. (2002). *The mathematics of marriage : dynamic nonlinear models.* Cambridge, Mass.; London, MIT.

Gottman, J. M. (1999). *The marriage clinic : a scientifically based marital therapy.* New York ; London, W. W. Norton.

Gottman, J. M. and R. W. Levenson (1992). 'Marital Processes Predictive Of Later Dissolution – Behavior, Physiology, And Health.' Journal Of Personality And Social Psychology 63(2): 221–233.

Gottman, J. M. and N. Silver (1999). *The seven principles for making marriage work.* London, Weidenfeld & Nicolson.

Harinck, F. and C. K. W. De Dreu (2004). 'Negotiating interests or values and reaching integrative agreements: The importance of time pressure and temporary impasses.' European Journal of Social Psychology 34(5): 595–611.

Harvard business review on negotiation and conflict resolution. (2000). Boston, Mass., Harvard Business School Press.

Harvard business review on decision making. (2001). Boston, Harvard Business School Press.

Hatfield, E., J. T. Cacioppo, et al. (1994). *Emotional contagion.* Cambridge; Paris, Cambridge University Press : Editions de la Maison des sciences de l'homme.

Heim, P., S. Murphy, et al. (2001). *In the company of women : turning workplace conflict into powerful alliances.* New York, Jeremy P. Tarcher/Putnam.

Holmes, T. R., L. A. Bond, et al. (2008). 'Mothers' beliefs about knowledge and mother-adolescent conflict.' Journal of Social and Personal Relationships 25(4): 561–586.

Isaacs, W. (1999). *Dialogue and the art of thinking together : a pioneering approach to communicating in business and in life.* New York, Currency.

Jackson, D. C., J. R. Malmstadt, et al. (2000). 'Suppression and enhancement of emotional responses to unpleasant pictures.' Psychophysiology 37(4): 515–522.

James, O. (2007). *They f*** you up : how to survive family life.* London, Bloomsbury.

Jehn, K. A. (1997). 'Qualitative analysis of conflict types and dimensions in organizational groups.' Administrative Science Quarterly 42(3): 530–557.

Kahane, A. (2007). *Solving tough problems. An Open Way of Talking, Listening, and Creating New Realities*, Berrett–Koehler.

Karpman, S. (1968). *'Fairly tales and script drama analysis.'* TAB 7(26): 39–43.

Kauklainen, A., C. Salmlvalli, et al. (2001). *'Overt and covert aggression in work settings in relation to the subjective well-being of employees.'* Aggressive Behavior 27(5): 360–371.

Keysers, C., B. Wicker, et al. (2004). *'A Touching Sight: SII/PV Activation during the Observation and Experience of Touch.'* Neuron 42(2): 335–346.

Kramer, R. M. (1999). *'Trust and distrust in organizations: Emerging perspectives, enduring questions.'* Annual Review of Psychology 50: 569–598.

Kubler-Ross, E. (1970) *'On Death and Dying.'* London, Routledge.

Langer, E. J. (1989). *Mindfulness. Reading*, Mass., Addison Wesley Pub. Co.

Lyubomirsky, S., K. M. Sheldon, et al. (2005). *'Pursuing happiness: The architecture of sustainable change.'* Review of General Psychology 9(2): 111–131.

Mar, R. A., K. Oatley, et al. (2006). *'Bookworms versus nerds: Exposure to fiction versus non-fiction, divergent associations with social ability, and the simulation of fictional social worlds.'* Journal of Research in Personality 40(5): 694–712.

Marche, T. A. and C. Peterson (1993). *'On the gender differential use of listener responsiveness.'* Sex Roles 29(11–12): 795–816.

McCullough, M. E. (2001). *'Forgiveness: Who does it and how do they do it?'* Current Directions In Psychological Science 10(6): 194–197.

McCullough, M. E., F. D. Fincham, et al. (2003). *'Forgiveness, forbearance, and time: The temporal unfolding of transgression-related interpersonal motivations.'* Journal Of Personality And Social Psychology 84(3): 540–557.

Mehrabian, A. (1967). *'Attitudes Inferred From Neutral Verbal Communications.'* Journal of Consulting Psychology 31(4): 414–417.

Mirvis, P. H. (2003). *To the desert and back : the dramatic story of the greatest change effort on record.* San Francisco, Calif., Chichester: Jossey-Bass; John Wiley.

Mruk, C. J. (1999). *Self-esteem: research, theory and practice.* London, Free Association Books.

Munduate, L., J. Ganaza, et al. (1999). *'Patterns of styles in conflict management and effectiveness.'* International Journal Of Conflict Management 10(1): 5–24.

Muraven, M., R. F. Baumeister, et al. (1999). *'Longitudinal improvement of self–regulation through practice: Building self-control strength through repeated exercise.'* Journal Of Social Psychology 139(4): 446–457.

Muraven, M., D. M. Tice, et al. (1998). *'Self-control as limited resource: Regulatory depletion patterns.'* Journal Of Personality And Social Psychology 74(3): 774–789.

O'Neill, B. (2007). *'Sorry to say.'* www.bbc.co.uk.

Ostell, A. and S. Oakland (1999). *'Absolutist thinking and health.'* British Journal of Medical Psychology 72: 239–250.

Osterman, K., K. Bjorkqvist, et al. (1999). *'Locus of control and three types of aggression.'* Aggressive Behavior 25(1): 61–65.

Pennebaker, J. W. and M. E. Francis (1996). *'Cognitive, emotional, and language processes in disclosure.'* Cognition & Emotion 10(6): 601–626.

Peterson, C. and M. E. P. Seligman (2004). *Character strengths and virtues : a handbook and classification.* Washington, DC; Oxford, American Psychological Association : Oxford University Press.

Petrie, K. J., R. J. Booth, et al. (1998). *'The immunological effects of thought suppression.'* Journal Of Personality And Social Psychology 75(5): 1264–1272.

Raiffa, H., J. Richardson, et al. (2003). *Negotiation analysis : the science and art of collaborative decision making.* Cambridge, Mass.; London, Belknap.

Richards, J. M., E. A. Butler, et al. (2003). *'Emotion regulation in romantic relationships: The cognitive consequences of concealing feelings.'* Journal Of Social And Personal Relationships 20(5): 599–620.

Richardson, R., J. and S. K. Thayer (1993). *The charisma factor : how to develop your natural leadership ability.* Englewood Cliffs, N.J.; London, Prentice Hall.

Rusbult, C. E. and I. M. Zembrodt (1983). *'Responses To Dissatisfaction In Romantic Involvements – A Multidimensional-Scaling Analysis.'* Journal of Experimental Social Psychology 19(3): 274–293.

Schopenhauer, A. and A. C. Grayling (2004). *The art of always being right : thirty-eight ways to win when you are defeated.* London, Gibson Square.

Scobie, G. E. W. and E. D. Scobie (1996). *'The components of forgiveness.'* International Journal Of Psychology 31(3–4): 3098–3098.

Simons, T. L. and R. S. Peterson (2000). *'Task conflict and relationship conflict in top management teams: The pivotal role of intragroup trust.'* Journal Of Applied Psychology 85(1): 102–111.

Smith, T. W. (1992). *'Hostility And Health – Current Status Of A Psychosomatic Hypothesis.'* Health Psychology 11(3): 139–150.

Sorenson, K. A., S. M. Russell, et al. (1993). *'Account-Making, Confiding, And Coping With The Ending Of A Close Relationship.'* Journal of Social Behavior and Personality 8(1): 73–86.

Stewart, I. and V. Joines (1991). *TA today : a new introduction to transactional analysis.* Nottingham, Lifespace.

Stone, D., B. Patton, et al. (2000). *Difficult conversations : how to discuss what matters most.* London, Penguin.

Strauss, N. (2005). *The game : undercover in the secret society of pickup artists.* Edinburgh, Canongate.

Tangney, J. P., R. F. Baumeister, et al. (2004). *'High self-control predicts good* adjustment, less pathology, better grades, and interpersonal success.' Journal Of Personality 72(2): 271–324.

Tannen, D. (1992). That's not what I mean! : how conversational style makes or breaks your relations with others. London, Virago.

Tashiro, T. and P. Frazier (2007). 'The Causal Effects of Emotion on Couples' Cognition and Behavior.' Journal Of Counseling Psychology 54(4): 409–422.

Towler, A. J. (2003). 'Effects of charismatic influence training on attitudes, behavior, and performance.' Personnel Psychology 56(2): 363–381.

van Baaren, R. B., R. W. Holland, et al. (2003). 'Mimicry for money: behavioural consequences of imitation.' Journal Of Experimental Social Psychology(39): 393–8.

van Oyen Witvliet, C., T. E. Ludwig, et al. (2001). 'Granting forgiveness or harboring grudges: Implications for emotion, physiology, and health.' Psychological Science 12(2): 117–123.

Wall, J. A. and R. R. Callister (1995). 'Conflict And Its Management.' Journal Of Management 21(3): 515–558.

Wayne, S. J. and G. R. Ferris (1990). 'Influence Tactics, Affect, And Exchange Quality In Supervisor Subordinate Interactions – A Laboratory Experiment And Field-Study.' Journal Of Applied Psychology 75(5): 487–499.

Wegner, D. M. (1994). 'Ironic Processes Of Mental Control.' Psychological Review 101(1): 34–52.

Wenzlaff, E. M. and D. M. Wegner (2000). 'Thought suppression.' Annual Review Of Psychology 51: 59–91.

Westen, D. (2007). The political brain: the role of emotion in deciding the fate of the nation. New York, PublicAffairs.

Wheeler, M. (2004). 'Anxious moments: Openings in negotiation.' Negotiation Journal 20(2): 153–169.

Willis, J. and A. Todorov (2006). 'First impressions: Making up your mind after a 100-ms exposure to a face.' Psychological Science 17(7): 592–598.

Zimbardo, P. G. (1981). Shyness : what it is, what to do about it. London, Pan.

Yankura, J. and W. Dryden (1994). Albert Ellis. London, Sage Publications.

Without whom

The Mind Gym: relationships was written by Octavius Black and Sebastian Bailey, co-founders of The Mind Gym. However, it would never have happened without the counsel, enterprise and remarkable commitment of many others.

First and foremost the very determined book team led by the irrepressible and talented writer Mandy Wheeler and supported at different stages by Dr Rebecca McGuire-Snieckus, Lizz Brocklesby, Sarah Vine, Kate Rew and Ambika Mavila.

The academic boards past and present chaired by the illustrious Professor Guy Claxton and including Professor Ilona Boniwell, Professor Janet Reibstein, Professor Michael West, Professor Ingrid Lunt and Emeritus Professor Peter Robinson.

The Mind Gym's current core team (in order of years, months, weeks and hours of unstinting dedication) Samantha Williams, Rachel Newton, Debbie Marshall-Lee, Pui-Wai Yuen, Alice Jackson, Rebecca McGuire-Snieckus, Matthew Gray, Danielle Heffernan, Hannah-Leigh Bovington, Jen Rolfe, Laura Barone, Andre Borgstrom, Laura Turk, Lizz Brocklesby, Nicola James Duff, Sian Edwards, Nick Sloper, Mark Corrigan, Sarah Donovan, Annastasia de Nobrega, Keith Webster, Chris Rosser, Carly Brescacin, Lucinda Everett, Hannah Roderick, Clare Kenny, Lindsay McSporran, Shirin Lock, Richard Graham, Russell Trow, Rob Johnston, Alice Stenhouse, Rachael Robinson, Nadia Gwyer, Sarah Royce-Greensill,

Chantelle Campher, Robert O'Grady, Samantha Felton, Ian Wheeler, Jaspal Bahra, Karen Sargent. And wise adviser, Chairman, David Roberts.

The pioneers who continue to embrace The Mind Gym and bring it into their organisations, not just occasionally but as a cornerstone for the development of their people and growth of their business. In particular, Lis Meikle, George Zielinski, John Nield, Julie Scott (RBS); John Castledine, Lisa Day (Pfizer); Alex Christou, Lisa Rose, Colin Sloman, Dan Flint, David Thomlinson (Accenture); Peter Turgoose, Margaret Ollerenshaw (Royal Mail); Sarah March, Jonathan Brown, Gail Preece (Orange); Stephan Thoma, Claire Magee (Google); Noel Hadden, Beate Heidler (Deutsche Bank); Julio Arquimbau (Barclays) and Elle Seaton, Genevieve Gowland (Barclays Capital); Matt Nixon, Deborah Binks-Moore, Rachel Lennon (Shell); Farida Gai, Helen Rogers, Clair Carpenter (HSBC); Rebecca Oxley, Trish Bussey, Vicky Hampson (Nike); Cathy Martin, Nick Clay, Bev Proctor, Bryan Robertson (RBS Insurance); Sue Round, Joanne McGuire (Sainsbury's); Adrianne Sale, Alex Thompson (Symbian); Sir Stuart Rose, Sharon Pavitt, Leigh Keating, Jane Daly, Paula West (Marks & Spencer); Andy Waller, Mel Gee Kee (Unilever); Chris Murray (Astra Zeneca).

Coaches who have delivered The Mind Gym summits, workouts, boosters, diagnostics and other mind-altering experiences in 686 organisations and 38 countries. In particular, Andrew Mallett, Andrew Pearson, Anisha Kaul, Anne Miller, Becky Heino, Cameron Blair, Catherine Nicholson, Catherine Semark, Cathy Ledwidge, Cathy Marshall, Chirag Jain, Claire Castell, Deborah Brown, Fernando Caramazana, Danny Easton, David Stevenson, Donna McGeorge, Douglas Martinez, Edwardyne Cowan, Frank O'Halloran, Gene Moncrief, George Rossi, Georgie Selleck, Gina Caceci, Jacqueline Farrington, Jane Palmer, Jean Burke, Jenny Flintoft, Jessica Chivers, Joanna Yates, Joff Marshall-Lee, John Ford, John Nicholson, Jonathan Hill, Jonna Sercombe, Julie Johnston, Justin Wise, Justyn Comer, Kate Sirrell, Karen Sigalas, Laurie Carrick, Leslie Solomon, Marian Thier, Mary Gregory, Matt Horan, Nicholas Holbrook, Nicole Scott, Noel Woodgate, Paul Calendrillo, Paul Turnbull, Phil Higgins, Philip Woodford, Renita Kalhorn, Reuben Milne, Sally Hinder, Sam Paulete, Samantha Aspinall, Samantha De Siena, Sandra Chewins, Sean Clemmit, Shona Garner, Simon Rollings, Stan Elson, Stephanie Hopper, Steven Dolan, Susan Mulholland, Tom Blaisse, Tony Brook, Tony Walker, Tracy Gunn.

Joanne Black for her generosity, kindness, unending patience and incisive advice on 'relationships' and one very special relationship in particular.

Juliet Bailey for her endless supply of source material and, along with Genevieve and Miranda, being the model of a loving relationship.

Tif Loehnis of Janklow Nesbit, without whom none of The Mind Gym books would ever have existed, and Jo Dickinson from Little, Brown whose exceptional judgement and sensitive advice makes her an editor any author would relish.

The greatest thanks of all are due to the hundreds of thousands of people who take part in The Mind Gym activities and share, every day, what they do and don't like. These honest (sometimes very honest) views are the basis on which The Mind Gym is constantly revised, refreshed and renewed. We hope that, as a reader of this book, you too will share your opinions and so make sure that The Mind Gym constantly improves and consistently gives you what you want. Well, as near as.

Index

AA engineers, 134
absolutist thinkers, 158–9, 247
accommodation (conflict resolution),
    141, 142, 145–6, 150–1, 152
acting out of character, 157
action plans, 233–4, 235
active care, 61–2
active-constructive, 61
admiration, lack of, 255
adolescents, 143–4
aggression, indirect, 185–97
Allen, Julie, 63
Allen, Woody, 36
alternative explanations, 31–2
America's Sweethearts (2001), 141, 143
anchoring, 179
anger, 50–1, 209
Animal House (1978), 63
apologies *see* Hardest word
appraisals, 144–8
Apprentice, The (US TV series), 178
Are you listening? (listening skills), 2,
    13, 15, 18, 20, 77, 78–93
  asking questions, 82–3, 90, 91
  critical listeners, 89–90, 92
  empathic listeners, 88–9, 92
  and the facts, 81–2
  filtered listening, 85–92
  focus, 79–81
  generous listeners, 86–8, 92
  solution-focused listening, 90–2
  the unsaid, 83–5

arguments
  argument-inducing language, 80–1
  repetitive, 214–16
  triggers, 254
  see also conflict resolution
'as if', acting, 243
assumptions, negative, 66
athletes, 51
attachment theory, 33–6
  anxious attachment, 34, 35, 36
  avoidant attachment, 34, 35, 36
  fearful attachment, 34, 35
  secure attachment, 34, 35, 36
attacks
  character, 117
  dialogic, 232, 233, 234–5, 236
attention
  centre of, 106–7
  see also Bids for attention
authenticity, 270–1
avoidance strategies (conflict
    resolution), 142, 146–7, 150–1
  conditional, 147
'avoider' types, 148

'back channel' responses, 79
bad experiences, minimising, 30–1
bad tempers, 39
bad vibes, 182–97
badmouthing people, 197
Baia, Ashley, 102–5
Barnes, Julian, 56

BATNA (Best Alternative To a
    Negotiated Agreement), 174–5,
    178
behavioural patterns
    breaking, 267–8, 269
    repeat, 14, 18, 21, 213, 214–24, 267
behavioural priming, 59
being let down, 32
belligerence, 117
Belushi, John, 63
benefit of the doubt, 31–3, 157, 161,
    271–2
bereavement, 262
Berne, Eric, 216, 219
Best Alternative To a Negotiated
    Agreement (BATNA), 174–5, 178
best intentions, 157
'between the lines', 84
biases, negotiator, 172
bids for attention, 13–14, 18, 20, 77,
    110–22, 216
    'away from bids', 112–14, 118–21–2
    'turning against bids', 112–15, 116–
        18, 121–2, 254
    'turning towards bids', 112, 113–16,
        121–2
bids for power, 136
black and white thinking, 158–9
blame
    false, 204
    passing on to others, 23, 166–7
Bloomberg, 134
body language
    dishonest, 176
    impact, 84
    inclusive, 106
boundaries, 272
Bowlby, John, 33
Brand, Russell, 99
Brault, Robert, 62
Brinkerhoff, Robert, 269
British Airways, 211
Brown, Gordon, 85
Bullshitter, The, 241–2
Bush, George, 38
Bush, George W., 55, 273
'But', saying, 163–6

caregivers, 33
Carey, Jim, 127
Carpenter, Mary Chapin, 198

Charrier, George O., 135
Carter, Jimmy, 98–9
centre of attention, 106–7
change
    personal, 32–3
    relationship, 10, 13–15, 266–9
    stages of, 262
character attacks, 117
character flaws, 161, 162, 200–1
Charlotte's Webb (2006), 143
Charm school (charisma), 15, 18, 20,
    77, 94–109
    and concentration, 97
    connection-making, 95–7
    and emotional recollections, 101–2
    generosity, 100–1
    hope, 94–5
    and impact word use, 97–9, 108–9
    passion, 95
    and putting others at the centre,
        106–7
    and story-telling, 102–5
    and surprise, 105
Charmer, The, 245–6
Check your impulse (self-control), 13,
    14, 18, 20, 23, 38–52
    and anger, 50–1
    assessing, 40–2
    avoidance strategies for, 50
    combining techniques, 50–1
    distraction techniques for, 50
    and finite effort, 46
    and flooding, 42–3
    focusing on the positive, 46–7
    and intention, 49
    and the ironic processes of mental
        control, 47–8
    jam tomorrow exercise for, 45–6
    practicing, 43–5, 51–2
    role models for, 51
    and writing things down, 48
Chesterton, G.K., 202
childhood experience, 33
children, 113
China, 200
choice, 6–7, 267–8
'click–whirr' phrases, 80–1
Clinton, Hillary, 102
Clooney, George, 267
closed questions, 83, 177
coal mining, 174–5

Cog's ladder, 135–6
collaboration, 142–3, 148, 150–3
Collins, Wilkie, 56
Coming together (long-lasting
    relationships), 10, 13–15, 77–138
  Are you listening?, 78–93
  Bids for attention, 77, 110–22
  Charm school, 77, 94–109
  Trust me, 123–38
communication
  improving your skills, 228–9
  responsive, 126–7
comparison-making, 28, 106
competing, 141–2, 144–5, 149–53
compromise, 142, 147–8, 150–2, 239
concentration, 79–81, 97
confidence, 243
confirming evidence, 55, 179
conflict, covert, 139, 185–97
'conflict explosive' types, 148–9
conflict resolution, 10, 13–15, 139,
    140–53, 154–68
  accommodation, 141, 142, 145–6,
      150–1, 152
  apologies, 139, 198–211
  avoidance strategies, 120–1, 142,
      146–7, 150–1
  collaboration, 142–3, 148, 150–3
  competitive, 141–2, 144–5, 149–53
  compromise, 142, 147–8, 150–2
  and mental agility, 140, 143, 149,
      152–3
  office politics, 182–97
  parent-adolescent relationships, 143–4
  preparing for, 268–9
  see also arguments
confrontation, 258
Confucius, 210
congruence, 97
connections, making, 95–7
consequences, 45–6, 246
contemptuousness, 117
contrariness, 117, 149
Control Freak, The, 71–2, 244
control issues, 206, 240
conversation cards, 68–9
Cool to be kind (giving people what
    they need), 14, 15, 18, 20, 23,
    53–62
  empathy, 53–60, 62
  kindness, 60–2

covert conflict, 139, 185–97
credibility, 127–9, 202–3
critical listeners, 89–90, 92
crowd dynamics, 134–6
Cruise, Tom, 105
Cuckoo, The, 253, 256
customer needs, 81–2
Cyborg, The, 247–8

de Dreu, C. K. W., 180
de Klerk, F. W., 231
De Niro, Robert, 57
deadlines, 245–6
Deal or no deal? (negotiation), 15, 18,
    21, 139, 169–81
  aftercare, 181
  appearing unthreatening, 180–1
  Best Alternative To a Negotiated
      Agreement (BATNA), 174–5,
      178
  collaborative negotiation, 170–1,
      180, 181
  competitive negotiation, 170, 171–2,
      180, 181
  consequences of, 175–6
  and deal speed, 176–7
  and decision-making traps, 179
  and interests, 172–3
  negotiator bias, 172
  and other people's perspectives,
      174
  and positions, 172–3
  and the power of knowledge,
      177–8
  sneaky advantage in, 172–6
  starting with 'no', 178–9
debate, 228
decision-making
  regarding gracious exits, 251–6
  traps, 179
defensive responses, 117, 155, 166–7
'demand–withdrawal' dance, 160–1
Dependency Paradox, 133
Depp, Johnny, 105
details, relationship, 110–11, 176, 274
Deutsche Bank, 4
dialogue, 225–36
  action plans, 233–4, 235
  attacks, 232, 233, 234–5, 236
  refusal to participate in, 235–6
  withdrawals, 232, 233, 234–5, 236

Different relationships, 10, 13, 213–75
    Gracious exits, 213, 251–65
    New beginnings, 213, 266–75
    Out of a rut, 213, 214–24
    Tough talk, 213, 225–36
    Tricky people, 213, 237–50
diligence, 127
Dilts, Robert, 55
discomfort, facing your, 69
disengaging see 'turning away from
    bids'
dismissiveness, 119
dissatisfaction, 256–8
distance, creating, 261
divorce, 111, 113–14, 119–20, 165
doctors, suing, 83
Dodo, The, 253, 254–5
domineering people, 117
Drama Triangles, 217
Draw the poison (arguments), 14, 18,
    21, 139, 154–68
Duck, Steve, 256
Dumper, The, 238–9

Eisenhower, Dwight, 98
elicitation questions, 101
Ellis, Albert, 67, 74
emotional 'hits', 216, 218–19
emotions
    flooding, 42–3
    stimulating, 101–2
    see also feelings
empathic listeners, 88–9, 92
'empathiser' types, 148
empathy, 18, 20, 23, 53–60, 62, 249
    and the meta-mirror, 55–8
    and negotiation, 177–8
    tactile, 59–60
    and trust, 130
ending relationships see Graceful exits
energy, 273–4
entrainment, 95–7, 105
Erin Brockovich (2000), 141, 143
escapism, 264
expectations, 32, 210
expertise, 128

facts, the, 81–2
familiarity
    and contempt, 125
    and trust, 123–5

fault finding, 163, 210
fear, 74, 206
fearful attachment style, 34, 35
feelings
    about relationship endings, 260–1,
        262
    acknowledging, 165
    assuming you understand other
        people's, 155–8
    changing other people's, 97
    see also emotions
Feeney, Brooke, 133
fiction, 54
Fight club, 13, 14, 18, 20, 139, 140–53
    accommodation, 141, 142, 145–6,
        150–1, 152
    avoidance strategies, 142, 146–7,
        150–1
    collaboration, 142, 143, 148, 150–2,
        153
    competing, 141, 142, 144–5, 149,
        150–1, 152–3
    compromise, 142, 147–8, 150–2
    and mental agility, 140, 143, 149,
        152–3
    power games, 152
'fight or flight' reaction, 152
first impressions, 83–4, 100–1
Fitzgerald, Ella, 63
flattery, 106
flooding, 42–3
fondness, lack of, 255
forgiveness, 32, 198–211
    benefits of, 207
    giving, 205–11
    marking, 209
    seeking, 198–205, 208, 211
formin', normin', performin', 135
Forster, E. M., 104
friends, 209, 264
future focus, 165

gaffes, 118
games see psychological games
gender difference, 79
General Electric, 181
generosity, 100–1
generous listeners, 86–8, 92
Gollwitzer, Peter, 49
good, the, looking for, 31–3, 157, 161,
    271–2

Gorbachev, Mikhail, 213
Gottman, John, 111, 113–14, 116, 119,
    131, 148–9, 255
Gracious exits (ending relationships),
    13, 14, 18, 21, 213, 251–65
    The Cuckoo, 253, 256
    decision-making regarding, 251–6
    The Dodo, 253, 254–5
    exit routes, 256–60
    happy endings, 260–1
    moving on from, 258–9, 261–5
    The Phoenix, 253–4
    repair attempts, 254–5, 258
    The Swan, 253, 255
Groundhog Day (1993), 215–16
guilt, 207
Guinness, Alec, 63

habits, 6, 267
Hanks, Tom, 63
Hardest word (apologies), 13, 14, 18,
    21, 139, 198–211
    adding credibility to, 202–3
    allowing time for, 204
    insincere, 202
    making amends, 203
    personal responsibility for, 199–200
    providing understanding, 201–2
    specificity in, 200–1
    when not to apologise, 204–5
Harrelson, Woody, 53
Heim, Pat, 191
high standards, 32, 210
Hoffman, Dustin, 216
Holmes, Tabitha, 143–4
Homes, Katie, 105
honesty, 176
hope, 94–5
Hubbard, Kin, 79

'I know best' attitudes, 155–7
'I smell trouble' (office politics), 18, 21,
    139, 182–97
ignoring others see 'turning away from
    bids'
impact making, 127
impact words, 97–9, 108–9
implementation intentions, 49
impulsivity see Check your impulse
indirect aggression, 185–97
inertia, 179

inner critics, 73–5
Innocent, 134
insecurity, 34, 35, 36, 270–1
insincerity, 202
insinuation, 162
intention
    best, 157
    guessing, 31–2
    implementation, 49
interests, 172–3
interference, pre-empting, 244
interpretations, 81, 155–7
interrupting, 167
intimacy
    and love maps, 130–1, 137–8
    'name and inquire' technique, 132–3
    and tentative invitations, 131–2
    and trust, 131–3, 137–8

Jackboot, The, 240–1
jam tomorrow exercise, 45–6
James, Oliver, 33
jealousy, 190–1
Jintao, Hu, 273
job offers, 178
Johnson, Boris, 99
Johnson, Samuel, 136
Jones, Joann, 61
judgement, deferring, 81

Karpman, Steven, 217
Kerry, John, 55
Keysers, Christian, 59–60
Khrushchev, Nikolai, 105
Kiecolt, Glaser & Glaser, 229
Kilmann, Ralph, 140
kindness, 60–2
Kipling, Rudyard, 31, 167
Know it All, The, 246–7
knowledge, 127, 177–8, 266
Kodak, 81–2
Kramer, Roderick, 128
Kubler–Ross, Elizabeth, 262

labelling, 161–3
law of unintended confusion, 273
leading questions, 177
Letterman, David, 63
Like me, love me, respect me (Mind
    Gym programme), 12, 15
listening skills see Are you listening?

long-lasting relationships *see* Coming
    together
loss, stages of, 262
love maps, 131, 137–8
loyalty, 255
lying, 242

Macmillan, Harold, 105
Maister, David, 132
making an impact, 127
Mandela, Nelson, 230–1
Mar, Raymond, 54
marriage
    and bids for attention, 110–11,
        113–14, 119–20
    mediation services for, 165–6
Marx, Groucho, 166
mediation, 165–6
memories, 101–2
mental agility, 6, 140, 143, 149, 152–3
mental control, ironic processes of,
    47–8
mental fitness, 5
meta-mirror, 55–8
micro signals *see* bids for attention
Miliband, David, 84–5
Mind Gym Foundation, 4
Mind Gym Online, 11, 274–5
Mind Gym programmes
    custom, 10–11, 16–19
    Like me, love me, respect me, 12, 15
    Relationship essentials, 12, 13
    Relationship repair kit, 12, 14
mindsets, positive, 162
mirror neurons, 59–60
missing information, 84–5
misunderstandings, 273
Monkhouse, Bob, 68
Mont Fleur process, 231
Mr Don't Mind Me, 242–3
Murphy, Susan, 191
Murray, Bill, 215
'myside bias', 54–5

Nadal, Rafael, 51
'name and inquire' technique, 132–3
'Name it, Claim it, Tame it', 220
names, using, 107
narratives, 104–5
needs *see* Cool to be kind; customer
    needs

negative loops, 160
neglect, 256
negotiation *see* Deal or no deal?
negotiator bias, 172
New beginnings, 13–15, 21, 213,
    266–75
'no', saying, 163–6, 247
non-fiction, 54
North, Colonel Oliver, 96–7

Oakland, Susan, 159
Obama, Barack, 102–5
objective behaviour, 81
observation, 81
Ocean's Eleven (2001), 142
office politics, 185–97, 272
    coping with, 192–7
oil, 174
'OK' profiles, 24–33, 34–7
Oliver, Jamie, 97
O'Neal, Ryan, 199
open questions, 82, 88, 177
optimism, 94–5, 263
organisational culture, competitive,
    193, 194–5
organisational restructuring, 270
Ostell, Alistair, 159
Out of a rut (repeat behavioural
    patterns), 14, 18, 21, 213, 214–24,
    267
    and psychological game playing,
        216–24
outcomes, 105
over-friendliness, 176
overshare, 131–2

pain barrier, breaking through, 69
para-language, 84
paranoia, 249
parent-adolescent relationships, rows,
    143–4
Parker, Dorothy, 143
passion, 95, 107–8
patience, 32
patterns of behaviour
    breaking, 267–8, 269
    repeating, 14, 18, 21, 213, 214–24,
        267
Pears, Ian, 56
peer relations, 152
Persecutor role, 217–19, 221

personal change, other people's
   resentment of, 32–3
personal responsibility, 6–7
   for break ups, 263
   for your mistakes, 199–200, 211
personal strengths, 30, 264
perspective-taking, 54–60, 174, 190–5
pessimism, 94, 263
Peterson, Christopher, 30
Pfeiffer, Michelle, 63
Philip, Prince, 118
Phoenix, The, 253–4
physical exercise, 107–8
Pitt, Brad, 63
politeness, 135–6
politics, 84–5, 98–9, 102–5, 213
positions, 172–3
'positive sentiment override', 124, 157–8
posture, 44–5
power, bids for, 136
power games, 152
power–dead–even rule, 191, 197
praise, 30
predicaments, 104
prejudice, 83–4
preparing for relationships see
   Relationship ready
Procter & Gamble, 135
productivity, 113
protagonists, 104, 106
psychological games, 216–24
   invites into/hooks, 221–4
   Persecutors, 217–19, 221
   Rescuers, 217, 219, 222
   roles/positions, 216–19, 221–2
   stopping play, 220–1, 223–4
   Victims, 217–19, 222
psychology, 2

questioning, 82–3, 90, 91, 246
   clarifying questions, 82
   closed questions, 83, 177
   direct questions, 176
   elicitation questions, 101
   fixed open questions, 82–3
   hypothetical questions, 82, 90
   leading questions, 177
   open questions, 82, 88, 177

Rackham, Neil, 81–2
Radcliffe, Paula, 51

Raiffa, Howard, 181
Ramsey, Gordon, 129
rating others (exercise), 36–7
Reagan, Ronald, 98–9, 213
recharging, 264
Reeves, Vic, 176
rejection, 67
Relationship essentials (Mind Gym
   programme), 12, 13
Relationship ready, 10, 13, 15, 20,
   23–75
   Check your impulse, 23, 38–52
   Cool to be kind, 53–62
   Right mind, 24–37
   Shy to shine, 63–75
Relationship repair kit (Mind Gym
   programme), 12, 14
reliability, 127
repair attempts, 203, 254–5, 258, 269
Rescuer role, 217, 219, 222
resilience, 197
resolutions, 47–8
responsiveness, 126–7
retreat see withdrawal
Rice, Condelezza, 273
Right mind, 13, 15, 18, 20, 23, 24–37
   'OK' profiles, 24–33, 34–7
righteous indignation, 206
rituals, trust-building, 134–5, 137
Rivers, Joan, 198
Roberts, Julia, 141–3
Roddick, Anita, 97
Rogers, Carl, 271–2
role models, 51
romance, 62
Roosevelt, Eleanor, 64
rose-tinted glasses, 263
rule of five, 173
Runaway Bride, The (1999), 142
Russia, 174

sales, listening skills, 81–2
sanitising, 269
satisfaction, 160–1
Sceptic, The, 248–9
Schwarzkopf, Norman, 97
security, 4–5, 34–6, 270–1
'seeing the best in people', 4–5, 31–2,
   157, 271–2
self-acknowledgement, 30
self-control see Check your impulse

self-criticism, 73–5
self-disclosure, 131–2
self-fulfilling prophecies, 4–5, 28
self-protection, 272
self-righteousness, 166–7, 199
self-value, 25–33
Seneca, 163
shadow meanings, 84
'shame attacking' experiences, 74
Shy to shine, 15, 18, 20, 23, 63–75
   causes of shyness, 69–74
   pervasive shyness, 64, 68–9
   recognising shyness in others, 66, 74
   shy extraverts, 63–4
   situational shyness, 64–7
   transitional shyness, 64, 67–8
siblings, 113
silent treatment, 119
Simpson, Homer, 38
small talk, 245
Smith, Will, 99
snobs, 128
sociability, 1
social inhibition, 72–3
social norms, 129–30
social nous, 129–30
social support, 133, 160, 209, 254, 264
solution-focused approaches, 30, 90–2
South Africa, 206, 230–1
spin, positive, 161, 162
status quo, 179
story-telling, 102–5, 106, 107
Stress Cadet, The, 239–40
subconscious mind, 216, 219, 220
subordinates, 152
sunk–cost, 179
superiority, sense of, 27
Supernanny, 145
surprise, 105
Swan, The, 253, 255
'switching', 119
systems, 5–6

tactile empathy, 59–60
talking
   over others, 167
   things through, 209
   yourself up, 29–30
teachers, 159
team building activities, 134, 135–6

team spirit, 135–6
tempers, 39
Thatcher, Keith, 63
Thatcher, Margaret, 63, 174–5
'thinking yourself smart', 58–9
Thomas, Kenneth, 140
'tongue tied' people, 72–3
Tough love, 10, 13, 14, 139–211
   Deal or no deal?, 139, 169–81
   Draw the poison, 139, 154–68
   Fight club, 139, 140–53
   Hardest word, 139, 198–211
   I smell trouble, 139, 182–97
Tough talk, 14, 18, 21, 213, 225–36
Toussaint, Loren, 208
toxic words, 163–6
Tricky people, 18, 21, 213, 237–50
   Mr Don't Mind Me, 242–3
   The Bullshitter, 241–2
   The Charmer, 245–6
   The Control Freak, 244
   The Cyborg, 247–8
   The Dumper, 238–9
   The Jackboot, 240–1
   The Know it All, 246–7
   The Sceptic, 248–9
   The Stress Cadet, 239–40
Truly, Madly, Deeply (1990), 263
Trump, Donald, 178
trust, 15, 18, 20, 77, 123–38
   and crowd dynamics, 134–6
   and familiarity, 123–5
   and intimacy, 131–3, 137–8
   lack of, 72, 123, 125–6
   and proximity, 124
   rapid establishment, 128–9
   rebuilding, 203
   sensible, 126–9
   sensitive, 126, 129–33
Truth and Reconciliation Commission, 206
'turning against bids', 112–15, 116–18, 121–2, 254
'turning away from bids', 112–14, 118–21–2
'turning towards bids', 112, 113–16, 121–2
Tutu, Archbishop, 206

'unconditional positive regard', 271–2
undervalued feelings, 117

Unilever, 134
universalisation, 158–61
'unsaid', the, 83–5
unthreatening appearances, 180–1
updating people, 127

valuing others, 25–9, 31–3, 246
Victim role, 217–19, 222
volunteer work, 69

Walmart, 134
Walsh, Willy, 211
wants, assessing, 227, 234
Watis, Tom, 161
web development, 182–96

Welch, Jack, 181
West, Mae, 39
White Men Can't Jump (1992), 53–4
Wilcox, Ella Wheeler, 274
Wilkinson, Johnny, 51
Williams, Robin, 105
'win/win' scenarios, 165, 170–1
Winterstone, Jeanette, 99
withdrawal (retreat)
    'demand–withdrawal' dance, 160–1
    in dialogue, 232–6, 269
Wood, Victoria, 63
Woods, Tiger, 51
Wright, Rev Jeremiah, 102
writing things down, 80